D0436165

WITHDRAWN

3 0700 11050 4171

CITIES OF AFFLUENCE AND ANGER

CITIES OF AFFLUENCE AND ANGER
A LITERARY GEOGRAPHY
OF MODERN ENGLISHNESS

PETER J. KALLINEY

UNIVERSITY OF VIRGINIA PRESS
CHARLOTTESVILLE AND LONDON

University of Virginia Press
© 2006 by the Rector and Visitors of the University of Virginia
All rights reserved
Printed in the United States of America on acid-free paper

First published 2007

9 8 7 6 5 4 3 2 1

Library of Congress Cataloging-in-Publication Data

Kalliney, Peter J., 1971–
    Cities of affluence and anger : a literary geography of modern Englishness /
Peter J. Kalliney.
        p.   cm.
    Includes bibliographical references and index.
    ISBN-13: 978-0-8139-2573-8 (acid-free paper)
    ISBN-13: 978-0-8139-2574-5 (pbk. : acid-free paper)
    1. English fiction—20th century—History and criticism.   2. National
characteristics, English, in literature.   3. Cities and towns in literature.
4. Social classes in literature.   5. Community in literature.   6. Commonwealth fiction (English)—History and criticism.   I. Title.
PR888.N3557K35   2006
820.9′355—dc22

                                                    2006013692

CONTENTS

ACKNOWLEDGMENTS

While researching and writing this book, I have benefited from the assistance of many people and institutions. Fellowships, grants, and release time from the University of Michigan, Oberlin College, the University of South Florida, and Mellon made this project possible. Many librarians, archivists, and colleagues have lent their expertise along the way: Kathy Arsenault, Merilyn Burke, and Virginia Champion at South Florida; Lynn Wiley at the University of Illinois; Susan Garrett and Tim Utter at the University of Michigan; Abraham Parrish at Yale; Katherine Lewis at Regent's Park; Eve Hostettler at Island History Trust; Elizabeth Hallock and David Wishner at E+D Architecture and Design; as well as David Gilbert and Rebecca Preston. Cathie Brettschneider and Ellen Satrom, my editors at the University of Virginia Press, and Ruth Melville, the copy editor, have been wonderfully supportive and responsive as I prepared my manuscript. Learning more about London and England—and more importantly, football—would have been impossible without good friends and gracious hosts: Corf, Big Si, Ekpe, Alan, Dom, James, Rich, With, and Gemma. I would also like to thank my students at Oberlin and South Florida, who have contributed a great deal to this book. I have discussed drafts, fragments, and ideas with more people than I can recall: Julie Buckner Armstrong, Michael Bérubé, Jed Esty, Grant Farred, John Hobbs, Elizabeth Hirsh, Lem Johnson, T. Scott McMillin, Patricia Rae, Rafael Reyes-Ruiz, Sonya Rose, Stephen Ross, Laura Runge, Erik Simon, Tim Van Compernolle, Rashmi Varma, and Sandy Zagarell. Jennifer Wicke and an anonymous reader for Virginia furnished me with exceptionally generous, detailed, and insightful criticism. I owe a special debt of gratitude to the scholars whose work and advice guided me through a mysterious process: Jim English, Jonathan Freedman, Patsy

Yaeger, and especially Simon Gikandi. I want to thank my parents, Sami Yousef and Elizabeth Edmunds Kalliney, for teaching me the value of education and persistence. Nedjma, my little star, has made the sometimes tedious process of revising more joyous than I could imagine. Finally, to Karen, my friend, partner, and closest collaborator: your patience, support, and intelligence humble and inspire me.

I am grateful to the Johns Hopkins University Press for permission to reprint portions of chapters 4 and 6 which originally appeared in *Modern Fiction Studies* 47.1 (2001) and 48.1 (2002), respectively.

CITIES OF AFFLUENCE AND ANGER

I. ENGLISH, ALL TOO ENGLISH
NATIONAL EXCEPTIONALISM AND
THE URBAN CLASS SYSTEM

In 1936 Victor Gollancz asked George Orwell to take a tour of England's northern industrial cities and write a documentary about his experiences among working-class people. The results of that journey were published a year later as *The Road to Wigan Pier,* carrying the imprint of Gollancz's Left Book Club. Although the subscription book society boasted some 38,000 regular members before the outbreak of World War II, Orwell's contribution is one of the few offerings to remain in continuous circulation, owing its durability partly to the fame of its author and partly to the text's searching, desperately funny critiques of English society. The book itself is a curious combination of autoethnography and autobiography: the first half offers an anthropological sketch of England's northern, working-class communities, documenting the effects of poverty on the country's millions of unemployed and underemployed families, while the second half, ostensibly explaining why socialism has not yet won the day in England, attacks the attitudes and mores of the middle classes, of which the author deems himself a "sufficiently typical" example (121). Written during the height of the Depression and on the eve of World War II, the book sits, uncomfortably, on the precipice of radical cultural change. During the next twenty-five years or so, England would participate in a world war and the cold war, elect its first majority Labour government, establish the basic foundations of a welfare state, and concede statehood and self-determination to most of its colonial territories. This conjunction of major political crises, both domestic and global, forced the English to perform a thorough self-examination in a relatively short period of time. Internally, the threat of unmitigated class conflict endangered already tenuous political stability. Internationally, the loss of an extensive overseas empire demanded a substantial reconsideration of English national identity: a discourse of intrinsic cultural particularity gradually replaced symbolic dependence on extrinsic colonial mastery. *The Road to Wigan Pier* clearly demonstrates its anxieties about this impending process—excited by the promise of widespread change but also nervous about the shape it might assume.

Orwell begins part 2, the book's autobiographical assessment of socialism in England, with his famous declaration that he "was born into what you might describe as the lower-upper-middle class." As a whole, the upper-middle class was a relic of sorts, well past its "heyday in the 'eighties and 'nineties." Late Victorian prosperity had long since given way to Georgian pessimism and nostalgia, with only Rudyard Kipling, whom Orwell calls the great "poet laureate" of the upper-middle class, reminding them of past glory. Orwell glosses the upper-middle class in terms of their approximate annual income, "the layer of society lying between £2000 and £300 a year." His own family, he mentions, was "not far from the bottom," hence his position in the lower-upper-middle class. These monetary figures, he hastens to add, are the most expedient way to convey his general meaning, but he insists that relying too much on income to determine one's class position can be a treacherous exercise:

> Nevertheless, the essential point about the English class-system is that it is *not* entirely explicable in terms of money. Roughly speaking it is a money-stratification, but it is also interpenetrated by a sort of shadowy caste-system; rather like a jerry-built modern bungalow haunted by medieval ghosts. . . . Probably there are countries where you can predict a man's opinions from his income, but it is never quite safe to do so in England; you have always got to take his traditions into consideration as well. (121–22)

While an individual's annual salary may give a rough indication of that person's relative position in the world, it can never adequately capture the intricacies of class politics and its relation to English national traditions. Orwell argues that unlike in other countries, where the size of a man's bank account might allow one to accurately guess his political orientation, England's convoluted social networks demand a more nuanced, culturally sensitive approach to the problem of class.

Cities of Affluence and Anger is an attempt to unpack Orwell's surprisingly rich metaphor of England's class system—and by implication, English national culture—as "rather like a jerry-built modern bungalow haunted by medieval ghosts." There is a vague but concrete feeling among contemporary scholars and political pundits that class politics is, or should be, in sharp decline. When John Major, throughout the early 1990s, unironically insisted that the goal of the Conservative Party was to create a "classless society," and when Tony Blair, during his address to the Labour Party conference of 1999, declared the class war "over," they were both echoing a refrain that prominent leftist academics had been arguing for years (to say nothing of more conservative politicians). For many scholars, the "old" rallying cry of class exploitation has been (or should be) replaced by a more inclusive, flexible, and heterogeneous coalition of social justice movements. Progressive intellectuals and activists have emphasized the need to create popular alliances among feminists, environmentalists, minority rights workers, gay rights advocates, and other progressive groups. But there is a latent anxiety, even as this new political landscape has emerged in the postwar period, that class politics still has some relevance. Rather like the ghost that seems so out of place in Orwell's modern bungalow—a spectral presence no one cares to acknowledge much less address by name—class politics haunts contemporary analyses of English culture. Dead but not buried, class lingers mostly as a "shadowy caste-system" of sorts in scholarly treatments of modern England, neglected by scholars who have probably grown weary of the subject after decades of debate.[1] As Peter Hitchcock argues, class is frequently mentioned alongside race, gender, and sexuality in contemporary academic discourse, but it remains radically undertheorized in comparison.[2] Contemporary academic studies of class politics are consistently apologetic, as if expressing an interest in class reflects an impoverished, antiquated sense of the field.[3] Most progressive scholars mention the class system as a form of exploitation, if only to cover their bases, but rarely does it feature as an object of heightened analytic or theoretical scrutiny.

My point is not that a class system still exists in some form, or simply that class politics still matters. What may most surprise readers of this book is how often twentieth-century texts, especially novels, take the articulation of class difference as a manifestly symbolic consideration, a contested site on which aesthetic objects perform substantive cultural work. In many respects, this book is less concerned with defining class politics as a social and political reality and more interested in thinking about it as a symbolic condition, as a contentious, unstable point around which cultural texts are structured.[4] Unlike much contemporary scholarship, which treats class as a relatively stable, known quantity, twentieth-century English fiction consistently mobilizes class politics as a way of theorizing social difference and imagining political agency in a rapidly changing cultural context. An acute sense of class conscious-ness, moreover, features not just in putatively working-class novels but in a wide variety of texts. The novels considered in this book, for instance, have a broad social and aesthetic range: I have included chapters on the high modernist *Mrs. Dalloway,* middlebrow country-house fiction such as *Howards End* and *Brideshead Revisited,* popular, working-class nov-els from the 1950s, and two experimental postcolonial texts, *The Golden Notebook* and *The Satanic Verses.* The novels themselves represent a cross section of twentieth-century English fiction; what they share, curiously, is their deployment of class difference as a site of fierce symbolic contes-tation.

Orwell's metaphor of the haunted house economically captures the slipperiness of class as a theoretical concept. England's class system, para-doxically, is both the house and its haunting, at once a tangible, material object and a spectral, ethereal presence, a thing belonging more properly to the spiritual plane. The foundations of the class system have a rough equivalent in the world of hard economics, but understanding the true significance of class demands an account of its intangible, shadowy, af-fective properties. In Marxist terms, we might say that Orwell's analogy articulates a tension between the material and ideological axes of class politics: class refers to the objective material conditions under which people live and struggle, yet it is also a way to project group solidarity (or difference) in a stratified society. The idea of class can describe the social circumstances through which capital organizes production and distrib-utes resources, but it can also be used to enunciate political sympathies and help galvanize people who may not occupy exactly the same social position. This book uses a variety of literary and cultural texts to help theorize the messiness of class politics in twentieth-century England. I suggest that this tension between class as a material condition and class as an ideological disposition becomes manifest through symbolic appa-ratuses, such as literary texts. Class as an objective relation and class as an ideological tool are relatively autonomous yet intimately related. Like the haunted house, these two axes of class politics are necessarily imbri-cated with one another, the tension between them exerting a determin-ing influence on complex symbolic structures, such as the novel.

The house in Orwell's metaphor is not an ordinary habitation but a modern bungalow, significant because it is not an indigenous architectural form. Originally, the bungalow came to England from India, where it was used first by Bengali peasants, then modified to accommodate British administrators. During the nineteenth century, it flourished in the English countryside—where many colonial officers retired—and from England was reexported to other colonies, particularly to Africa, where it was thought a suitable residence for Europeans living in the tropics.[5] For the purposes of this project, Orwell's metaphor is instructive because it underscores the deep, structural connection between the class system in England and the changing fortunes of British imperialism. In an economic sense, of course, British capitalism was fully integrated in and dependent on a vast network of colonial possessions. The metropolitan class system, as such, should be seen as a very specialized, localized division of labor that was contingent on a much broader set of economic and political arrangements, of which colonial space was an equally important component. Politically, the empire functioned as a kind of social safety net for all classes of English society, in which a discourse of material scarcity dominated long stretches of the late nineteenth and early twentieth centuries. When the cyclical labor market contracted, for instance, many of the poverty-stricken working class made their way to the settler colonies, relieving the burden on the domestic economy. For Orwell's lower-upper-middle class, securing a job in the civil service or the military was the easiest way to maintain a lifestyle that would have been financially impossible in the metropole: lots of land for hunting and riding, inexpensive servants, and palatial homes were feasible in the colonies but not at home. By the late nineteenth century, the concept of Englishness had become so dependent on imperialism that it had become difficult to articulate a form of national identity without referring to it. As Orwell himself argues, abandoning the imperial project would "reduce England to a cold and unimportant little island where we should all have to work very hard and live mainly on herrings and potatoes" (159–60). Decolonization would have dire material and ideological consequences for England, threatening its material security and mortally wounding its national self-esteem. England's economic viability and political authority were dependent on an extrinsic imperial geography, without which it would be reduced to a meager diet, bad weather, and global insignificance.

During the *longue durée* of imperial contraction that was the twentieth century, domestic class politics became increasingly more important to the discourse of national identity because it offered a way to
articulate a version of English cultural exceptionalism or "insiderism."[6]
The threat, and later the reality, of imperial decline forced the English
to turn inward, to perform a thorough inventory of Englishness in the
absence of an expansive imperial imaginary. Strangely enough, it was a
domestic class system—which was itself in the process of a major reconfiguration due, in part, to the waning of empire—that allowed the English to reframe the discourse of national identity through a social system
that was intrinsically and mysteriously unique to England. There may
be some countries, as Orwell opines, "where you can predict a man's
opinions from his income, but it is never quite safe to do so in England."
In the twentieth century, England's murky, unpredictable class politics,
basically economic but also "interpenetrated" with a "shadowy caste-
system" embedded in tradition and affect, was transformed into a kind of
national patrimony, a social and ideological marker of intrinsic cultural
peculiarity. Throughout this long period of national self-examination,
England's class system continued to function as a discourse of wealth,
status, and hierarchy, but, paradoxically, it also became a way to project
a shared culture and a common social vocabulary. Although class as
a set of social practices was by no means insulated from the nation's
program of overseas conquest—domestic class politics was intertwined
in the rise and fall of empire—it was ideologically transformed into an
eccentric, highly localized system that differentiated England from both
its European neighbors and the colonial periphery. Anthropological ex-
aminations and thick descriptions of the domestic class system, which
began with late nineteenth-century antipoverty campaigns, continuing
with Mass Observation (and *The Road to Wigan Pier*) between the wars,
and again resurfacing with the New Left in the 1950s, provided the country with a sophisticated discourse of national distinctiveness.[7] Despite
the continuing existence of class difference and the lingering threat of
class war throughout the century, class also became a discursive site on
which the English could reframe a highly provisional national unity in
the face of imperial collapse.

My argument on the discursive connection between English cultural
exceptionalism and class politics presupposes and builds upon recent
scholarly work on national identity in Britain and the postcolonial world.[8]
My first premise is that the historical, material, and cultural realities of

Britain and England can be considered only in the context of imperialism. Whatever Britishness and Englishness may be, their construction is necessarily relational and comparative. In *Maps of Englishness: Writing Identity in the Culture of Colonialism,* Simon Gikandi makes exactly this point when he insists that "Britain can only be comprehended in relation to its colonial others" (33). As Linda Colley has argued, this construction of national consciousness effectively predates the material reality of conquest, beginning when imperial expansion was little more than a fantasy. England's relationship with its colonial others, especially with its closest neighbors, the Celtic nations, has been variable and problematic.[9] The idea of Britain—as opposed to England, whose physical boundaries have remained fairly constant—is itself inherently flexible, expanding and contracting to meet the changing demands of imperial rule. Legal definitions of who is and who is not a British subject have changed as often as the coordinates of imperial sovereignty. Whereas the idea of Britain has been reworked politically and legally over a period of centuries, the idea of a restrictive English culture became increasingly more important as imperialism lost its teeth in the past hundred years.

The difference between Britishness and Englishness has always been difficult to define and maintain, primarily because they are relational categories in a state of perpetual flux. Ian Baucom has recently attempted, quite persuasively, to disentangle Englishness from Britishness by considering England's connection to empire; he argues that Englishness is a contradictory structure, emerging "at once as an embrace and a repudiation of the imperial beyond" (7). In the twentieth century, the idea of a bounded, exclusive Englishness came to be thought and rethought, sometimes competing with and replacing the idea of Britain, which had an expansive geographic frame supported by an extensible set of legal and cultural institutions. Jed Esty, in *A Shrinking Island: Modernism and National Culture in England,* has documented this change during the modernist period, illustrating how cultural objects functioned as a crucial discursive arena in which this transition has been imagined and implemented. My project refines and extends this line of argumentation, exploring how class became a particularly important site through which to articulate a more geographically and culturally restrictive sense of Englishness over the course of the twentieth century. By situating an emerging discourse of English exceptionalism in the context of imperial disintegration, I hope to demonstrate how the idea of a provisional, relational national unity became a culturally productive, and fiercely contested, narrative during the twentieth century. New definitions of class politics—and a domestic geography of class—became vital spaces in which to imagine English national coherence.

Postcolonial immigration was the decisive occurrence and postcolonial literature an important imaginative project with which this discourse of English exceptionalism was both aligned and contested. As many scholars of postwar Britain have discussed, the idea of a restrictive English culture has been used to defend the national geography against the "invasion" of alien, nonwhite subjects.[10] Rather than focus on such reactionary efforts, which have been exhaustively treated by other scholars, I emphasize the ways that postcolonial literature has challenged the logic of cultural exclusivity by participating in, rather than rejecting, the discourse of national exceptionalism. Many immigrant narratives, instead of renouncing the idea of English culture altogether, have reformulated Englishness as a more complicated and inclusive narrative process. Recognizing and participating in an indigenous field of social difference—often glossed as the urban class system—is one of the ways that postcolonial writers have contested ethnically restrictive definitions of English culture. Postcolonial literature has been instrumental in "reviving" a national cultural scene in the postwar period; it would be impossible to analyze contemporary English literary culture without accounting for the rise of postcolonial fiction. The increasing symbolic importance of the city in the discourse of cultural distinctiveness has been at the heart of this transition, for postcolonial texts have been able to make a claim on Englishness by marking urban space as ethnically diverse. As I shall argue, both modernist and postcolonial literature have engaged in debates about national identity by drawing the boundaries of a modern cultural polity around the urban landscape.

Ethnographic studies of England's social structure, which are at the heart of this new reified Englishness, often begin by sketching the outlines of the normative family home, so Orwell's decision to represent the class system as a house is typical of its genre in many respects. During the extended period of imperial decline, and later England's immersion in global capital markets, plotting the coordinates of indigenous domestic spaces became a common trope for reconceptualizing national domestic space: the family home emerged as a popular site for rethinking the geographic boundaries of Englishness in a moment of forced self-examination. The study of domestic space allowed a range of writers to mark class difference and reposition internal hierarchies—middle-class reformers and progressive thinkers usually emphasized the dire conditions in which many working-class families were forced to live, thereby negatively positing the middle-class home as a normative social arrangement—but it also provided a metaphor for reinventing national geography in the absence of an extrinsic imperial system. Whereas the family home, both as an architectural symbol and as a social project, was something the English proposed to export to the colonies during the high period of imperialism, during the twentieth century domestic space became an imaginative geography of intrinsic Englishness, a location of cultural uniqueness entirely separate from the imperial beyond.[11] Space, broadly speaking, emerged as a crucial discursive category through which the English staged cultural peculiarity and distinctiveness. For these reasons, this book studies the literary representations of domesticity and urban space in an attempt to grapple with the cultural reformation of national geography during the previous century.

In more general terms, this paradoxical attempt to cite class difference as a marker of collective identity coincides with a heightened literary awareness of and investment in urban England. Gradually, over the course of the century, English literature draws more and more frequently upon images of the urban landscape—and less often upon rural England and depictions of country life—to mark the boundaries of national culture.[12] Although the tropes of the satanic mill and the insalubrious slum persist, twentieth-century fiction increasingly reads the city as emblematic of modern England. A wide range of literary texts use the triumphs and failures of urban life to characterize the essential conditions of national culture. Even Orwell, who spends so much of *The Road to Wigan Pier* exposing the abominable conditions in which ordinary working-class families of the industrial north are condemned to live, insists that there is something indisputably satisfying about the urbanized, working-class family:

> In a working-class home . . . you breathe a warm, decent, deeply human atmosphere which is not so easy to find elsewhere. I should say that a manual worker, if he is drawing good wages—an "if" which gets bigger and bigger—has a better chance of being happy than an "educated" man. His home life seems to fall more naturally into a sane and comely shape. I have often been struck by the peculiar easy completeness, the perfect symmetry as it were, of a working-class interior at its best. Especially on winter evenings after tea, when the

fire glows in the open range and dances mirrored in the steel fender, when Father, in shirt-sleeves, sits in the rocking chair at one side of the fire reading the racing finals, and Mother sits on the other with her sewing, and the children are happy with a pennorth of mint humbugs, and the dog lolls roasting himself on the rag mat—it is a good place to be in, provided that you can be not only in it but sufficiently *of* it to be taken for granted. (116–17)

Secure in a compact social world, immune to the neuroses, social pretensions, and material ambitions of the middle classes, the working-class family epitomizes what is right and decent about England—in other words, everything about English culture worth preserving during a period of rapid change. Orwell adduces physical proximity and familial compatibility as evidence of the "perfect symmetry" embodied in working-class domesticity. As the middle-class ethnographer, Orwell cannot help mentioning the sense of alienation with which he confronts this scene: he may find himself temporarily in this space, but he will never be "sufficiently *of* it to be taken for granted." Orwell's ontological insistence on the humble perfection of working-class domestic space underscores the paradox of modern Englishness, or what Esty calls a "second-order universalism": it is at once unique and typical, anomalous among nations but taken for granted within the cultural and geographical confines of England (191).

It is worth noting that Orwell's deeply romantic depiction of working-class domesticity is premised on the general vitality of urban life, whose bedrock is the patriarch/manual worker figure. The "easy completeness" Orwell attributes to the family home is grounded in a language of class difference, but it also depends on the infinite repeatability of the setting. As he insists, "This scene is still reduplicated in a majority of English homes"; the alienation of the middle-class ethnographer fades rapidly, replaced by a clear sense that the working-class family functions as a collective national symbol (117). The specificity of the nuclear working-class family morphs easily into the universality of English culture. This conscious invocation of working-class life in its urban environs is not ancillary to but constitutive of Orwell's attempt to mark off the particularity of Englishness. He overtly rejects images of the "classless" family and a village setting—tropes of Englishness that were very much available to him and other writers of his generation—in favor of an urbanized scene with visible class markings. Though not all the texts I consider in this book adopt Orwell's celebratory line, there is a clear trend toward representing England, and the English national character, by calling attention to the trappings of urban signs of class difference. England's class system (once a source of considerable moral and political anxiety) and its large cities (often cited as a blemish on "England's green and pleasant land") became increasingly appealing as tropes of cultural legibility and distinctiveness. This book, then, is primarily concerned with the complex relationship between class, the city, and the literary production of modern Englishness. Its overarching goal is to map the imaginative and material reordering of space in twentieth-century England.

MEMORIES OF CLASS

In *Knowledge and Class: A Marxian Critique of Political Economy*, Stephen A. Resnick and Richard Wolff almost flippantly remark, "*Class* is an adjective, not a noun" (159). Class is not a material object, they suggest, but a modifier, a way to describe relationships between things. In an equally telling allusion to the theoretical evasiveness of class, P. N. Furbank quips, "The appropriate discipline for studying 'class' is not sociology but rhetoric" (qtd. in Cannadine vii). If rhetoric is indeed the proper discipline in which to consider class politics, we might say that the study of class in twentieth-century English culture is dialectical in a discursive sense, constituted by a narrative of steady ascent and a counternarrative of rapid decline. There is a rich tradition of sociological and historical writing in Britain, dating back to the middle of the nineteenth century at least, in which class functions as a privileged analytic category. For the first wave of British New Left scholars of the 1950s— especially E. P. Thompson, Raymond Williams, and Richard Hoggart— progressive intellectual work usually began (and concluded) with the study of class relationships. In more recent times, however—since the 1970s or so—this style of political critique has been pinned back in a rather defensive position, periodically raising its voice to insist that class "still matters." A strong backlash against the preeminence of class in leftist circles began with the "second generation" of New Left scholars, including figures like Tom Nairn and Perry Anderson. This counternarrative, of course, implies that class politics is somehow in descent or retreat as a result of changing material and ideological conditions. Some advocates of this position merely assert that class was a prescriptive and overvalued term for describing a more complicated nexus of social oppression, insisting that progressive politics should be mobilized against a broader range of exclusionary practices such as racism, discrimination on the basis of gender or sexual orientation, and classism. Other participants in this debate—including some of the most ardent supporters of research on class politics—have argued that class itself, as a way to describe material conditions and ideological systems, is no longer as important as it once was, that class no longer has the explanatory potential it did at an earlier moment.

What is most surprising is not that these different camps disagree about the relative consequence of class as a theoretical category, but that both groups structure their arguments around the idea that class politics has reached a point of crisis. The position that the class system and our ways of theorizing it are in turmoil provides a shared rhetorical strategy in arguments for and against the relative merits of class-based political analysis. Although these two factions seem diametrically opposed, they share a fundamental sense that the class system, and by extension English culture as a whole, has reached an impasse. The implications of this rhetorical confrontation speak to deeper anxieties in English culture throughout the twentieth century.

The polemics around class politics, and this deepening sense of an intractable crisis, reflect a more systematic interrogation of English national culture during the period of imperial contraction. It is no accident that the most politically committed, sustained, and brilliant efforts to study England's convoluted class system, particularly its working class, were produced by the New Left thinkers of the 1950s and 1960s, precisely when the empire was disintegrating rapidly. Scholarship on the working class helped articulate an important critique of capitalism and English political history, but it also functioned as a discourse of cultural distinctiveness during a moment of national self-reflection. For progressive intellectuals, telling a story about the rise of class politics and writing ethnographies of class difference were also ways to reinvent a shared national history separate, at least in appearance, from an imperial imaginary. This particular brand of class politics was, as Orwell suggests, something intrinsically English, a system that distinguished the English from their colonies as well as from their imperialist rivals. In contrast, the backlash against this manner of reading English history and culture is supported by the suspicion, fear, or hope that English culture really sits in a parlous state, that England has in fact become the cold and unimportant island Orwell foretold at the close of its imperial chapter.

These attempts to demystify class politics or displace it from its privileged position also reflect an attempt to attack the mythology of English cultural uniqueness. As a whole, this discursive wrangling over class politics implies much more than a fight for the academic left's moral high ground: it is structured by far deeper struggles over the past and present definitions of English culture.

The three germinal texts of the British New Left—*The Uses of Literacy* (1957), by Richard Hoggart; *Culture and Society: 1780–1950* (1958), by Raymond Williams; and *The Making of the English Working Class* (1963), by E. P. Thompson—offer an unflinching commitment to and some of the most sophisticated analyses of a politics of class. Moreover, these texts display many of the strengths and limitations of postwar work on the English class system. Rather than provide a thorough retrospective of the New Left or a genealogy of contemporary progressive scholarship—or even provide extensive readings of the texts themselves—I will instead situate their attempts to establish indigenous intellectual and political traditions in the context of postwar imperial contraction. These texts should be read as part of a long intellectual movement in which class politics became a way to reframe a discourse of English cultural particularity. The movement's crystallization at this precise historical juncture makes a great deal of sense given the sinking trajectory of English imperialism. Although the work of the British New Left has been rightly criticized for its silence on questions of empire, race, and sexuality, their efforts to disentangle Englishness from a discourse of imperial rule can also be read as sympathetic to a platform of decolonization. Their investment in salvaging a distinctive form of Englishness was not the same as an interest in simply preserving it unreconstructed—it also represented an attempt to profoundly rethink the parameters of an intrinsic cultural tradition for use in a progressive political agenda.[13]

The Uses of Literacy begins with a detailed ethnography of the urban working class, and in so doing it provides a straightforward advertisement for the cultural peculiarity of the English class system. Hoggart resists narrowly Marxist or highly theoretical definitions of the working class, adroitly skipping over questions such as a person's relation to the means of production. Similarly, in an effort to counteract the "middle-class Marxist's view" of working-class life, he consciously avoids the image of the heroic indigent laborer or the self-improving political activist, the figures with which a middle-class audience would be most familiar. Instead, the book tries "to evoke the atmosphere, the quality, of their lives by describing their setting and their attitudes" (3, 5). Indeed, the first half of *The Uses of Literacy* depicts, in detail too great to convey in this space, a whole range of working-class habits, tastes, and preferences: it provides ethnographic accounts of working-class speech, domestic space, leisure activities, reading habits, religious practices, mores, and philosophies of life. In many respects, the book is an attempt to record both the fascinating complexity and the frustrating conformity of working-class culture as the author sees it. While some working-class habits provide a formidable prophylactic against the penetration of commodity capitalism, they can also lead to a stupefying, passive uniformity and resistance to progressive thought. Having grown up in a working-class family, Hoggart admits that finding the proper perspective from which to consider the problem proved a vexing question: he writes that he tends to be "unwarrantedly sharp towards those features in working-class life of which [he] disapprove[s]" and conversely overeager to celebrate those features he deems meritorious (4–5).

Like Orwell, but with much more detail and direct knowledge, Hoggart lovingly renders a sketch of working-class family life (which I discuss at greater length in chap. 4). Just beyond the home, though, Hoggart insists that the working-class neighborhood provides an ingenious, highly sophisticated support network designed to fit the particular social and material needs of its inhabitants. "To a visitor," he admits, such densely packed "proletarian areas" must seem "understandably depressing": the outsider confronts children ragged and underfed; uniform, shoddy houses crammed together; grimy pubs; flyblown corner shops; and the odor of the local gasworks. "To the insider," however, these "small worlds" are sources of inestimable comfort, "each as homogeneous and well-defined as a village." Residents know their environs and its inhabitants intimately: the shops that offer credit, the families who earn just a little more money than their neighbors, the men who are generous with their wives, the women who keep tidy homes, or the children likely to get into mischief. He marks urban space as immutably working class and ineffably English: whereas the "bosses' cars whirr away at five o'clock to converted farm houses ten miles out in the hills," the local men "stream up into their district" at the end of their shifts (38). Hoggart's description of the urban neighborhood is instructive, taking the overworked trope of the "well-defined" village community and transforming it into an urban, working-class form. The countryside, with its converted farmhouses and pretentious, bourgeois residents, now represents an ersatz Englishness.

Only the industrial, working-class districts are inhabited by people fully integrated with and representative of their environment.

The book's ethnographic sections are not merely an attempt to locate cultural value in working-class social practices but also a way to consider the argument that postwar prosperity—the wide availability and affordability of mass consumer products—has irreversibly changed the attitudes and habits of working-class people. What struck Hoggart most during his research was not the extent to which "fifty years of popular papers and cinema" had affected working-class habits, but the degree to which his subjects had remained relatively unaffected by such changes (13). Despite this position, there is still a fear, in both the argument and the form of the book, that working-class life was in fact experiencing a radical transformation, that *The Uses of Literacy* represents a desperate effort to validate and preserve a way of life at the moment of its extinction. The second half of the book examines these new, quite alarming cultural trends: the commercialization (and attenuation) of indigenous cultural traditions (in song, dance, and the press), the split of working-class culture caused by increased educational opportunities for some, and widespread apathy to party politics. Newer forms of popular culture, Hoggart argues, are damaging, not because they are insufficiently highbrow, but because "they make it harder for people without an intellectual bent to become wise in their own way" (262). A "genuine class culture," undoubtedly exclusive and pernicious on its own terms, is being replaced by "a poorer kind of culture," or what he calls a "classless" society of mass communication and generalized forms of leisure (265–66). The problem is not that working-class people now have access to a better standard of living, but that such changes encourage the working class "to lose, culturally, much that was valuable and to gain less than their new situation should have allowed" (4).

There is a great deal to be said about this argument and its attempts to debunk the facile attractions of commodity culture. For better or worse, it has set the paradigm for much work in cultural studies, which is always ready to critique capitalism and frequently surveys working-class practices for examples of resistance. For the purposes of this project, however, what interests me most is Hoggart's coupling of working-class ethnography, in which he sketches the complexity and uniqueness of working-class practices, and the sense that working-class culture faces a dramatic crisis. Even as the text narrates the richness of working-class social structures, Hoggart shows a persistent fear that they are on the verge of rapid dissolution. Given the chance, working-class life presents a viable, indigenous discourse of national vigor. *The Uses of Literacy* provides a highly differentiated map of domestic space, repeatedly emphasizing the uniqueness and persistence of working-class traditions in the face of increasing outside pressures. Although Hoggart recognizes the divisiveness of a class-bound society, he is reluctant to relinquish this idea of cultural distinctiveness, preferring instead to turn it into a kind of communal heritage.

If *The Uses of Literacy* offers an ethnographic treasure trove of English peculiarity, replete with celebrations of national ingenuity and moments of deep self-doubt, *Culture and Society* provides its analogue in the sphere of high culture, presenting a fairly comprehensive intellectual history of nineteenth- and twentieth-century England. Like Hoggart, Williams myopically focuses on English traditions to the exclusion of other cultures. In the introduction to a later edition of the book, Williams defends his decision to concentrate solely on indigenous writers, though he agrees that the book must be read "alongside those other traditions, which bear, sometimes in common ways, sometimes with quite different approaches, on the same themes." Nevertheless, he remained sure, some twenty-five years after its initial publication, that *Culture and Society* "could only be formed, in its particular method, around this particular experience and tradition." The reason for this restrictive genealogy, he argues, is that the "new social and cultural relationships" he describes in the book "were part of that historically decisive transition" we now call the Industrial Revolution. This process of change, in its novelty, intensity, comprehensiveness, and permanence, had affected England more deeply than other nations (x–xi). These strands of English exceptionalism may seem naive or even repressive in our contemporary intellectual climate, but such critiques miss the stakes implied by his position. *Culture and Society* is not an attempt to dismiss the effects of other cultures on England or to ignore the contributions of non-English subjects to national institutions. Instead, the book tries to reclaim a few progressive elements from an essentially oppressive, hierarchical culture. Although the book includes essays on several conservative or even reactionary thinkers, Williams makes a concerted effort to recuperate some latent progressive thread in their work. This project must have seemed quite urgent at the time, for Williams repeatedly draws comparisons between the crises of the Industrial Revolution and the postwar, cold war moment. Above all, *Culture and Society* is an attempt to fashion a truly corporate culture, a culture that proceeds on the basis of common access to cultural materials and participation in the political process. Like Hoggart's interest in recording the intricacies of working-class life, Williams's investment in the English intellectual tradition represents an effort to redraw the boundaries of national culture during a period of crisis. The book's exclusive cultural parameters should be read not only as a product of England's imperial ideology, which they certainly are in several respects, but also as a way to imagine a democratic English culture quite apart from its imperial legacy.

Of the three germinal New Left texts, *The Making of the English Working Class* offers perhaps the most thorough and spirited defense of English self-reliance, ingenuity, and cultural integrity. In place of Hoggart's ethnographic techniques or Williams's intellectual history, Thompson favors a historical approach, studying the working class at the moment of its emergence between 1780 and 1832. In contrast to *The Uses of Literacy,* it targets the activities of insurgent working-class militants, examining evidence of class consciousness as it was expressed "in traditions, value-systems, ideas, and institutional forms" (10). With the explicit aim of emphasizing working-class agency rather than passivity, Thompson argues throughout that the working class "was present at its own making," an active participant in the historical evolution of class as an ever-changing set of social relationships (9). The book affirms the value of working-class institutions, citing their indigenous, egalitarian traditions as a resource from which contemporary political activists can draw sustenance. Although he acknowledges that the working class was sharply divided at different times, and also that it gained cohesion by pitting its interests "against their rulers and employers," Thompson argues that working-class culture represents a shared collective history (11). Class may be the exclusive property of those who make and remake it, but Thompson's project also attempts to turn that particular history into common intellectual property. Because the working class suffered repression in so many ways, "their institutions acquired a peculiar toughness and resilience." The class system as a whole, he argues, "acquired a peculiar resonance in English life: everything, from their schools to their shops, their chapels to their amusements, was turned into a battle-ground of class" (831–32). To borrow a phrase from *Culture and Society,* class is, for Thompson, a "whole way of life," a system that inundates English culture with the values, ideas, and social forms of a class society.

This pressing need to assert English exceptionalism, and the desire to read class in the mundane institutions of daily life, not only reflect a progressive assertion of the importance of class politics but also function as a way to reframe the whole discourse of Englishness. Rather than fall back on the stock images of English life, many of which were thoroughly enmeshed in and blind to a politics of class hierarchy and imperialism, these New Left thinkers tried to turn class into an inherent national attribute, even a shared resource out of which an indigenous cultural narrative could be fashioned. Of course, the idea of class difference was still able to convey a sense of rank, privilege, and authority, or conversely, subjection, oppression, and indigence, as well as militancy and political awareness. But at the hands of these theorists, it was also becoming a system through which the English were able to mark the political and social boundaries of a corporate, indigenous culture distinct, in theory, from English imperialism.[14] This language of impending, intractable crisis, which New Left texts reiterate at an astounding rate, also should be read in the context of a pressing question: how would England define itself as a postimperial nation? It is possible to render a cynical judgment of their efforts by pointing out their collective reluctance to consider the problems of race and imperialism, but I think we can also read their attempts a little more sympathetically as genuine efforts to rehabilitate a sense of national coherence that would not dwell on imperialist symbols.[15]

The backlash against this style of reading class was in many ways prefigured by these writers themselves. In the work of Hoggart and Williams in particular, there is an intense anxiety that the working class, as it has been known, is rapidly disappearing, or that its habits, ways of thinking, and modes of existence are being inexorably transformed by modern society, especially commodity capitalism. *The Uses of Literacy* is deeply pessimistic about mass publications that, to Hoggart's mind, seek to create a "culturally classless society" through immersion in a vapid popular culture. Williams, too, wrote *Culture and Society* in order to draw comparisons between different periods of rapid change and transition, namely the Industrial Revolution and the "post-1945 crisis of belief and affiliation" (xii). Williams fears that working-class culture, which he glosses as innately collective and democratic, may be losing out to bourgeois culture, whose outstanding attributes are individualism, inequity, and downright selfishness (328–29). By the early 1960s, many leftists strongly suspected that welfare state reforms, which had all but banished the most deleterious effects of poverty, were eroding the political intransigence and vitiating the cultural distinctiveness of the working class. Clumsy terms like "embourgeoisiement" and "deproletarianisation" were widely adopted to describe the improved material conditions enjoyed by even the poorest strata of society during the moment of postwar prosperity.[16] The popular myth of the "affluent worker," used to confirm working-class contentment and complicity, gained ever-wider currency, supported by an unprecedented rise in the standard of living for most working-class families.[17]

The concern that class differences were being attenuated by working-class affluence and the dominance of commodity culture allows us to historicize modern English literature in fundamentally new ways. As Michael McKeon argues in *The Origins of the English Novel, 1600–1740*, the form of the English novel during the eighteenth century was determined by its ability to mediate social flux. The tensions embedded in the development of commercial culture were prime concerns of early English fiction: "The social significance of the English novel at the time of its origins lies in its ability to mediate—to represent as well as contain—the revolutionary clash between status and class orientations and the attendant crisis of status inconsistency" (173–74). In the eighteenth century, England's landed classes were anxious that the infiltration of their ranks by social inferiors, like merchants, was diluting the sense of status to which they felt entitled. In the twentieth century, however, a far different class dynamic comes into play. The narrative of working-class affluence cannot be explained by the idea that the middle classes were anxious about infiltration from below. Rather, the fear is that the working classes themselves, and England as a whole, lose something distinctive yet intangible when class differences disappear.[18] Although the coordinates of this collective narrative were outlined most clearly by the first generation of New Left scholars, it is my contention that this way of representing class politics had been adopted by a wide range of cultural workers during the twentieth century. By the middle of the century, it became possible to see the existence of class difference as a way not only to imagine an intraclass collective identity but also to rethink national peculiarity against the threat, and later the actuality, of imperial contraction. The complexity and cultural richness of the class system allowed the English to posit an intrinsic cultural coherence just as the extrinsic geography of empire was made unavailable (or repudiated) as a symbol of national unity and greatness.

The position that the importance of class was declining, as both a material reality and a basis for collective political action, already appears in the early work of New Left scholars. At the hands of frustrated leftists, signs of material comfort and political apathy were used to excoriate the English working class and progressive activists in general. Most famous were the rancorous attacks launched against Thompson by Perry Anderson and Tom Nairn in the pages of *New Left Review*. In an effort to counteract Thompson's supposedly naive adoration of the working class and its traditions, they pile invective on invective against English parochialism, conservatism, and the national absence of cerebral or skeletal fortitude. Nairn, for instance, bemoans "English separateness and provincialism; English backwardness and traditionalism; English religiosity and moralistic vapouring, paltry English 'empiricism,' or the instinctive distrust of reason." [19] Not to be outdone, Anderson, in "Origins of the Present Crisis," attacks the whole of English culture, claiming that a "supine bourgeoisie produced a subordinate proletariat," resulting in a society mired in a "thick pall of simultaneous philistinism (towards ideas) and mystagogy (towards institutions), for which England has justly won an international reputation" (40, 43).

These kinds of pyrotechnics, of course, need to be situated in the wake of 1956 (after the invasion of Hungary and the 20th International, at which the Communist Party finally owned up to Stalinist atrocities), when public bloodletting had become ritual among the left. The tenor of their denunciations, however, speaks as much to the crisis of English national identity as it does to the dissolution of the Communist Party. It is apparent that Anderson and Nairn were eager to deride a toothless working-class polity, but they were perhaps more interested in the project of deriding English culture altogether: for Anderson, England has justly earned its "international reputation" for slothfulness and diffidence. If Hoggart, Williams, and Thompson are deeply invested in the relative autonomy and resilience of working-class traditions as an expression of indigenous culture, Nairn and Anderson are equally invested in claiming the *failures* of the working class and its political allies as unique embodiments of Englishness. In *Languages of Class*, Gareth Stedman Jones summarizes, a little too neatly, the New Left project as "different attempts to marry a broadly Marxist conception of the working class to what Thompson called 'the peculiarities of the English'" (7). It is important to read this articulation of cultural distinctiveness as a constitutive premise, rather than an accidental by-product, of New Left writers' work on the problem of class politics. To say that this parochial interest in the

English class system was blind to the politics of empire is true but inadequate: their work might profitably be read as an attempt to invent a set of progressive political symbols that did not rely on England's imperialist identity.

In more recent scholarship, these spectacular polemics have mutated into more benign, stark realizations that the working class has "ceased to be a vital historical force" (Dimock and Gilmore 1). Homi Bhabha states the case against scholarship on class most succinctly when he remarks that "class identity is autoreferential" in Marxist theory, obscuring and "surmounting other instances of social difference" (222). Leftists still committed to the "old" politics of class frequently blame continental theorists, such as Louis Althusser, Nicos Poulantzas, Etienne Balibar, Ernesto Laclau, and Chantal Mouffe, for replacing empirical analysis of class with the study of discourse and ideology.[20] The "crisis" is no longer whether or not the working class has the ability to defeat its antagonists. Instead, Laclau and Moffe critique the "whole conception of socialism which rests upon the ontological centrality of the working class" (2). Sketching this highly schematic genealogy of British scholarship on class demonstrates how coextensive the discourses of class and Englishness have become. The praise of working-class ingenuity goes hand in hand with such moments of bitter reproach and despair. In reading these discussions of class as evidence of a wider concern with redefining Englishness without the baggage of imperialism, I do not intend to dismiss these as serious inquiries into the nature of class itself. But it is impossible to read these debates from our current vantage point without seeing how they were embedded in a discourse of English cultural distinctiveness— for better or worse. The rise and fall of class as a critical narrative has in many ways become inextricable from a wider discourse of national particularity during a period when England was forced to abandon its identification with imperial power.

The stakes in this process become clear when scholars see class as a theoretical barrier to thinking about other pressing issues such as national identity, race, ethnicity, gender, and sexuality. By showing how the discourses of urban class politics and national exceptionalism have become so completely dependent on one another, I hope that class may once again become a productive way to enhance our understanding of other theoretical concerns. Chapters 3, 4, and 5, for instance, show how the material and imaginative staging of gender and sexuality in twentieth-century literature are supported by elaborate rituals of class difference and Englishness. Likewise, the final two chapters discuss postwar class politics in order to theorize how postcolonial literature participates in and contests the construction of national distinctiveness. Placing class at the heart of my discussion does not represent an attempt to celebrate it at the expense of other theoretical considerations, but instead to situate the cultural and aesthetic implications of urban class politics in the articulation of modern English national identity.

These agonizing exchanges between some of England's most important scholars about the relative merits of class politics illustrate how Englishness has come to be associated with a bewildering combination of endearing quirks and exasperating afflictions. While Thompson is eager to bask in the militant glow of the English working class, Nairn and Anderson are just as interested in allowing the defeats and compromises of the working class to stand for blemishes on English society as a whole. The strain of national exceptionalism I describe in this book emerges in these provocative oscillations between seemingly irreconcilable extremes. As my discussion of *The Road to Wigan Pier* suggests, writers such as Orwell regularly described Englishness as a curiously intense mixture of pride and shame in national traditions. His boasts about the resourcefulness and ingenuity of the working class appear side by side with lamentations about the pathetic state of English culture. This once-proud nation, he reminds us, teeters on the brink of political and social collapse. The sharp split in the New Left between those who want to celebrate and those who want to deemphasize the importance of the working class likewise hints at the nearly paralyzing ambivalence with which many writers approach the problem of national identity. Rueful lamentations about English culture often slide into hesitant articulations of national distinctiveness. In this respect, this bipolar discourse of national identity is clearly very different from more celebratory or defensive forms of nationalism with which it might be conflated. Raymond Williams once remarked that the English, when in doubt, imagine a pendulum.[21] Though the discourses of national exceptionalism and patriotic nationalism may occasionally draw on one another, the texts to which I turn usually describe Englishness as a bemusing conjunction of affiliation and abjection. In *The Satanic Verses,* Rushdie even uses this ambivalent form of Englishness to protest against more virulent, exclusionary brands of aggressively patriotic nationalism he identifies in the "New Right" discourse of the 1980s. For the most part, the writers I consider in this book describe Englishness as an occasionally delightful, sometimes embarrassing, usually frustrating condition to which they are inescapably confined.

Apart from their importance as testaments to indigenous cultural institutions, the foundational texts of the British New Left also tell us something striking about class politics as a system of representation. In their efforts to establish the inherent value of working-class cultural forms, these texts articulate a distinct tension between the material and immaterial qualities of class politics. They depict, in some detail, the material conditions in, against, and through which working-class agents make themselves as individual subjects and enter into larger collectives. The primary determinant of class difference is, after all, one's position in an economic system. But these texts also demonstrate how the parameters of class can be rethought as shared cultural heritage. Moreover, the desire to see both political and cultural value in the structures of working-class life is itself an ideological move, directed primarily against the long tradition of reading the working class as a site of cultural impoverishment. This aspect of class politics, though clearly related to material circumstances, constitutes a field of intangible or ideological activity. The function of belief or affect, though potentially having an impact on the material conditions and actual choices of individual agents and groups, is not material in itself: it does not describe the historical or economic relationships in which people are engaged. The way these theorists represent class politics in England, then, involves a complex negotiation between class as a material reality and class as a way to galvanize disparate political agents. In short, the idea of class is useful precisely because it is mobile and polyvalent: at different times, class appears under the guise of a social narrative, an ideology, an imaginative fiction, a concrete social reality, a marker of difference, a sign of solidarity, a language of conflict, or a discourse of cooperation and commonality. This kind of flexibility and ambiguity in the application of class as a theoretical concept can be both productive and troublesome, allowing us to explore the complexity and unpredictability of the political field.

This book uses a heterogeneous collection of cultural texts to situate the deployment of class in twentieth-century English fiction. I draw on Althusser's description of the social field as constituted by the interaction between three distinct but interrelated modes: the real, the imaginary, and the symbolic (categories he borrows from Jacques Lacan). The real denotes the existence of material or economic relations. Such "determinate conditions" constitute a reality so complex as to be functionally indecipherable and inaccessible in their immediacy.[22] It is only through the symbolic order—language, signs, discourse, syntax—that we can describe or represent our material existence. Symbolic representations, however, are never politically neutral or entirely free from ideological considerations. The imaginary is the term Althusser develops to capture these intangible, affective, or ideological conditions—the way in which we represent and have the world represented to us. Althusser famously describes ideology as "a 'Representation' of the Imaginary Relationship of Individuals to their Real Conditions of Existence"; in other words, ideology is a representational system that mediates the relationship between the individual and the world ("Ideology" 162). An ideological apparatus, as we might guess, is an institution that teaches us how to behave in a manner consistent with a set of ideological premises, which then become our own ideological convictions—structures such as the family, religious institutions, or schools. In this sense, the "imaginary" has no less "reality" than the category of the real—in fact, Althusser argues that ideology "always exists in an apparatus, and its practice, or practices. This existence is material" (166). To borrow a term from Raymond Williams, the imaginary is the "structure of feeling"[23] whereby individual subjects position themselves in the social world, or the affective systems through which we understand our many social functions—commitments to family, God, education, law, political reform, and the like.

As this short discussion illustrates, the narrative of class difference in twentieth-century English culture has both real and imaginary components. It purports, especially in its histories and ethnographies, to document the real, material conditions of the modern class system. But these discourses of class are similarly shaped by the articulation of ideological predispositions. The statement that the class war is over, just like the argument that working-class culture represents a repository of cultural distinctiveness, is supported by inherently ideological assumptions. The most sophisticated analyses of class, in fact, are those that do not shy away from these kinds of questions but instead make transparent their ideological positions and incorporate them into a coherent argumentative frame.

It is in symbolic systems that we can perceive most readily the tension between class as a set of material circumstances and class as an ideological or affective structure. The symbolic order both stages and attempts to resolve the radical discontinuity of class as a function of determinate conditions and class as a way to theorize political consciousness. I read aesthetic objects and other cultural texts as discursive sites through which the tension between the real and the imaginary finds articulation. Fiction does not simply reflect this tension but actively engages in the management, production, and even resolution of such symbolic contingencies. This is another way of saying, in Peter Hitchcock's words, that "the class content of the working class [or any class] is not identical with its representation," or that the articulation of class in the symbolic order is necessarily problematic.[24] Class is relational in a social sense (the class system being directly involved in the production of social difference) and in a symbolic sense (the discursive articulation of class always negotiates the multivalent operations of class politics in both the real and the imaginary modes). To this end, I agree with Terry Eagleton and Pierre Macherey when they argue that the literary text, "far from constituting some unified plentitude of meaning, bears inscribed within it the marks of certain determinate absences which twist its various significations into conflict and contradiction."[25] This observation on textual indeterminacy, which now approximates a standard critical practice in our postdeconstruction moment, has a special bearing on the way I understand the utility of class politics in the process of interpreting aesthetic objects. I read the novel as a discursive field of operation whose parameters are determined by the specific interactions between the real and imaginary modes. The textual object is a symbolic articulation of this tension, or an attempt to represent, manage, and even resolve this particular set of contradictions.

My interest in asking class to perform this type of critical work does not indicate a desire to read individual texts as simple conveyances of "bourgeois" ideology or working-class values, reducing textual complexities to mere symptoms of ideological apparatuses or material conditions. Instead, it reflects an attempt to both theorize the symbolic richness of class and also consider the strong connection between the discourse of English particularity and the cultural significance of class politics. Even when the problem of class sparks the interest of literary critics, it is far too often treated as if its aesthetic rendering were a self-evident process, as if the aesthetic distillation of class were the same as the thing itself.[26] Even if social class were a relatively straightforward historical reality, literary critics would still require some kind of theoretical apparatus to consider how class becomes operational in its narrative or conceptual condition. But class, of course, is not straightforward at all, and my eagerness to complicate our understanding of its symbolic function is indicative of my interest in treating it as a site of rhetorical contest. In England during the past century or so, this type of discursive jousting, as it were, has been waged primarily through the language of national identity. The usefulness of class as an attribute of national uniqueness is predicated on its capacity to productively negotiate the difficulties embedded in its rhetorical deployment. If this manner of reading cultural texts strikes the reader as too restrictive—I realize that the novel, for instance, is much more than a vehicle for imagining political subjectivity and articulating the distinctiveness of the English at a particular historical moment—I hope the book as a whole will make clear how urgent these projects seemed to cultural workers in twentieth-century England.

MAPPING CULTURE

With the rise of "globalization" as a shorthand term for the political and material reorganization of transnational economic flows and the academic study of that process, the present moment is not, perhaps, the most auspicious time to embark on the study of national space. The political sovereignty, legal authority, and spatial integrity of the nation-state, we are told, have been compromised by the expansion of international systems of control and regulation.[27] The cultural boundaries of the nation, likewise, have become quite permeable under the regime of "empire." Metaphors such as "flows," "networks," and "deterritorialization," which rely on disembedded, delocalized theories of geographic relationships and political structures, now feature prominently in most inquires into the nature of globalization. This has resulted in an acute "crisis of cognitive mapping"[28] in our theoretical apparatus, in which our critical vocabulary for considering geography and spatial relationships is in the midst of a radical renovation.

In contrast, this book concentrates on specific geographic zones and spatial practices in twentieth-century England. I examine how literary texts use whole cities, individual neighborhoods, public areas, and private spaces to articulate a form of national distinctiveness through a unique class system. Additionally, I focus on the ways in which architects, urban planners, developers, and politicians have themselves engaged and influenced this project. However, my inclination to read local spatial practices as sites through which the nation has been lived and imaginatively produced is not an attempt to retreat into the theoretical or practical comfort of the local, to imagine "the local" as hermetically sealed from the unfolding of more expansive geographic processes. In other words, I want to move the discussion beyond the familiar coordinates of "space vs. place," "global vs. local," or "public vs. private."[29] Rather, ever-widening circuits of international exchange produce new kinds of, and often intensify, local *cultural* differences. Economic and political globalization has proceeded cheek by jowl with an alarming rise in the expression of national, regional, and ethnic cultural difference, often accompanied by stunning violence and brutality. Even as the state is losing political and juridical authority, the nation—especially in countries where the nation-state once provided coherent legal and cultural boundaries—has been partially disaggregated from the state and become even more important, and more expressive, as a cultural object. Regional and subregional difference, or what in the context of England I have called cultural exceptionalism, has not been eradicated by the emergence of transnational space but instead has been reenergized and deployed as a tactical response to globalization. Typically, it is highly specific, relatively bounded locations through which larger social and political bodies—such as the nation—can be mobilized most effectively. My readings, which concentrate on individual geographic sites and spatial practices, are an attempt to show how local spaces, and the cultural attributes with which they are endowed, are embedded in and produced by a global set of relationships filtered through a national consciousness.

In the case of England, a long history of overseas exploration, conquest, and subsequent geographic retraction has determined a national investment in a discourse of local particularity. In *Out of Place: Englishness, Empire, and the Locations of Identity,* for instance, Ian Baucom contends that "from the time that the British Empire was little more than a hypothesis, the concepts of Britishness and Englishness have existed only in some or other relation to imperialism, generally in dual relation of affirmation and denial" (40). As I have argued in this introductory chapter, the threat, and later the actuality, of imperial decline during the past century forced the English to overhaul this set of national symbols, moving swiftly from the concept of an extensive British authority to an intensive national exceptionalism. This process, moreover, resulted in a radical material and ideological transformation of the English landscape, a rethinking of not only national symbols but domestic space itself. In the absence of an imperial expanse, the English turned inward, confronting the loss of colonial sovereignty by renovating an indigenous geography. When imperialism could no longer guarantee material security, military self-confidence, or political stability, domestic space became the site through which the nation staged its cultural distinctiveness and attempted to manage its social contradictions.

One of the most surprising consequences of this transition was the emergence of the city as an important location in the discourse of intrinsic cultural forms. Although nineteenth-century writers, especially those in the Romantic tradition, frequently use the pastoral mode to plot the geographical coordinates of English culture, twentieth-century novelists increasingly began turning to urban settings to rethink the boundaries of an indigenous cultural polity. Because of its strong material and ideological links to imperialism, the pastoral idyll became more and more unworkable, especially in highbrow literature, as a setting through which to explore contemporary (rather than historical) cultural particularity. During the postwar period, moreover, some of the most important claims on and critiques of English peculiarity were made by postcolonial immigrants, who settled primarily in urban areas. The project of "tropicalizing" metropolitan cities, as *The Satanic Verses* claims to do, is as invested in the cultural distinctiveness of English space—London, in this instance—as its literary antecedents. The novel's aim of deconstructing England's nationalist propaganda during the 1980s relies on its insistence that London is uniquely and unequivocally multicultural. The ability of the city to act as a symbolic location of modern national uniqueness represents a subtle but noticeable cultural shift, reflecting not only the fact that "[t]he country and the city are changing historical realities," as Williams reminds us in *The Country and the City*, but also the changing relationship between national and imperial space (289).

This book concentrates on three broad historical phases in order to explore the relationship between domestic social geography and a waning empire. Chapters 2 and 3 place turn-of-the-century land reform debates in the context of two conflicts of imperialist aggression—the Boer War and World War I—and a growing sense of imperial crisis. Early twentieth-century campaigns to alleviate urban blight and reduce extreme poverty grew out of late Victorian moral crusades, but several military defeats at the start of the South African War (1899–1902) gave their cause particular urgency. Fearing the collapse of empire, advocates for land reform argued that England's continued stability would depend on its ability to reduce or even eradicate domestic inequities. The second broad historical period is the three decades following World War II, characterized by the domestic establishment of the welfare state, the rapid dissolution of empire, and the first waves of large-scale immigration from the former colonies. Welfare state reforms—which included a systemic reconstruction of urban areas—were based on an elaborate system of economic, political, and social planning designed to increase national self-sufficiency. This emphasis on rehabilitating domestic space should be viewed through the wider lens of imperial contraction, which encouraged the English to reconsider the potential of national geography and domestic culture. The third historical period, roughly commencing with the 1980s, can be characterized by England's immersion in an emerging global economy and its abandonment of the welfare state model. The Thatcher administration rapidly dismantled the basic institutions of the welfare state in order to facilitate England's participation in international financial markets. London in particular has been able to prosper in the global marketplace precisely because it could successfully sell itself as a unique cultural center and an ideal location for the financial industry. Taken as a whole, this historical trajectory traces the different incarnations of modern English cultural exceptionalism and describes its continuing relevance during this current phase of global exchange.

Chapter 2 situates the changing generic parameters of late pastoral fiction in the context of land reform discourse during the early part of the century, connecting the decline of the country-house novel with imperial crises and domestic class conflict. Whereas earlier versions of the country-house novel turned an essentialized version of rural England into a portable cultural object—something to export to the colonies as a form of linguistic and moral instruction—these later examples of pastoral fiction are far less convinced of England's political viability and moral imperative. E. M. Forster's *Howards End* (1910) and Evelyn Waugh's *Brideshead Revisited* (1944) systematically expose the fragility of the pastoral conceit, instead using the country-house form to rethink English cultural geography in the absence of an extrinsic colonial space. Rather than projecting cultural uniformity and political stability, both novels call attention to the presence of domestic strife in an attempt to perform a kind of national "salvage work."[30] No longer secure in

England's imperial position, these estate novels fasten their gaze on domestic problems as a way to imagine long-term cultural coherence.

Chapter 3 combines an examination of London's imperialist architecture, especially in its public parks, with a reading of the spatial and aesthetic politics of Virginia Woolf's *Mrs. Dalloway* (1925). This chapter draws connections between the novel's attack on English imperialist ideology and its commitment to modernist narrative strategies. By making a series of direct and indirect pleasures available to working-class, metropolitan men in particular—pleasures such as sports, sexual fantasies, and entertaining spectacles like parades and exhibitions—London's public spaces actively encouraged men to imagine themselves as vicarious participants in the imperial project. The novel is an explicit attempt to critique England's pernicious class system and its commitment to an imperialist agenda. The novel's stream-of-consciousness narrative, which manufactures symbolic connections (rather than direct social bonds) between its large cast of characters, depends on the compact physical geography and social diversity of London's public space to effect its critique of the urban class system. But the text's self-conscious technical experimentation should also be read as an attempt to "domesticate" modernist aesthetic difficulty. Through its use of aesthetic experimentation as a means of interrogating England's class system and its commitment to imperialism, the novel effectively anglicizes avant-garde principles, translating the demand for aesthetic novelty into the political lexicon of the English.

The next chapter turns to the 1950s and the cultural politics of the welfare state. Through readings of John Osborne's *Look Back in Anger* (1956) and Alan Sillitoe's *Saturday Night and Sunday Morning* (1958), I demonstrate how the texts of the Angry Young Men refashion the conventions of domestic narrative—historically gendered feminine—to articulate a specifically masculine style of class anger. The chapter situates their adaptation of domestic literary forms by examining material and cultural shifts during the high period of the welfare state, relating postwar urban planning strategies and actual domestic architecture to the popular narrative of working-class affluence. I read the rhetorical display of masculine affect as the complex negotiation of an unstable gender position—in which both exaggerated heterosexuality and the domestic responsibilities implied by marriage and a family are highly esteemed—and the continuing existence of undiminished class anger under conditions of material prosperity. Furthermore, these texts demonstrate how quotidian spatial practices—such as those performed in the family home—inform the discursive staging of masculinity and political dissent within the material and ideological circumstances of the welfare state. This unusual combination of relative material security and increasing class consciousness, made possible by the postwar economic boom and the welfare state political consensus, manifests the potential contradiction between class as a reflection of material conditions and class as an ideological tool. Materially, we might say, Angry protagonists eagerly participate in welfare-state prosperity; affectively, they are anxious that economic improvements may have come at the cost of more systematic political reform.

The fifth chapter, on *The Golden Notebook* (1962), reads Doris Lessing's novel as a nascent postcolonial, feminist satire of Angry domestic fiction. Rather than use the domestic form to consolidate an excessively masculine version of indigenous class politics, the novel subverts the trope of cultural domesticity, turning narratives of English exceptionalism against themselves. Working with the formal conventions of ethnographic writing on the working class practiced by writers such as Orwell and Hoggart, the novel interprets domestic space—both real and metaphorical—as the site of a destructive, disabling peculiarity. Reversing the spatial and temporal ordering of imperialist texts like *Heart of Darkness,* the narrative imagines the English home as the epicenter of mental illness and the emerging representational crisis we now call postmodernism. By exploding this domestic trope, novels such as *The Golden Notebook* demonstrate that narratives of English cultural distinctiveness, even when they can be disengaged from elitist and imperialist politics, still rely on a whole set of exclusionary ideological assumptions. Lessing turns such narratives of English exceptionalism into admissions of crippling parochialism.

In the final chapter, I turn to *The Satanic Verses* (1988), one of the most celebrated texts of the postcolonial corpus, to assess the compatibility of postcolonial theory and recent scholarship on globalization. The 1980s offer a particularly fruitful moment to consider this problem: the historical conjunction of London's emergence as a global city and the revival of jingoistic nationalism during this period show how narratives of British patriotism and English cultural distinctiveness, whose symbols often draw freely on an imperialist past, appear in an emerging transnational politics of space. For its part, Salman Rushdie's novel uses a narrative of international travel to resist the rising tide of nationalist rhetoric in England. To escape from the nightmare of immigration—marked by metropolitan racism, discrimination, and poverty—the novel offers a narrative of intercontinental travel, proposing a "globalized" political subjectivity as an antidote to the ills of the postcolonial condition. The text's frame of international mobility, however, relies on and reproduces the conflicts between international capital and labor. Its deployment of physical mobility as a trope through which the protagonist can fulfill his quest for intellectual and spiritual renewal depends on a problematic mobility of class and culture. It is the task of postcolonial theory to adapt to this emerging geographic system and the responsibility of globalization theory to critique these new ways of imagining political subjectivity.

As these chapter synopses suggest, English fiction increasingly, though not exclusively, glosses national space as the global city of London. If fin de siècle London was an object of national suspicion and resentment,[31] contemporary fiction tends to represent London through tropes of social diversity and cultural competition—by implication, a space worth fighting for. Postcolonial fiction, with its investment in "colonizing" England, often journeys to the symbolic heart of metropolitan space. Texts such as *The Lonely Londoners* (1956), Sam Selvon's novel about postwar West Indian immigrants, show that arrival at and familiarity with London rank among the foremost "pleasures of exile," to use George Lamming's phrase. Sir Galahad, one of the novel's main characters, recaptures the sense of exhilaration from his maiden voyage every time he sees London's sights:

> Always, from the first time he went there to see Eros and the lights, that circus [Piccadilly Circus] have a magnet for him, that circus represent life, that circus is the beginning and the ending of the world. Every time he go there, he have the same feeling like when he see it the first night, drink coca-cola, any time is guinness time, bovril and the fireworks, a million flashing lights, gay laughter, the wide doors of theatres, the huge posters, everready batteries, rich people going into tall hotels, people going to the theatre, people sitting and standing and walking and talking and laughing and buses and cars and Galahad Esquire, in all this, standing there in the big city, in London. Oh Lord. (90)

Despite the endemic racism and poverty Galahad and his fellow immigrants confront in the metropole, London's sheer magnetism proves irresistible. Life in the capital represents modern existence: for Galahad, at least, its teeming energy represents "the beginning and ending of the world." The city's dominance as the symbolic head of national culture becomes something of a paradox. London simultaneously stands in for the body of the country, yet it retains a special distinctiveness of its own.[32] At once synonymous with England and unique, its service as an international flag bearer of Englishness distinguishes it from the rest of the nation. Selvon's choice of title is tactical: the novel's characters are very much Londoners, whether or not their fellow metropolitans accept them as such. And London's uniqueness is very much a postcolonial condition, for its ability to serve as a site of modern Englishness depends on its social diversity and cultural heterogeneity. Galahad's blackness and relative indigence are as integral to metropolitan space as the whiteness and wealth of his fellow pleasure seekers in Piccadilly Circus.

This emphasis on London implies many of the tensions I hope to set in motion during the ensuing discussions. At different times, the three most common meanings of metropolitan—urban space, imperial capital, and cultural center—work with and against one another. In somewhat different contexts, both Williams and Esty use the term "metropolitan perception" to allude to the specific collocation of forces at work in the European centers of imperial power, which were also the centers of modernist culture: home vs. world, national vs. imperial, center vs. periphery, domestic vs. cosmopolitan, and, for my purposes, class as social difference vs. class as cultural attribute.[33] London is uniquely English and manifestly cosmopolitan, the center of an expansive imperial—and later global—as well as a more restrictive national space. Although Williams and Esty confine their discussions of metropolitan perception to the modernist period for the most part, this book discusses how postcolonial writing represents, and is determined by, this engagement with metropolitan space. While modernist literature represents and critiques London as a primarily imperial incarnation of the urban environment, postcolonial novels, I argue, participate in the project of imagining London as a postimperial city. Postcolonial literature's investment in London, moreover, allows the city to retain, and perhaps consolidate, its position as locus of global cultural production even as it loses its dominant slot in an imperial hierarchy. In other words, London's position as a center of global cultural production is not strictly a form of political/economic neoimperialism: the incorporation of anticolonial texts and intellectuals into the cultural mix helped London cement its position as a global city.[34] If London was the space in which the English celebrated their imperial dominance, as I discuss in chapter 3, it was also the city through which they came to understand themselves, at least in cultural terms, as a postimperial nation.

Postcolonial literature's investment in both London and English national identity speaks to the deeper ironies of the process I am describing. London, once the administrative and financial center of a vast empire, becomes the location through which postcolonial writers participate in, even predominate, the discourse of English cultural exceptionalism. By tracing an aesthetic investment in urban space, particularly London, throughout the twentieth century, I read modernist and "metropolitan-postcolonial" literature as part of the same literary and historical trajectory. Modernist interest in the city, exemplified by *Mrs. Dalloway*'s depiction of London, made the urban environment more widely available as a language of English national identity. Postcolonial texts, including *The Lonely Londoners, The Golden Notebook,* and *The Satanic Verses,* freely incorporate and revise the urban aesthetics of their modernist predecessors. Without ignoring the important differences between modernist and postcolonial writing, it makes a good deal of sense to read these two literary moments as contiguous, not diametrically opposed to one another. London plays an understandably pivotal role in this narrative.

In this respect, the plural form of "cities" in my title is slightly misleading. The symbolic construction of Englishness as an intricate, mysterious urban class system has been accomplished primarily through depictions of greater London, both modernist and postcolonial. But I rely on the plural form to indicate the variegated social dimensions of urban space itself. Each of the texts I examine in this study foregrounds the existence of class difference by depicting contrasting modes of inhabiting and traveling through the urban environment. *Mrs. Dalloway*'s innovative aesthetics, for instance, are enabled by the social diversity, prospect of relative anonymity, and compact physical geography of London. Similarly, when *The Satanic Verses* reworks the conventions of travel narrative, it does so in response to the changing class conditions implied by the heightened global movement of people and commodities. Both novels are willing to argue over the political and cultural maps of local, national, and even global spaces. They treat social geography, in other words, as plastic, as something that can be made and remade by its consumers. To the extent that literary texts offer creative orderings of geographic relationships, every narrative has a stake in the social vocabulary of space.

Retrospectively, we can read the twentieth century as an extended period of intensive aesthetic experimentation, a process enabled, in part, by the changing material and cultural geography of domestic space.

In consequence, this book reads space as a means of cultural production.[35] Redrawing the geographic and cultural boundaries of the nation has been an important theme in twentieth-century English literature. To the degree to which these texts are committed to articulating an indigenous cultural particularity, they are also transforming specific geographic spaces into scenes of cultural production. I read technologies of space as more than disciplinary apparatuses,[36] modes of producing gender,[37] ways of organizing systems of production,[38] or methods of securing colonial hegemony.[39] Although they can and do perform all these functions, spatial technologies—particularly ways of imagining and using specific geographic sites—can also "produce," or be actively involved in the production of, cultural objects. Precisely because forms of spatial organization express power, or because space is a site of contestation, the act of plotting itself positions people and objects in spatial relationships with symbolic effect.[40] If most contemporary geographers now read space as "an ever-shifting social geometry of power and signification," we should remember that narratives about space are important sites of signification themselves (Massey 3). Nowhere has this been more apparent than in England and Britain, where the national and cultural boundaries—and the imagery used to configure them—have expanded and contracted so dramatically in the last century or so. The steady transition from an extrinsic imperialist geography to an intrinsic discourse of national distinctiveness has been accomplished *by* cultural objects but also *through* the class politics of urban space. As the following chapters show, geographic sites as diverse as the country house, the public park, the metropolitan home, and immigrant neighborhoods have all been implicated in debates about the nature of modern Englishness. The attempt to narrate a cultural form of Englishness, in short, is also an attempt to rethink the nation's material, geographic boundaries. Of course, urban space—and the class politics used to define it—were not the only discursive sites through which a form of modern Englishness was articulated. But taken together, I believe they provide a productive way to situate the aesthetic conditions of twentieth-century cultural exceptionalism.

2. BROKEN FENCES
FORSTER, WAUGH, AND THE GARDEN CITIES

A cursory survey of nineteenth-century fiction indicates that few English writers were willing to represent the urban class system as a site of national cohesion. Read selectively, the novels of Charles Dickens, Elizabeth Gaskell, William Makepeace Thackeray, and Thomas Hardy, for instance, imply that the cultural and political differences arising from the class system and industrialism may ultimately threaten the long-term stability of the nation. In *Sybil; or, The Two Nations* (1845), to take the most pointed example, Benjamin Disraeli describes a society in which the rich and poor form two distinct cultural and political entities, "between whom there is no intercourse and no sympathy; who are as ignorant of each other's habits, thoughts, and feelings, as if they were dwellers in different zones, or inhabitants of different planets; who are formed by a different breeding, are fed by a different food, are ordered by different manners, and are not governed by the same laws" (67). The list of writers who thought the urban class system an intractable obstacle to cultural unity and political peace could be extended indefinitely if we were to include other genres: a group as diverse as Thomas Carlyle, John Ruskin, Matthew Arnold, Friedrich Engels, Cecil Rhodes, Henry Mayhew, William Morris, and William Booth (of the Salvation Army) all argued, at different moments and for quite different reasons, that class divisions, and the urban-industrial conditions that perpetuated divergent class interests, were bound to unhinge the nation sooner or later.

Victorian fears about class antagonisms and a debilitating urban environment routinely cited England's northern industrial districts as the concrete result of unchecked economic development. By the turn of the century, however, London had largely replaced the industrial north as the locus of urban anxieties. Less industrial in character—but, it is interesting to note, far more imperial in its orientation—London's sheer size and penchant for growth outpaced the ability of reformers and ideologues to come to grips with its manifest social conflicts. Distinguishing between the cause of the disease and its symptoms, though, was no simple task. While many commentators blamed the poor themselves, describing them as a moral and even genetic liability to the nation, more progressive reformers insisted that the conditions of life in urban districts were the cause of the malaise. A profusion of quasi-scientific studies at the turn of the century purported to disentangle causes from effects: armchair sociologists constructed elaborate maps that coded neighborhoods by economic means; amateur ethnographers scrutinized working-class families for conformity with, or deviance from, middle-class standards; phrenologists, eugenicists, and other proponents of scientific racism measured cranial capacity of the poor to quantify biological degeneracy and predilection for criminality; and journalists, fueling the moral panic, dutifully reported the results of such dubious research. Nearly everyone, regardless of political orientation, agreed that London and its teeming poor constituted a potential threat to national security.[1]

A series of humiliating defeats at the start of the Boer War (1899–1902) led to growing speculation that England was no longer capable of producing healthy, intelligent, and responsible soldiers. In Manchester, an astounding eight out of eleven army recruits were turned away after failing the basic physical examination, and the figures from London's poor areas did not lag far behind.[2] The fact that Britain's highly professionalized forces were being pushed to the limit by a disorganized, underfunded militia prompted many to forecast the imminent end of empire. Urban, working-class districts, the breeding grounds from which the majority of soldiers were drawn, became a suspect source of manpower. But these concerns over army recruitment were part of broader conversations about the social health of the urban working class.[3] In part, public debates about the urban environment were also a way to argue about the importance of imperialism. To take one of the most famous examples, even the title of *The Heart of the Empire: Discussions of Problems of Modern City Life in England. With an Essay on Imperialism* (1901), Charles Masterman's documentary on London's slum districts, makes obvious the relationship between the urban class system and imperialism. Masterman describes second-generation Londoners as "a characteristic *physical* type of town dweller: stunted, narrow-chested, easily wearied; yet voluble, excitable, with little ballast, stamina, or endurance," characteristics leading inexorably to "almost universal decay."[4] The challenge of colonial governance necessitated a healthy, disciplined working class in England. Discussions about urban poverty, irrespective of the political orientation of the participants, were framed by an acute awareness of imperialism and its effect on England's class politics.

Fin-de-siècle literary representations of London also helped clarify the direct connection between urban poverty and the possibility of imperial retraction. Capitalizing on the popularity of adventure stories, a wide variety of late Victorian writers turned the slums of London's East End into a domestic colony, stocked with exotic creatures and alien, hostile races. As Joseph McLaughlin demonstrates in *Writing the Urban Jungle: Reading Empire in London from Doyle to Eliot,* writers such as Arthur Conan Doyle, Margaret Harkness, Arthur Morrison, and Jack London applied the narrative template of imperial romance and ethnographic travel writing to the heart of metropolitan space, thick with intrepid explorers and hostile natives. *The Secret Agent* (1907), by Joseph Conrad, represents the culmination of this metropolitan decay minigenre. Ostensibly a story about anarchists in London, the novel goes out of its way to satirize political dissidents for their patent inefficacy. Conrad's anarchists are not the lean, hungry ideologues we might expect, but instead a pack of lazy, grossly corpulent, exceptionally harmless misfits. As more than one reader has noticed, nearly all the anarchists, and even the counterinsurgents who spy on them, are physically deformed by obesity or other maladies—"marred," in the narrator's mocking words, "by too much flesh" (101). More than anything else, such revolutionaries, "the enemies of discipline and fatigue mostly" (57), are the product of bad breeding, the visible signs of physical and racial deterioration in urban areas. As McLaughlin and James English point out, *The Secret Agent* is less concerned with tangible signs of political unrest—its misshapen anarchists never commit any acts of violence—than with social anarchy and cultural disintegration. English in particular underscores the connection between Conrad's consistent, viscerally comic deployment of physical debility and popular understandings of racial deterioration exemplified by the city, especially London, the bloated imperial command center.[5] But it is worth reiterating that the crisis of urban fitness was informed by more general conversations about England's imperial future. Rot at the heart of empire, most agreed, would spread quickly to the colonial extremities.

In this chapter and the next, I situate two strains of modernist literature—first, the estate novels of E. M. Forster and Evelyn Waugh, and next, the urban, high modernist novel, represented by *Mrs. Dalloway*—in the context of debates sparked by turn-of-the-century anxieties about racial deterioration, city dwellers, and the persistence of class inequity. Some reacted to this sense of crisis by calling for a renovation of urban space itself: more green space, where the poor could exercise and recuperate, and more architectural testaments to England's military accomplishments, which would generate enthusiasm for the imperial project and encourage England's most physically fit subjects to volunteer themselves for duty abroad. As I discuss in the next chapter, London's monumental district—the region bracketed by Whitehall, Buckingham Palace, Hyde Park, and Regent's Park—was a kind of imperial playground at the metropolitan core, conceived as a space in which the English could both display their puissance and train men for potential service.

My immediate concern, however, is with the more radical land reform platforms launched at the turn of the century. Horrified by the conditions in slums and galled by unbounded suburban expansion in the southeast, reformers such as Ebenezer Howard and his followers demanded rationally planned, democratically governed, socially just "Garden Cities" to be built throughout the countryside. Garden Cities, Howard insisted, would combine the best features of urban and country living: high wages, cultural events, and social diversity from the city, with low rents, clean air, and green space from village life. His plans called for a network of urban nodes, agriculturally self-sufficient and industrially integrated in the national economy, to be constructed in depressed rural areas. Garden Cities would offer the poverty-stricken a chance to escape urban slums while simultaneously braking the unplanned suburbs then sprouting throughout the southeast. Only coherent planning strategies, Howard insisted, could restore balance and equity to England's domestic space.

This desire to mitigate or resolve the social conflicts embedded in the urban class system should be read alongside impassioned discussions about England's future as an imperial power. The Garden City movement was an explicit attempt to reconsider the geographic class conditions necessary for political harmony—and hence domestic security—at a moment of imperial uncertainty. Howard's emphasis on self-reliance, in other words, was an early effort to imagine England as a *postimperial* nation. When it became clear that imperial expansion, which had long functioned as a political and social safety valve, was unduly taxing the country's resources, reformers such as Howard argued that careful husbanding of domestic assets could ensure political and social stability as the nation turned away from expansionist policies.[6] His vision for resolving class conflict and urban poverty also functioned as a plan for domestic stability during a phase of speculative imperial retreat.

We can discern in the country-house novels of Forster and Waugh a special attention to this discourse of land reform and metropolitan class tensions. Plans for geographic reform gave such novels a social vocabulary with which to assess the vibrancy of national culture. The plot of *Howards End* (1910), for instance, offers a remarkable piece of social engineering, in which representatives of the landed gentry, the industrial bourgeoisie, middle-class liberals, and the urban, lower-middle class all compromise to fashion a new, more socially just future in the countryside. Such forms of cooperation, the novel suggests, are the only legitimate response to England's many social contradictions. *Brideshead Revisited: The Sacred and Profane Memories of Captain Charles Ryder* (1944), though far more pessimistic about the future of England—and the future of the country-house novel—likewise emphasizes the threat of class war. In the words of its narrator, Charles Ryder, the novel is the "last . . . of its kind, the last of a splendid series" (179). The novel marks the accomplishments and mourns the passing of the rural aristocracy "at the moment of [its] extinction" (226–27). Class insurgents, we are led to believe, have usurped control of the country estate, and, by proxy, the nation. In this respect, both novels adapt the country-house genre to openly question the viability of narrowly pastoral solutions to England's present dilemmas. If, as Raymond Williams argues so persuasively in *The Country and the City,* country-house literature tends to obfuscate social conflicts by relying on the trope of bucolic harmony, the novels of Forster and Waugh represent a noteworthy development. Both texts foreground the presence of class anger, offering counternarratives to the myth of harmonious village life. While Forster is invested in proposing a progressive solution to England's urban-imperial crises, Waugh is eager to claim the bankruptcy of national culture as a way to satirize plans for reform.

Because the discourse of land reform made explicit the material and imaginative connections between domestic geography and imperialist ideology, estate novels even vaguely aware of contemporary politics could no longer rely on the fiction of a singular, hermetically sealed

English culture centered in the countryside. If earlier examples of pastoral literature sought to particularize "Little England" as a way to consolidate the nation's unique place at the head of the imperial system, this latest generation of country-house novels is less secure about England's position and more ambivalent about its moral imperative. By articulating both the uniqueness and the pedagogical portability of English culture, the pastoral helped consolidate the intrinsic value of domestic culture in the context of the nation's geographical expansion. The rise of the country-house novel, roughly coincident with the rise of an overseas empire, allowed England to narrate its particularity within the hierarchy of imperial relationships—an essential Englishness was clearest in rustic life—while simultaneously promulgating the universality of England's moral condition. In other words, the pastoral device was not only a means of self-representation but also an educational export to the colonies, where it could serve as a textbook of English values. It helped the English represent themselves as culturally distinct from and yet politically bound to the rest of the empire.[7]

Written during a period when imperial designs and domestic stability were threatened by conflicts both local and global, it makes sense that novels such as *Howards End* and *Brideshead Revisited* attempt to seriously rethink the conventions of the genre. Neither text places much faith in the moral security of the ruling classes—these novels make it clear that the stability of the rural order was illusory—and I set this political hesitancy in the context of increasing trepidation over the country's imperial agenda. These texts use the country-house genre to redraw the spatial coordinates and cultural signposts of a postimperial England before the material collapse of empire. With the nation's imperial future in doubt, these novels turn inward to perform a cultural inventory; if England could no longer rely on its empire to mitigate class conflict or consolidate a national identity, it would have to resolve political differences at home to ensure future political stability. The liberal, reformist Forster, as we shall see, is far more enthusiastic about dismantling class differences than Waugh, who depicts Englishness as threatened by vanishing social distinctions. In part, these texts emphasize the existence of class differences to articulate new versions of cultural exceptionalism. Whereas Forster sees the abolition of class privilege as a way to ensure a healthy, active old age for the postimperial nation, Waugh sees the same prospect as a fitting death sentence for a national body already in the advanced stages of decay. More than just a stereotypical symbol of

English culture, which had become inescapably yoked to the country's imperial identity, the class system, ironically, was becoming one of the most salient reminders of national unity. Both Forster and Waugh cite class difference as a distinctive marker of English peculiarity, setting the English apart from their European competitors as well as the imperial beyond.

METROPOLITAN DEGENERACY AND THE IMPERIAL FANTASTIC

There have been dozens of scholarly books and articles, many published in the last fifteen years, offering historical accounts of Ebenezer Howard and the Garden City Association, England's most well known land reform advocates in the twentieth century. Given the emergence of postcolonial studies, what is most surprising in these accounts is their near-total obliviousness to how imperialism influenced land reform proposals in Britain.[8] I mention this critical lacuna for two reasons. First, it is important to understand that turn-of-the-century political reformers campaigned to alleviate the plight of the urban poor. Although this platform grew out of Victorian poverty relief efforts and other radical political agendas, the project acquired a sense of urgency when England confronted the prospect of military defeat in the colonies. Second, the new class of geographic experts—architects, land surveyors, and urban planners—whose ranks swelled during the early part of the century, were at the center of a growing professional network spread across the breadth of the empire.[9] Architects and planners, starved of commissions at home, often gained experience or built their portfolios by apprenticing and practicing in the colonies before returning to England. As Edward Said has pointed out, cartography and spatial discipline have always been at the heart of colonial domination: "Geography was essentially the material underpinning for knowledge about the Orient. All latent and unchanging characteristics of the Orient stood upon, were rooted in, its geography" (*Orientalism* 216). This busy professional traffic between metropole and colonies should not be overlooked when we historicize debates about domestic land reform.

While the geographic sciences were an essential component of imperialist endeavors, they also enabled the English to internalize a fairly complex vocabulary of domestic racial difference during the Victorian period. By the middle of the nineteenth century, it was already becoming common to describe the urban poor, especially in London, as a deficient, alien race.[10] With the advent of ethnographic techniques and the popularization of social Darwinism, the English had developed an extensive social imaginary of race that they could apply to their own working class (Masterman, for instance, repeatedly refers to all urban dwellers—not only the working class—as a new, degenerate race). The most unsympathetic observers faulted the poor themselves for their pitiable state, citing everything from moral turpitude and biological inferiority to sheer indolence as reasons for their descent into squalor. The reformist elements of the middle class, meanwhile, typically pointed to environmental factors, blaming the insalubrious conditions of urban slums for the physical and moral deterioration of the working class. No one in a position of authority, however, questioned the fundamental premise that the urban poor constituted a cancerous, foreign body in the heart of the metropole. As Richard Soloway points out, the "uninspiring performance" of the military in South Africa only confirmed suspicions of racial degeneracy, provoking "a veritable orgy of criticism, enquiry and analysis focusing on the alarming possibility that the race was somehow decaying" (137).[11] A gaggle of physicians, scientists, churchmen, journalists, and ethnographers scrambled to quantify, both in words and statistics, the extent of the crisis in the years leading up to the Great War. Widespread concern over the condition of the urban poor mobilized a whole series of related anxieties about the alienating effects of modern city life and the threat of violent class conflict, as well as the moral integrity and political efficacy of imperialism.

Although this crisis of fitness was informed by deeper fears about class, race, and imperial decline, the discourse of degeneracy also made a series of vicarious pleasures available to the English by documenting the proximity of foreign dangers so close to home. As McLaughlin notes, hearty explorers such as Sherlock Holmes were able to traverse the inscrutable, hostile landscape of the city, protecting the indigenous population from the "invasion of 'foreign substances' into individual and national bodies" (20). Similarly, reformers such as William Booth, founder of the Salvation Army, refashioned travel literature and ethnography to narrate their "adventures" among the "savage" urban poor. *In Darkest England and the Way Out,* Booth's account of his time in the East End, uses Henry Stanley's extraordinarily popular *In Darkest Africa* as a literary model for his domestic narrative crusade. The trope of explicitly racialized heroism in these texts depends on the ability to exaggerate the menace of urban slums and to skillfully manage, even master, such alien terrain. Just as these texts rely on and exacerbate popular anxieties about racial deterioration, they also market themselves by encouraging imaginative participation in the thrills of exploration and conquest.

Writings such as these stage, perhaps by unconscious association, the material and ideological connection between imperialism and a domestic geography of class. If anthropologists once studied remote indigenous groups in order to confirm the gap between the imperial and colonized subject, urban slum narratives reenact this difference on domestic terms, reducing the geographic and cultural distance between the observer and subject. Urban ethnographies were becoming, by the turn of the century, a way to narrate the intricacies, ironies, and fantasy life of urban culture. As Judith Walkowitz demonstrates in her remarkable study of the "Ripper" phenomenon, sensationalistic accounts of East End prostitution and flophouses in Victorian newspapers permitted middle-class readers to assert their difference from working-class city dwellers. But the mass popularity of these stories can also be read as a consolidation of the national imaginary around an urban class fantasy, one that paradoxically narrates a story of cultural particularity even as it emphasizes social dissimilarity. Such urban ethnographies both mark the presence of unassimilated class difference and provide a discursive site that allowed the English to develop a complex, highly differentiated language of cultural distinctiveness.

IMPERIALISM AND THE COUNTRY BEAUTIFUL

Although most reformers agreed that the security of the nation was threatened by the immediate prospect of racial degeneration and urban anarchy, opinions varied when it came to fashioning solutions. Architects, as opposed to urban planners and other radical reformers, tended to support more conservative and less coordinated plans for change. In general, they favored construction projects of a more celebratory and instructional sort. Individual buildings and monuments in public places (such as parks and squares) would beautify the urban environment and inspire racial and national pride, as well as teach practical moral lessons. Jealous of the broad vistas and imperial grandeur of such cities as Paris, Brussels, and Vienna, the architectural establishment campaigned to emulate these continental models. Throughout the early part of the century, leading publications such as *The Builder, Journal of the Royal*

Institute of British Architects, and *Architectural Review* endorsed plans to redevelop central London as an "Imperial Quarter" (see Metcalf). All the most famous commissions of this period, such as the redesign of the Strand, the reconstruction of the Bank of England, the Victoria Memorial, and Aston Webb's plan for a rebuilt Mall (not completed),[12] paid tribute to England's imperial position. As the costs associated with maintaining a vast empire became more apparent in the early part of the century, architects at home sought to resolve this tension by reimagining metropolitan space in more explicitly imperial terms.[13] In my next chapter, I take a closer look at London's imperial districts through the narrative eyes of *Mrs. Dalloway* and *The Lonely Londoners.*

The same group of builders and designers who were the leading advocates of an imperial architecture were also deeply committed, in both an architectural and an ideological sense, to the English "country beautiful" movement. Architects such as Edwin Lutyens and Herbert Baker were modifying the principles of the country house to consolidate British political superiority in India and South Africa while simultaneously designing stately residences in England's Home Counties.[14] During the period when Lutyens oversaw construction of the Viceroy's House in New Delhi, he continued to draw plans for country homes in England. These connections were not mere historical coincidences: as Anthony King demonstrates in his study of the bungalow, architects were employing colonial housing styles (and imperial profits) to rejuvenate the countryside ideal in southeast England.[15]

I am suggesting that there were strong material, aesthetic, and ideological connections between Britain's imperial project and the articulation of domestic pastoralism. Professional architects were actively contributing to imperial rule through government building projects in the colonies as well as designing a more impressive, imperial metropolitan center. The same architects and their patrons were aggressively marketing the country-house ideal. Throughout his long career, Lutyens was the darling of *Country Life,* a journal dedicated to faux ruralism. There was no contradiction between Lutyens's role as an imperial architect and as a spokesperson for pastoral values. It is hardly coincidental that this movement gathered momentum at this precise historical juncture: persistent affirmations of country living were directly linked to a growing sense of imperial crisis.[16] Just as Lutyens's work in Delhi represented an attempt to legitimate and naturalize British rule in India, his commitment to pastoral architecture was a way to proclaim the greatness of an England embodied in its country homes.

THE SOCIABLE CITY

The most vocal agitators for radical land reform agreed that inhospitable cities were to blame for the national crisis, but they were less invested in preserving the countryside than in using it to help eradicate class-based exploitation. Howard and his followers at the Garden Cities Association continually squabbled with the Royal Institute of British Architects (RIBA), a group largely committed to both an imperial London and the country beautiful. Howard, in contrast, had little enthusiasm for patriotism and empire and no patience with RIBA's brand of elitism. Instead, he argued that the abundance of inexpensive rural land should be used to build clean, efficient, socially just cities. This debate between rural preservationists (who also tended to be staunch defenders of empire) and land reformers informs the ideological conflicts staged in such country-house novels as *Howards End* and *Brideshead Revisited*.

Howard's theories about the composition of cities were important for two reasons. First, he was one of the earliest thinkers to argue that space is a product of social forces and should be fashioned to accommodate human needs. He recognized that the built environment does not mirror a natural order but instead reflects political choices and arrangements. At the turn of the century, long before the creation of social geography as an academic discipline, he argued that the social division of labor is articulated in and reproduced by the geographic separation of the country and the city. Howard's thinking moved beyond the rigid geographic determinism that preceded him and helped initiate the modern discourse of urban planning. His basic arguments form the foundation of modern spatial theory and are essential for any politically sophisticated understanding of social geography in capitalist societies. Second, Howard's plans were also part of an early effort to imagine England as a postimperial nation, a fact totally ignored by current accounts of urban planning. No longer assured of the relatively peaceful dispersal of surplus people and capital through the imperial system, the English were beginning to turn inward, concentrating on self-sufficiency and national ingenuity. In a slightly different context, Jed Esty calls this project "salvage work," a concerted effort to recover the cultural identity of a nation on the brink of imperial dissolution ("National Objects"). Unable to rely on

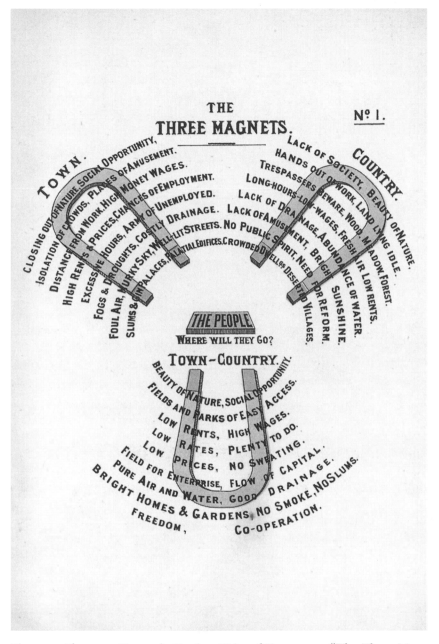

Figure 1. Ebenezer Howard, *Garden Cities of To-morrow,* "The Three Magnets." Howard argued that carefully planned Garden Cities could combine the best features of urban and county life. (From Ebenezer Howard, *To-morrow: A Peaceful Path to Real Reform,* 1898; repr., London: Routledge, 2003)

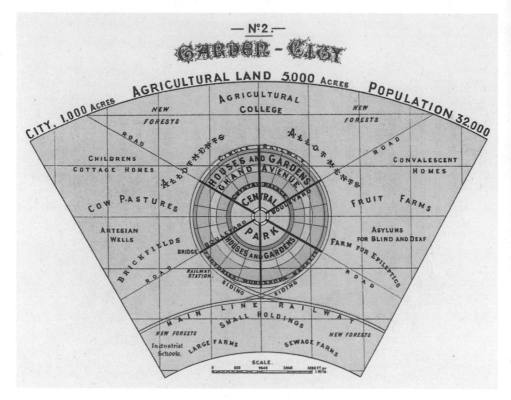

Figure 2. Ebenezer Howard, *Garden Cities of To-morrow,* "Garden City Diagram." Howard hoped to limit the expansion of Garden Cities by providing inviolable "green belts" around each town cluster. (From Ebenezer Howard, *To-morrow: A Peaceful Path to Real Reform,* 1898; repr., London: Routledge, 2003)

imperial dominance for a sense of political security or cultural superiority, groups such as the Garden City Association (later the Town and Country Planning Association) began to redraw the boundaries of Englishness within a more limited geographic field.

Turn-of-the-century urban planning functioned as a site for rethinking the physical and metaphorical boundaries of indigenous culture, blending a language of self-sufficiency with an emphasis on domestic space. Although Howard found the socialist icons Robert Owen and William Morris very compelling, he did not support a naive return-to-the-land scheme or any attempts to recapture an edenic, mythical "Merrie England."[17] Instead, he insisted that town and country *"must*

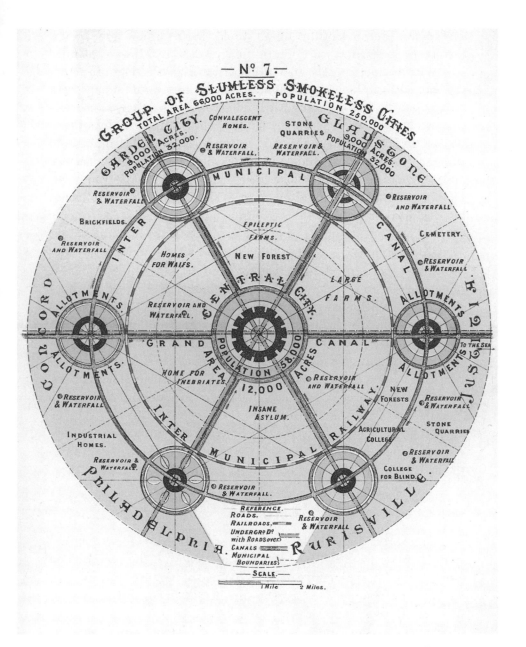

Figure 3. Ebenezer Howard, *Garden Cities of To-morrow,* "Group of Slumless, Smokeless Cities." Howard envisioned Garden Cities as interconnected nodes, each self-sufficient but commercially integrated in circuits of regional exchange. (From Ebenezer Howard, *To-morrow: A Peaceful Path to Real Reform,* 1898; repr., London: Routledge, 2003)

be married," and out of this union would "spring a new hope, a new life, a new civilization" (48). From the crowded city Howard planned to extract its chief appeals: an active social world, varied leisure activities, and relatively high wages. Similarly, the country would supply green space, clean air, and low rents. Most importantly, all land would be held in trust: individuals owned shares in the venture, but the idea of land ownership (and speculation) would be eliminated. Profits from rises in property value or increased productivity would revert to the collective, and stakeholders could liquidate their shares at any time. Strongly influenced by anarchist philosophers Peter Kropotkin and Elisée Reclus, Howard was committed to the abolition of privately held land, hoping that Garden Cities could achieve this ambitious goal without recourse to violent revolution. Howard's ideas were not widely applied until after World War II, when extensive damage from the Blitz and the collapse of empire offered an opportunity to renovate national space. Without the colonies to help manage or displace domestic political problems, reformers such as Howard were convinced that England's national health depended on the resolution of class conflict. His rejection of pastoralism should be read as an unwillingness to accept either England's dependence on an imperialist ideology or domestic social hierarchies. Forster, like Howard, believed passionately in the need to address class inequity. *Howards End,* written in the early part of the century, also repudiates the countryside ideal by underscoring the potential for national land reform, reconsidering the values of the countryside and the nation once domestic class conflict could no longer be dispersed into colonial space.

WHERE HOWARD MEETS HIS END

In a complex reading of *Howards End,* Fredric Jameson argues that Forster's poetics—his quasi-modernist style—relies on the premise that "imperialism" has something definitively "bad or negative" about it, that it should not be understood as a "positive achievement and an enlargement of our sensorium" except when it is transformed into aesthetic objects. For Forster, and for the modernists at large, imperialism is a troubling blind spot that haunts their project, though most cannot or will not acknowledge it directly, preferring instead to turn empire into a poetic process. The problem of imperialism, in other words, emerges as formal or stylistic innovation. In Forster's case, Jameson reads modernist poetics as an attempt to resolve the representational problems presented by an economic system in which the distance between metropolitan consumption and colonial production becomes unfathomable. Against imperialism, Jameson argues, Forster turns to "the national daily life" of England, achieving a kind of "self-subsisting totality" by transforming "chance contacts, coincidence, the contingent and random encounters between isolated subjects, into a utopian glimpse of achieved community" ("Modernism and Imperialism" 58).

I, too, want to emphasize how Forster orchestrates these chance encounters to fabricate an "achieved [national] community" in *Howards End*. Unlike Jameson, however, I do not read the novel's utopian ending—which, incidentally, resembles many features of the Garden City—as an attempt to romanticize the pastoral, insisting on a return to some lost or vanishing rural order. It does not, in other words, merely assert the primacy of a knowable place (the countryside) or a knowable community against the problem of modern "flux," represented by London and the unpalatable imperialism with which it is associated in the novel. Instead, the narrative uses the conventions of the pastoral to resolve domestic class conflict in an effort to rethink English national culture as distinct from the imperial project. Rather than use the great-house aesthetic as a way to consolidate the political and moral connection between England's countryside and its imperial identity, Forster commissions the country-estate genre to confront internecine fighting and restore England's political health.

As Lionel Trilling pointed out many years ago, reading *Howards End* as "a novel about England's future" depends on the knowledge that "it is a story of class war" (88).[18] The narrative brings together a diverse set of characters in competition for the small estate after which the novel is named. Early in the story, the aristocratic Mrs. Wilcox, whose family has owned the farm for generations, dies. This sets the plot in motion, with representatives of antagonistic class interests all making claims on the homestead. Ruth Wilcox informally bequeaths the property to Margaret Schlegel, a family friend and a member of the enlightened middle class. Henry Wilcox, the ruthless, uncouth, bourgeois widower, sets out to cheat Margaret Schlegel out of this inheritance, but ends up marrying her instead. Even Leonard Bast, a murky character of ambiguous class origins, has a say in the future of Howards End through a series of unlikely plot twists. In essence, the narrative resolution offers a complicated piece of social engineering in which the preservation of national integrity is effected through class compromise and land reform. The novel suggests that the future of the countryside, and indeed the nation, will only be secured through radical political restructuring of national space. Though Forster may have been attracted to the aesthetics of the pastoral, his novel also concedes that its continued relevance will depend on its ability to reorganize the nation's geographic and political boundaries.

If we read *Howards End* selectively, we could easily argue that it merely recycles some of the more conservative tropes of country-house writing, serving up a coherent national space in order to stave off the unpleasantness and unfathomability of urban poverty and imperialism. Like others before him, Forster appears to sentimentalize a lost England by revealing the countryside at its most peaceful. In passages such as the one below, he does little to disguise the fondness he feels for England's few remaining peaceful, rural enclaves:

> If one wanted to show a foreigner England, perhaps the wisest course would be to take him to the final section of the Purbeck hills, and stand him on their summit, a few miles to the east of Corfe. Then system after system of our island would roll together under his feet. Beneath him is the valley of the Frome, and all the wild lands that come tossing down from Dorchester, black and gold, to mirror their gorse in the expanses of Poole. The valley of the Stour is beyond, unaccountable stream, dirty at Blandford, pure at Wimborne—the Stour, sliding out of fat fields, to marry the Avon . . . invisible, but far to the north the trained eye may see Clearbury Ring that guards it, and the imagination may leap beyond that onto Salisbury Plain itself, and beyond the Plain to all the glorious downs of central England. . . . The reason fails, like a wave on the Swanage beach; the imagination swells, spreads and deepens, until it becomes geographic and encircles England. (152–53)

Forster foregrounds the uniqueness of England in the opening sentence by asking us to imagine ourselves as foreigners. The particularity of English culture is mirrored by the singularity of its island geography. Seemingly untouched by human labor or industrialism, "system after system" of edenic beauty encircle the country. Rivers, lakes, valleys, plains, downs, forests, and beaches lie before the mind's eye until nature confounds reason. The apprehension of this splendor spatializes our imagination, and our faculties must become "geographic" in order to comprehend

England and its cultural boundaries. The essence of the country—the individual features of the countryside slide easily into a general impression of the nation—is contained by Forster's invocation of a unified geographic system. This spatial conceit borrows heavily from the pastoral literary tradition and underscores the genre's ability to naturalize an entire cultural order.

As it stands, these kinds of passages are consistent with country-house novels that seek to locate an essentialized sense of Englishness in the nation's natural landscape. Sequences such as this place the novel squarely in the pastoral tradition and suggest that it is a fairly conservative addition to the canon. But if we continue to read, and read a little more closely, Forster includes some newer, less predictable phrases in this section. The following quotation fills in the second set of ellipses from the last excerpt:

> . . . and beyond the Plain to all the glorious downs of central England. Nor is suburbia absent. Bournemouth's ignoble coast cowers to the right, heralding the pine trees that mean, for all their beauty, red houses, and the Stock Exchange, and extend to the gates of London itself. So tremendous is the City's trail! . . . How many ships, railways, and roads! What incredible variety of men working beneath that lucent sky to what final end! The reason fails. . . . (152–53)

In this image of the national geography, neither suburbia nor the city is absent. Though these spaces may not contain the elemental beauty of central England's "glorious downs," neither is the city reduced to the figure of the satanic mill or filthy slum. Forster includes England's ships, railways, and roads among his list of geographic treasures, writing urban, suburban, and rural areas into the same economic and geographic system. These passages, like the novel as a whole, are deeply invested in national cartography, but I want to emphasize the diversity of this vision. If the novel depicts a crisis in English culture, it is not the threat posed by an expanding urban geography or declining imperial fortunes: cities and industry are part of the country's national capital and are tributes to its ingenuity. In one of the novel's many authorial asides, Forster even suggests that the literary "cult" of the countryside may have run its course: "To speak against London is no longer fashionable. The earth as an artistic cult has had its day, and the literature of the near future will probably ignore the country and seek inspiration from the town" (105).

Survival does not depend on the victory of the country over the city; as the plot implies, national stability requires the successful reconciliation of competing class interests and geographic realities.

While the novel politely refuses to romanticize the countryside in service of a reactionary political agenda, it adamantly rejects the innate value of the country house as a symbol of national cultural unity. Despite the superficial charms of Howards End, the novel makes it clear that the country-beautiful ideal was an unworkable solution to England's many political problems.[19] Forster implies, for example, that the countryside has fallen into disrepair. As Henry Wilcox, who vacates Howards End immediately after Ruth's death, explains to Margaret, the house

> is impossibly small. Endless drawbacks. . . . Well, Howards End is one of those converted farms. They don't really do, spend what you will on them. We messed away with a garage all among the wych-elm roots, and last year we enclosed a bit of the meadow and attempted a rockery. . . . You remember, or your sister will remember, the farm with those abominable guinea-fowls, and the hedge that the old woman never would cut properly, so that it all went thin at the bottom. And, inside the house, the beams—and the staircase through a door— picturesque enough, but not a place to live in. . . . And the position wasn't right either. The neighborhood's getting suburban. (127)

For all practical purposes, the house has little value in its present condition. It is a relic. An exasperated Wilcox tries to rent out the premises but finds no permanent tenants. For a good part of the novel, the house serves as a warehouse for the possessions of the homeless Schlegel sisters—hardly the romantic seat of an aristocratic family and highly suggestive of the family's lack of enthusiasm for the countryside in the Home Counties, which, as Henry mentions, is being rapidly converted into undifferentiated suburbia.[20] Later in the novel, after her marriage to Henry, even Margaret admits, "His objections to the house were plain as daylight now" (182). This is not to suggest that the novel abandons the cultural utility of the country house as a metaphor for a larger social project, but that its status as a mere symbol is no longer plausible as a representation of continuity. Instead, the novel opens up the figure of the country house to ongoing critique: rather than serve as a marker of stasis or unreconstructed tradition, it becomes a site of active social struggle and political negotiation. The house and its grounds are more than just a symbol of England's mythical past—they represent a contested present and a possible future, resuscitating the symbolic value of the country-house narrative to rearticulate a unique domestic culture in the face of social and political turmoil.

Despite this subtle change of attitude, Forster nevertheless reserves a special kind of nostalgia for the countryside. Although the novel openly acknowledges the impracticality of return to some lost rural order, the pastoral idyll still expresses a longing for cohesion; "only connect," the novel's oft-quoted epigraph, anticipates such a reading (21). Ruth Wilcox, whose family once owned Howards End, is the narrative's only extant link to this halcyon past. When we first meet her, it is as if her very being rises organically from the landscape: "She seemed to belong not to the young people and their motor, but to the house, and to the tree that overshadowed it" (36). The novel makes it clear that she has "only one passion in life—her house" (88), but it also suggests that her ability to act as a guarantor of cultural continuity is thwarted by modern social conflict. Although the early pages of *Howards End* depict Ruth Wilcox as a revered, beneficent symbol of national unity, her premature demise also suggests that this moment has passed with her. Her death plunges this rural order into chaos: she inexplicably wills the property to Margaret Schlegel, more acquaintance than close friend. This thrusts Margaret to the center of the narrative, opening the door for Henry's deception (he conceals his wife's codicil) and his later marriage to Margaret, eventually leading to the story's denouement. The passing of Ruth Wilcox turns the estate—and, by proxy, the future of England—into a bone of contention.

The novel's highly schematic plot, then, focuses on the disposition of the country house, and by implication the nation. Each character competes for the estate in the name of different class interests. HenryWilcox, the rapacious and unapologetic capitalist who "steals" Howards End from his future wife, clearly symbolizes England's wealthy bourgeoisie, who have financial clout but lack cultural sophistication and a social conscience. If Ruth Wilcox stands for a dying aristocratic order, the Schlegel sisters, Margaret and Helen, represent England's liberal, cultured, urban upper-middle class. Though far from politically outspoken, the pair have a reformist liberal philosophy; they understand the basic implications of England's imperialist aggression and class divisions, and they espouse a more enlightened, progressive political philosophy. They take a special interest in Leonard Bast, an autodidactic clerk whom they meet by chance. The novel implies that the sisters have the position, knowledge, and desire to reconcile competing political interests, acting as mediators between the ingenious but exasperating Wilcox and the impecunious Bast. Their politics rely on a sense of fairness, so important to the middle class during this period, while their idealism gives them the necessary wisdom and perspective to recognize the extent of the national predicament, symbolized by the struggle for Howards End.[21] If anything threatens Howards End, it is the class antagonism between interests represented by people like Wilcox and Bast. Unlike many earlier versions of the estate novel, in which the preservation of the countryside, and hence the nation, depends on maintaining the hegemony of the ruling classes and preserving the legitimacy of inheritance, *Howards End* offers a cross-class reconciliation of a decidedly modern sort. The text suggests that the continuing relevance of the country manor will depend not on its power to mobilize the myth of social stability and cultural unity but instead on its ability to actively resolve contemporary political crises. Forster's greatest insight, however, is not his reliance on a broadly reformist political philosophy, but his desire to connect the problem of urban blight with the logistics of imperialism. As the novel's depiction of the Wilcox family demonstrates, Britain's imperialist ambitions had a direct effect on the political geography of England.

THE COLONIAL SPIRIT

Through the figure of Henry Wilcox, the novel explores the strong material and ideological connections between the countryside ideal and England's imperial project. Forster suggests that men such as Wilcox have come to replace England's historical ruling classes, repeatedly emphasizing the political and geographical implications of their ascendancy. In "Origins of the Present Crisis," Perry Anderson argues that England's bourgeoisie never confronted the aristocracy as it did in other feudal societies. The "bourgeois revolution" in Britain was "the most mediated, and least pure . . . of any major European country" (28). For the most part, industrial and financial capitalists merely insinuated themselves into the remnants of a more traditional gentry. They did not accomplish this transformation without conflict or social cost to both classes, but by the turn of the twentieth century this "new" coalition of dominant classes was effectively running the nation. *Howards End* explores the confrontations between capitalists like Wilcox; a dying aristocracy, symbolized by his first wife; and the cultured, idealistic middle classes.

The Wilcox family represents this semirusticated capitalist class almost perfectly, dramatizing the social and geographic upheavals that accompanied their rise to power. Helen, Margaret's younger sister, holds no illusions about the family or the principles on which they stand. There is a palpable sense of indignation in her voice as she describes a typical breakfast at Howards End: "Mr Wilcox reading the *Times* . . . Charles was talking to [his brother] about Stocks and Shares." This scene quickly dispels her misconceptions about the family's pretensions toward the life of the country gentry, leading her to the temporary conclusion that "the whole Wilcox family was a fraud, just a wall of newspapers and motor-cars and golf-clubs" (39). Unlike the gentry who preceded them, the family has no substantive economic or historical ties to specific locations. As Judith Weissman observes, they "travel around England buying and selling houses with new ease and abandon," coming and going as it suits them (434). Later in the novel, as the family acquires yet more properties, Helen sarcastically remarks that "the Wilcoxes collect houses as [a child] collects tadpoles" (155). To her great disappointment, Margaret learns shortly after her marriage that Henry has no intention of living at Howards End. The narrator, by way of explanation, offers Margaret this bit of advice: "But the Wilcoxes have no part in the place, nor in any place. It is not their names that recur in the parish register. It is not their ghosts that sigh among the alders at evening. They have swept into the valley and swept out of it, leaving a little dust and a little money behind" (218). The sooner she realizes that she has married into a nomadic family, the sooner she will be able to adjust to her new life. Social and physical mobility define their lifestyle. They think nothing of having a wedding in Wales and traveling by car back to London the following morning (remember, this is the early 1900s). After her marriage, Margaret complains that Henry refuses to decide on a permanent residence (226). Their power and sense of social status come from their ability to manipulate, traverse, and reconstruct the environment in pursuit of leisure and money.

As Andrew Thacker argues in *Moving through Modernity: Space and Geography in Modernism,* the pivotal role of the automobile in the novel captures most succinctly the relationship between the Wilcoxes' social position and their imperialist attitude toward space.[22] When Margaret first spends time with Ruth Wilcox, Henry and his daughter, Evie, are traveling throughout the northern countryside by car. At this time, the automobile was strictly a luxury item, yet the Wilcoxes already own several and keep a chauffeur on hand, using their cars frequently and recklessly. Margaret calls it "the colonial spirit." No one in the family is able to "live near, or near the possessions of, any other Wilcox" (182). As a consequence, they each set off for new territories to conquer. Weissman argues that there is a direct connection between cars, colonialism, and the transformation of England's rural districts: "Cars and empire and the destruction of the English village are inseparable," she posits. Because the country had no indigenous oil supplies at that time, "the English needed their empire to get the oil to run their cars" (434). Thacker points out that the sharp increase in automobile ownership was commonly figured as an immediate threat to village life. Historically speaking, we can explain the Wilcoxes' nomadism, or their desire to dominate space, by understanding how their class fraction maintained its economic and social hegemony.

Forster makes every attempt to make plain this connection between motorcars and imperialism, the two great passions of the Wilcox clan. In the scenes immediately preceding Bast's death, the unfortunate man watches Charles whir by at the wheel of a car. The narrator contrasts Charles to Bast by describing the former as an "Imperial" type, healthy, vigorous, perpetually in motion (276). As the novel continues, we learn that Margaret's use of "colonial spirit" to describe the family ethos speaks to a deeper truth. Paul, the younger son, who stands to inherit nothing of his father's fortune, goes to Nigeria in search of his own fortune. Margaret, though ambivalent about England's imperial interests, admires him for the hard work he is willing to do in difficult conditions: "beastly work—dull country, dishonest natives, an eternal fidget over fresh water and food. A nation who can produce men of that sort may well be proud. No wonder England has become an Empire" (108). Elsewhere, Margaret argues that the Wilcoxes are the kind of industrious people who "keep England going" (237). Charles, the elder brother, fought in the Boer War and now works for his father's concern. For his part, Henry builds his fortune—and doubles it in the few years after his wife's death—by running the Imperial and West African Rubber Company, one of the vast imperial projects designed to bring raw materials back to Europe for manufacturing. Until Margaret's first visit to his offices, "Henry had implied his business rather than described it, and the formlessness and vagueness that one associates with Africa itself had hitherto brooded over the main sources of his wealth." With that first trip, however, she becomes uneasily aware that she is the direct beneficiary of those colonial dealings:

> And even when she penetrated to the inner depths she found only the ordinary table and Turkey carpet, and though the map over the fireplace did depict a helping of West Africa it was a very ordinary map. Another map hung opposite, on which the whole continent appeared, looking like a whale marked out for blubber, and by its side was a door, shut, but Henry's voice came through it . . . perhaps she was seeing the Imperial side of the company rather than its West African, and Imperialism always had been one of her difficulties. (175)

Wilcox, of course, shares none of his wife's trepidation over imperial exploitation. The more we learn about his ventures, the more his involvement in Africa looks unsavory—as if he takes real pleasure in it—and less a matter of sound business practices. In his London home, he entertains guests underneath a giant map of Africa and boasts of "carv[ing] money out of Greece and Africa, and [buying] forests from the natives for a few bottles of gin" (243–44). Helen, who comes to despise the family, critiques them frequently for their blind faith in conquest and abstract notions of progress.

With this in mind, we are in a much better position to understand the class position of the Wilcoxes and what they represent in the novel. They have no illusions about Howards End and no attachment to it or what it symbolizes to Mrs. Wilcox and the Schlegel sisters. They would be just as happy anywhere in England, or anywhere in the world, so long as it offered amenities and access to financial opportunities. They live a class position through economic exploitation of and spatial domination over England and its colonial possessions. Jameson suggests that Henry's colonial ventures support the novel's ability to romanticize England's countryside ("Modernism and Imperialism"). The text, however, does not lend itself easily to such an interpretation. It does not, as we might expect, turn rural England into a pastoral idyll; in fact, it takes pains to highlight the flimsiness of that conceit, calling the Wilcoxes "destroyer[s]" who pave "the way for cosmopolitanism" (276). In effect, Henry "recolonizes" England: he takes the techniques he and others developed to exploit the colonies and imports them back to the metropole.[23] The Wilcoxes run their lives on the premise that the landscape is malleable, an entity that can be manipulated to meet their needs and fulfill their desires. Because they respect neither places nor the people inhabiting them, the Wilcoxes are able to apply their business acumen spatially, to remake the earth—at least what parts of it they control—after their own image. They do not romanticize the countryside as an empty vessel of ancient values. Instead, they treat rural England, like the rest of the world, as an active social and geographical entity full of opportunities and obstacles. They have time for neither rural preservationists nor idealistic reformers. But the novel also suggests that their imperial designs are unsustainable; for all his determination, Wilcox cannot indefinitely support his ambitious dreams. Eventually, we are reminded at the novel's conclusion, England's survival will depend on its capacity to turn inward and resolve internal social conflict. Although the novel is quite critical of the Wilcox family, Forster's reformist designs suggest that their industriousness and resources, stripped of imperialist ambitions, could be successfully drafted into a program of class reconciliation.

For Forster, capitalists such as the Wilcoxes represent the greatest threat to the countryside and national culture as a whole, but they also have the ingenuity and leverage to effect positive changes if given guidance and the right circumstances. When Ruth Wilcox dies, the future of Howards End remains an open question. She leaves the property to Margaret, who, though a Londoner, seems interested in preserving the spirit of the place. But this does not mean she will leave it unchanged: she realizes that the countryside—by implication, the nation—must adapt if it is to survive, hinting that an influx of capital and energy might stand it in good stead. Although Henry temporarily cheats her out of this inheritance, the same act brings the pair together in marriage, forming an unstable union between the reformist middle class and the remorseless bourgeoisie. To this mix, Forster adds one unlikely participant: Bast, an indigent, London insurance clerk of the lower-middle class, proximate to abject poverty yet precariously perched above it.

The novel clearly associates Bast with the types of physical deterioration then thought endemic to urban life. The narrator places him on the precipice of "the abyss," a direct reference to Masterman's *From the Abyss: Of Its Inhabitants by One of Them* (1902)—an allusion most readers of the period would have grasped immediately. In fact, the novel establishes this connection between urban dwellers, like Bast, and the national crisis of "degeneracy" very early. As the narrator follows the hapless character into his flat, one of the neighbors comments on the declining birth rate in Manchester, linking Bast's depressing existence to the problem of bad breeding (57). We then get a tour of his domestic space, "reeking with metallic fumes." His meal consists of fatty, freckled beef tongue flanked by installments of reconstituted soup and pineapple (61–62). Bast's official cause of death, of course, is a weak heart, further suggesting the plight of the unhealthy urbanite. Even Margaret, usually the voice of optimism, concludes "that our race is degenerating" (146). By contrast, she describes the Wilcoxes as hearty English stock who "breed and . . . work," concluding that the world will "never be a bad one" so long as "men like my husband and his sons govern it" (237). The healthy, adventurous Wilcoxes are the antithesis of physically weak and genetically suspect figures of Bast's ilk. Tibby, Margaret and Helen's brother, describes people like Bast as the types who "cause Mr Wilcox to write letters to the papers complaining of our national degeneracy" (220). Yet he is part of the intelligent, educated poor who want desperately, in the eyes of the Schlegel sisters, to improve themselves. They meet him by chance at a concert, and he becomes an object of fascination and debate for them. Should his sort be given money, books, education, opportunities, or simply pity? Unlikely as it sounds, he figures more and more prominently in the plot as it progresses, dogging the imperious Wilcoxes at every turn. In the end, he, too, has a great deal to say about the future of the estate.

It must be said at the outset that the novel's conclusion offers one of the more fantastically unrealistic solutions to England's national crisis, but perhaps this makes it all the more interesting. As Jameson suggests, the novel resolves the condition of England through a series of chance encounters and unlikely twists of fate. Helen Schlegel, unwed, becomes pregnant by Bast. The propinquity of scandal to his family's name unnerves Henry, but he initially promises any assistance he can offer. Helen makes only one request: that she and her sister spend one final night at Howards End, where the Schlegel family possessions are being stored. He balks at this proposal, correctly guessing that she may wish to prolong her stay indefinitely: "If she wants to sleep one night, she may want to sleep two. We shall never get her out of the house, perhaps" (262). When the two sisters ignore his prohibition, he summons Charles, his heir, ordering him to remove them from the house. In an attempt to execute his father's wishes, Charles happens upon Bast, who has come to apologize for his role in the affair, and precipitates his humiliating death under a shelf of toppled books—the self-taught man is killed by the instruments of his advancement. Charles gets sent down for manslaughter, propelling the Wilcox clan into disarray and Henry into lethargic semiretirement. Curiously, Helen stays at Howards End, has her child, and the four—Margaret, Henry, Helen, and the infant—remain at the house to resuscitate the farm. Together, they will fashion a new life on the small estate.

We can detect, in this conclusion, Forster turning away from England's culture of imperialism and toward its indigenous national heritage. The Wilcoxes' need to dominate space, both domestic and imperial, is checked by the Schlegels' enlightened reformism. If England insists on aggressive colonial expansion, it will be brought to ruin; this ruthless competitiveness will only hasten national decline, perhaps through war with Germany, its imperialist rival.[24] Instead, the narrative encourages us to mine national life for cultural resources, suggesting that the pastoral has the potential to rejuvenate the country. With the Wilcoxes' capital and the Schlegels' intelligent compassion, England could revive its national fortunes by becoming more self-reliant. The wealthy, imperialist, robustly masculine capitalists will provide resources and energy, while the reformist, cosmopolitan, sensitively feminine middle class will supply ethical guidance, wisdom, and a sense of moral purpose. The eventual heir will be the lower-middle classes and, by extension, even the working class. Helen's child will be given opportunities denied its father.

But this invocation of national heritage does not simply represent a return to some prelapsarian rural order. This reformist impulse, expressed as a desire to mitigate class antagonisms, is also a way to make England viable as a postimperial nation. The principal characters are all engaged in a struggle to define the future of Howards End and the nation itself. Henry, concerned with "the rights of property," remains determined to control the future of the estate. His collapse at the end of the novel implies not only the undesirability of his political insensitivity but also the impending abandonment of his imperial aspirations. Margaret, on the other hand, has a strong love for the countryside and hopes that she can preserve it through guile and creativity. Even the marginal Bast has his say, for his class envy threatens to undermine the whole project. The novel simultaneously transforms and is constrained by its use of the country-house genre. It is clear, for instance, that we are meant to understand that Howards End represents something more than itself—that it stands in for the national cultural condition. But it is equally clear that the novel revises the conventional limitations of the form. It refuses to romanticize the countryside and openly acknowledges the imminent threat of violent class struggle, using the pastoral as a vehicle for considering political restitution. In the hands of Forster, England's pastoral national heritage is not static but a cultural resource out of which he hopes to resolve domestic political tensions and thereby enable England's survival. *Howards End,* like the work of land reformers such as Ebenezer Howard, is a profound attempt to imagine Englishness as a postimperial condition.

This tension between the country-house form and rapidly changing historical circumstances is important for *Brideshead Revisited* and its problematic relationship to the pastoral tradition. Although Waugh, who writes in the 1940s, remains interested in the aesthetic parameters of the country-house genre, his novel openly acknowledges that the material, political, and aesthetic conditions required for "traditional" estate narratives have ceased to exist. Waugh's satire is informed not only by arguments about land reform and the maintenance of an overseas empire but also by a vexed relationship with modernist literature. Readers approach the novel expecting to find a certain degree of comfort or satisfaction in its quaint deployment of the country-house form. We anticipate, in other words, that the novel will fend off modernism's narrative complexity by reinvigorating the country-house tradition. Instead, readers find neither. Although the text uses the rural estate to critique modernist narrative innovation, the novel ultimately suggests that the days of a vibrant pastoral literature have passed. Like Forster, Waugh reworks the country-house novel to address contemporary political and aesthetic concerns. Unlike Forster, however, Waugh sees no future for rural England, imperial England, or the country-house genre. For him, both rustic communities and the pastoral genre have met an untimely end.

NOSTALGIA TIMES TWO

Written on the eve of World War II and published in 1944, *Brideshead* has the aura of a much older novel. In part, the novel feels so out of step with its contemporaries because it seems to recall a moment when the charm of the countryside had not yet been compromised by meddlesome urban planners and loutish suburban homesteaders. Unlike *Howards End,* whose narrative depicts the conflicts created by an aggressive bourgeoisie and lower-middle class *ressentiment, Brideshead* chronicles the lives of the Flyte family, a clan of West Country Roman Catholics—a dying breed by the 1930s. They let their money, as one character observes, "sit quiet": they still extract land rent from their tenant farmers, while their liquid assets, managed by a prestigious firm in London, are tied up in long-term investments with safe but modest returns (174). They send their sons, Brideshead (who takes his name from their estate) and Sebastian, to Oxford, while their daughter receives a fabulous coming-out ball in London, the last "of its kind . . . the last of a splendid series" (179). They move among a set far beyond the reach of the boorish Wilcoxes, a group so small and selective that it cannot maintain itself in the face of increasingly fierce competition from other social classes.

The text also feels so much older because the themes of obsolescence and remembrance of better times saturate the narrative. By the moment of the novel's composition, it implies, the golden era of the aristocracy and its rural hegemony has passed. The narrator remembers such a time fondly, but he is equally clear that it has long since lapsed into memory. The Marchmain mansion at St. James, where the family holds Julia's ball, was one of only "half a dozen London houses which could be called 'historic'" any longer (179). The narrator, army captain Charles Ryder, tellingly makes his living as an architectural painter. He first falls in love with the family by succumbing to the rustic charms of their home and its grounds, admiring the "buildings that grew silently with the centuries, catching and keeping the best of each generation." His professional success during the 1930s has more to do with a keen eye and a sense of timing than any particular aesthetic gifts. He describes the buildings he paints as the ones in which "England abounded" in "the last decade of their grandeur." He counts himself fortunate that "Englishmen seemed for the first time to become conscious of what before was taken for granted, and to salute their achievements at the moment of extinction." Those great houses seem to disappear one after the other, only "a few paces" separating his arrival from that of the auctioneers (226–27). England's renewed enthusiasm for architectural painting was, ironically, a belated response to years of profound indifference to the fate of the countryside itself.

By structuring the narrative's symbolic economy around the theme of memory, the text employs a distinctive narrative strategy. As Ryder sits down to write the novel, everything has already happened. He underscores the finality and the inevitability of the events he transcribes; nothing could have been done to alter the past. There is no element of chance, contingency, or choice in the story he relates. In fact, very little transpires in the book: the plot is curious because almost nothing happens. "My theme is memory," he begins book 2. He reduces his life to these recollections, declaring simply "we possess nothing certainly except the past" (225). He bears witness, through the Flytes and the estate, to a slow, painful decommissioning of the country manor as the novel wears on. It would be easy to read this device as a simple formula for nostalgia, but this interpretation cannot fully explain the narrative's ingenious, unconventional structure. It lacks, for instance, a central conflict. There is no real battle for the countryside or England, no real protagonist apart from the estate itself. The ostensible setting of the novel is England during World War II, but Ryder narrates almost entirely in retrospect. He frames the novel with passages from the present, describing his ignominious return to Brideshead—hence the book's title—with his regiment. The battle for England's rural spaces, then, has already been waged and lost. Apart from the novel's discussions of religious faith and Roman Catholicism, the story is "empty."

I call *Brideshead*'s always-already narrative quality *nostalgia for nostalgia*. I differentiate it from "simple" nostalgia because it announces two distinct modes of desire. In the first instance, the text communicates a straightforward longing for a lost pastoral eden. The novel mourns the passing of an older, aristocratic order, wishing to preserve the last remnants of England's countryside. It freely acknowledges, however, that the impending demise of the empire and the arrival of the welfare state in the aftermath of World War II—and the widespread adoption of urban planning à la Ebenezer Howard, the bane of every rural preservationist—will spell the end of the countryside as he imagines it. The text implies that idealistic planners and bureaucrats will now have the power to effect massive geographic and political change. In this respect, the text distinguishes itself little from the more uninteresting works of England's pastoral literary tradition, which continually lament the disappearance of the countryside. Although the basic historical conditions have been updated, the trope of the vanishing countryside remains consistent with its predecessors.[25]

But this novel carries with it another kind of longing: the yearning for an earlier *cultural* moment when such styles of fiction were aesthetically viable. By late 1930s, as novels like *Brideshead* and *Lady Chatterley's Lover* demonstrate, such direct forms of narrative desire had been aesthetically compromised by the advent of high modernism and the rise of an avant-garde literature in the previous fifty years. In addition to simple nostalgia, the text fashions a more conflicted kind of desire through which it seeks to recall a more straightforward, less complicated cultural moment. Waugh's narrative telescope, in essence, has a bifocal lens. As much as for the countryside itself, the novels pines for the time when one could write serious literature about the loss of rustic England, implicitly blaming the modernists for the precipitous decline of the country-house genre. This superabundance of nostalgia compensates for an essential narrative paucity; an exercise in self-sabotage, it repeatedly stages the futility of its project, simultaneously remembering an earlier moment and acknowledging the impossibility of its restoration. The text's multiple levels of desire and its anxieties about the modernist project perhaps explain why Waugh himself and some of his most admiring critics rush to deny the presence of nostalgia in the text.[26] In fact, I read the novel's painfully empty narrative as an extremely skillful parody of high modernist texts, like *Ulysses* or *Mrs. Dalloway,* in which nothing "happens." As much as the text laments the collapse of England's great houses and families, its sadness comes from the aesthetic vacuum into which it steps.

THE AGE OF HOOPER

Before examining *Brideshead*'s aesthetics of nostalgia in more detail, I want to briefly discuss the novel's use of class conflict as a central narrative motor. The novel's deployment of class war is unusual in two respects: not only does the text depict the aristocracy as a pitiful, helpless, persecuted class fraction, but it also suggests that they are driven to the brink of extinction by a new sociopolitical menace, otherwise known as the welfare state. For the most part, aristocrats have only themselves to blame for their marginality; a few cranks and down-at-the-heel profligates remain of this once great class, stripped of their land, political influence, and even their symbolic cultural position. By the time the narrator sits down to imagine the novel, the aristocracy is not simply under siege but has been fully displaced. If the total ineptitude of the ruling class makes this an atypical country-house narrative, its usurper, the welfare state, is without precedent. The ranks of the aristocracy are not threatened by poor crops, disloyal tenants, or a crisis in primogeniture but by the onset of World War II and Britain's political consensus of the 1940s. Under the auspices of the welfare state, the novel laments, a greedy, undereducated bourgeoisie have conspired with the working classes to effectively oust the aristocracy. Worse yet, the likes of Howard and his land-reform lobby are in the ascendant, ensuring that the country estates so beloved by Waugh will not survive long in this new political landscape. The welfare state, along with all the changes it implies, becomes a political and cultural signpost for the aristocracy's rapid decline and the inevitable dissolution of its cultural legacy, the country house.[27]

Partly because the narrative offers no active conflict, the novel offers no real protagonist in the conventional sense. If there is any kind of hero, it is the house itself: the narrator intently records its beauty as a way to protest its physical and ideological destruction. The house, and by extension the family who inhabit it, seem to stand in for an entire social order, or what Williams calls, ironically, the "knowable community." *Brideshead,* however, stretches this synecdoche to its absolute limits. We quickly realize that the family no longer has the ability to stand in for a larger social group or class fraction: the text continually draws our attention to the marginality and utter isolation of the Flytes. The elder son and heir, Brideshead, is an aloof bachelor until the end of the novel, when he concocts a disastrous marriage to an impecunious, middle-class widow too advanced in years to produce any offspring. Julia, the only daughter, marries a very bourgeois member of Parliament whose opportunist politics involve muckraking with the trade unions (to boot, he is Canadian, not English). Clearly outside their social set, he bristles at the marriage settlement offered by the family's solicitors, who insist on committing Julia's ample dowry to trust: "What do I want with trustee stock?," he rages. "I make money work for me," he assures her, demanding "fifteen or twenty per cent" return on his investments rather than the paltry "three and a half" stipulated by her family's lawyers (190). Sebastian, the younger son, is feckless in the extreme, drinking himself to death in Morocco. No one from this family, it seems, has the competency or desire to inherit Brideshead; the aristocracy's inadequacies and historical obsolescence make them unfit to look after their own interests. Their social exclusivity only exacerbates the problem, ensuring the ultimate ruin of the family and their ancestral estate. The narrative offers a kind of satiric sympathy for the Flytes, describing their class position by depicting them as outsiders, a self-destructive and misunderstood minority.

The estate comes closest to approximating the role of a melodramatic protagonist against whom the fates conspire. It develops an unconscious subjectivity, maturing gracefully over the years in spite of its ignorant inhabitants, achieving a state of peace and fulfillment. Readers encounter endless descriptions of each room—its decor, function, and furnishings, architectural features—and the magnificent grounds. If we can call the estate a protagonist of sorts, the narrator names the main antagonist, wryly, "the age of Hooper." As Ryder bids farewell to his deepest love, he blames the untimely demise of Brideshead on this shadowy character, Hooper: "The builders did not know the uses to which their work would descend; they made a new house with the stones of the old castle; year by year, generation after generation, they enriched and extended it; year by year the great harvest of timber in the park grew to ripeness; until, in sudden frost, came the age of Hooper; the place was desolate and the work all brought to nothing; *Quomodo sedet sola civitas.* Vanity of vanities, all is vanity" (350–51). The beauty of the historic estate, which was established during the Elizabethan period, is virtually unappreciated by the Flytes themselves. The product of an extended era, of generations who planned with the surety of the ruling class, it represents so much more than the dynastic family who inhabits it: permanence and magnitude in the midst of decay and contraction. It stands in for an entire moral, ideological, even narrative order. But what, we may ask, is the age of Hooper, and why does it have the power and authority to destroy everything beloved by the narrator?

Hooper, readers discover early in the text, is a young officer in Ryder's company. Ryder calls him as "a sallow youth" with "a flat Midland accent" (7). Though he appears to have attained a military commission, the narrator says he enlisted "reluctantly, under compulsion, after he had made every feeble effort in his power to obtain deferment." Apart from these half-hearted descriptions—he also alludes to his inferior's bland, rather pedestrian incompetence—Ryder offers us little substantive commentary on why this otherwise nondescript soldier captures his fascination. We come to understand that Hooper is young, middle class, from a less fashionable part of the country, and insufficiently educated. His intellectual training has not furnished him with knowledge of the country's great military achievements and regal history "but, instead, a profusion of detail about humane legislation and recent industrial change." Without further explanation, Hooper becomes to Ryder "a symbol . . . of Young England, so that whenever I read some public utterance proclaiming what Youth demanded in the Future and what the world owed Youth, I would test these general statements by substituting 'Hooper' and seeing if they still seemed as plausible" (9). He represents everything mediocre, mundane, and trite. The estate has been requisitioned for use by the army for training, but in Ryder's eyes they do so in the spirit of Hooper: urine and garbage everywhere, the ornate woodwork and art obliterated beyond repair, the lawns and hedges ruined by target practice and drunken lorry operators. The young army officer becomes a symbol for the arrival of the welfare state, and the narrator is far from enamored with the political reorganization it implies.

But Ryder's complaint, embedded in a discourse of insurmountable class difference, paradoxically operates by foregrounding the cultural uniqueness of England by virtue of its class system. The novel's ironic layers depend on emphasizing the absurdity of the situation: the aristocracy, primarily through its negligence, arrogance, and turpitude, is partly responsible for creating the conditions that have led to its own demise. Hooper stands for "Young England" precisely because he is a class symbol, a condensed image of the national predicament. In effect, the metaphor satirizes England for its unique brand of Englishness. Waugh's use of class conflict as the main narrative engine makes this an unusual country-house novel, especially one written on the eve of World War II. As Simon Featherstone argues, the war helped consolidate the trope of national unity so common in pastoral literature. Following Williams and John Barrell, Featherstone suggests that this metaphorical use of the pastoral, especially at times of political crisis, masks the presence of social dissent by imposing images of continuity and collective action. But, he suggests, it also "explores the contradictions of culture and class even as it seeks to deny them."[28] Waugh, in contrast, uses the country-house novel both to present a vision of national unity, now lost, and to announce the presence of an indomitable enemy, the insipid Hooper and all he represents. Unlike many pastoral narratives, *Brideshead* promulgates a message of imminent social collapse. But this annunciation, steeped in ironic reflections, works by insisting that class problems are the most salient feature of England's particularity, the unique result of England's cultural genius and myopia.

If we probe more deeply into the meaning of Waugh's neat synecdoche, we come to understand that Hooper stands in for a political arrangement as well as a social group. As a class, Hooper represents the mass of nonaristocrats: the middle classes and even the working class presumably. More importantly, on the eve of the war, he symbolizes the dominant ideological ethos of the day. The broad political consensus of the welfare state became most explicit in the postwar settlement, but as Alan Sinfield argues, it began as a wartime pledge to the working class.[29] Many viewed the welfare state as a political compromise between the working class and business interests, managed primarily by the upper-middle class. On the eve of wartime mobilization, "[r]adical social change was generally anticipated" in health care, pensions, education, and housing (14–15). Resolving class conflict in England, under the auspices of a socially conscious, democratic bureaucracy, became an important component of repositioning national identity in an age of geopolitical transition. As early as 1939, before conscription had begun, the ruling Tories established the rudiments of the British welfare state. Later on, the war itself demonstrated that a Keynesian-style "planned economy" could work to the medium-term benefit of both capital and labor, securing economic growth during the postwar reconstruction and decolonization.[30] The very troubled 1930s would give way to a more austere but socially just 1940s.[31]

Not surprisingly, writers and cultural elites such as Waugh were less than enthusiastic about the ascendancy of egalitarian politics, further expedited by the onset of war. Sinfield notes that Waugh, in *Unconditional Surrender* (1961), "rather gleefully points out . . . that even under the wartime restrictions he and his friends had ways of getting oysters, salmon, gulls' eggs, caviare and French cheeses." About life during the Labour government of 1945–51, when the age of Hooper peaked, Waugh glibly recalls that the "kingdom seemed to be under enemy occupation" (qtd. in Sinfield 13). In short, Waugh and his class fraction represent a small but determined group of conscientious objectors to the new political consensus, defining their politics from a minority position. Waugh acknowledges that his opponents now set the terms of the political debate, and his vociferous protests are circumscribed by his self-appointed position on the margins.

This transaction is particularly interesting because the ruling classes, once proud owners of the country manor, have had their cultural property—the country-house novel—seized. *Brideshead* narrates the cultural and political marginality of the aristocracy, adding layer upon layer of irony by underscoring the extent and rapidity of its displacement. Rather than enabling narrative action, this marginality tends to undermine the ability of the text to construct the plot as a temporally organized progression of events. As outsiders to England's social and political landscape, the Flytes are totally passive; the family and their narrator, Ryder, have been made historically and narratologically redundant. Everything has happened before Ryder embarks on his story, and he emphasizes this from the outset. It is not simply that we know the end of the tale before it really begins, but that so little is at stake in the telling. We read lengthy descriptions of the family's eccentricities, cocktail hour habits, religious practices, and of course their estate. The family's position on the political margins consolidates the novel's deployment of class relationships as a sign of the national predicament, and the framing device gives Ryder's storytelling a strong sense of inevitability. By the present of the narrative, the age of the Flytes has passed. Events have conspired to reduce the actual and symbolic influence of England's aristocracy, and no one has the ability or motivation to rectify the situation.

In place of a more dynamic narrative, Waugh substitutes an excessive nostalgia. The golden age, he reminds us at every turn, has passed, now irretrievably lost, accessible only in quasi-historical fiction such as his own, and only to those privileged enough to have experienced it (if only by proxy, as is the case with Ryder). Waugh even inscribes a sense of longing in the title. In his own way, Waugh provides a remarkably detailed historical account of how the aristocracy lived and understood their class position during this period. For most readers, his nostalgia, laced with bittersweet irony, is an ambivalent attempt to recognize the achievements—and failures—of an indulgent and wasteful minority. But the novel is, narratologically speaking, rather sophisticated. Because little happens—the characters, for the most part, do not recognize the crisis before them, face no difficult choices, and would have been powerless to remedy the situation even if they had been more self-aware—the family is victimized by forces beyond their control and comprehension. Within the logic of the narrative, the Flytes resemble pathetic heroes, objects of a persistent, fairly gentle form of satire (at least by Waugh's vicious standards). Through this narrative inactivity, Waugh laments much more than the passing of a functional aristocracy. *Brideshead* marks a break in the pastoral literary tradition. Waugh believes himself the heir of this great tradition, but he also writes himself as the end of the line. Before his work came scores of poems, novels, essays, and memoirs of variable quality, each assuming its place in a knowable community of texts, England's canon of pastoral literature. After *Brideshead,*

this type of literature does not die, but it operates at a different intellectual pitch and cultural register. In the 1950s, most of this kind of fiction
began appearing under the guise of "degraded romance,"[32] and a few
decades later, as BBC-style, drama-of-manners television miniseries.[33]
This novel helps define the fault line between highbrow literature and
more commercial art. The novel's lack of plot is a kind of parodic imitation of high modernist texts. Even the theme of religious conversion
offers a play on modernist "epiphanies," a common climaxing device
in stream-of-consciousness narratives. Although it rejects the linguistic
and technical experimentation we find in such novels, it is a plot-poor,
satirically melodramatic pastiche of its self-consciously experimental
counterparts.

In many ways, the novel is the last of its kind. It is, peripherally, a
canonical novel, the last of its type read attentively by critics. Kazuo
Ishiguro's *The Remains of the Day* is a possible exception to this observation, but its consistent use of irony, memory, and narrative inevitability recalls those qualities in *Brideshead,* thereby emphasizing, I would
argue, the continuing difficulty of deploying the estate novel as an earnest literary enterprise. By the 1950s England's cultural coordinates were
markedly different. The elite literature of the last fifty years—the kind
taken more seriously by academics and cultural experts—is far more
urban in focus, far less celebratory of England's past, and more cognizant of diverse social groups. We can read *Brideshead*'s odd narrative,
then, as a negotiation between the traditional form of the country-house
novel, the political manifestation of the welfare state and decolonization,
and the effects of modernism on literary culture. The form of the novel
actualizes the relationship between these complementary historical conditions by narrating its own paralysis. Even while the novel resists the
political dominance of the welfare state and the aesthetic supremacy of
more formally experimental brands of modernism, the narrative is unable or unwilling to formulate a viable response beyond its insistent and
singular satire.

With this in mind, we can access the cultural significance of the text's
essential narrative lack. This nostalgia for nostalgia alludes to both aesthetic and national forms of longing. Not only does the novel mourn
the extinction of a social institution—the country-house novel—but
it also remembers an earlier cultural moment. This narrative emptiness
asks us, as readers, to remember a time when genuine representations of
conflict could plausibly structure this kind of literary endeavor—when

the narrative resolution could be suspended until the conclusion. Here, however, the future has been decided before the story begins. The narrative plays out, through its portrayal of a dying aristocracy, the aesthetic condition of the country-house genre. The narrative resists the supremacy of modernism and the displacement of this older literary tradition, but its narrative lack also acknowledges the imminence of its own historical vanishing. The circumstances in which the novel emerges delimit its narrative void and, in a sense, give it a comprehensible structure. Waugh makes little attempt to portray fully self-aware characters: they are denied political agency and moral authority. Their fall is inevitable; their incompetence and lack of political savvy may have hastened their obsolescence, but nothing could have preserved their position. The narrative is not really tragic. The characters do not commit errors in judgment. Events happen to these individuals, who contribute very little to their own destruction. The story's always-already temporal frame suggests that there is little at stake. Effectively, there are no options left for these figures, no choices to make, and no conflicts to resolve. Waugh asks us to recall a time when the countryside was a "real" literary place, a setting through which the pastoral could perform substantive political and cultural work.

As I turn, in the following two chapters, to the high modernist *Mrs. Dalloway* and then to the midcentury texts of the Angry Young Men, several of the ideological problems lurking behind the scenes of these manorial dramas—the difficulty of representing masculine prerogatives and the failure of men to reproduce their conditions of existence—will come center stage. In *Howards End*, for example, I have emphasized how the project of class compromise guides the unfolding of the story, but the novel also depicts a confrontation between the Wilcoxes, coded English/imperial/masculine, and the Schlegels, their cosmopolitan/liberal/feminine counterparts. The inheritance plot makes the family a site of ideological bartering: the Schlegels cash in some of their cosmopolitan chips for a stake in the English homestead, while the Wilcoxes swap their aggressive imperialism for a less risky, more equitable future. Bast, and to a lesser extent Charles Wilcox, are the unfortunate casualties of this confrontation over reproductive privileges.

Brideshead, in contrast, presides over a self-obsolescing aesthetic. The queer undertones of the Ryder-Sebastian relationship, along with the barren marriage of Brideshead, echo around the estate's empty, soon-to-be-condemned halls. Where Forster extends the possibility of a new mortgage on revised terms, Waugh concludes with an unambiguous foreclosure, symbolized by these reproductive failures. As these novels are well aware, any social formation needs to reproduce both its material and its ideological conditions of existence. In a curious way, *Brideshead*'s ironic tone comes close to pursuing an anti-ideological aesthetic: it cannot imagine the conditions necessary for its own reproduction, offering, by virtue of its satiric insistence, a negation of ideological "recruiting," the central function of ideological apparatuses. Waugh's country house, as both a material apparatus and a cultural device, is no longer able to guarantee the conditions necessary for its own reproduction. As my reading of *Mrs. Dalloway* will suggest, the representational challenges posed by class conflict and national culture coalesce in surprising ways around the problem of masculinity in its modern, urban condition.

3. STRANGERS IN THE PARK
WOOLF, SELVON, AND
THE TRAFFIC IN MODERNISM

In an essay on Oxford Street, the longtime center of London's gaudy, cut-price shopping district, Virginia Woolf casually remarks that "the charm of modern London is that it is not built to last; it is built to pass." Woolf surprisingly chooses Oxford Street, rather than one of London's innumerable historic sites, as an emblem of the capital precisely because it foregrounds the transitory qualities of modern urban life. London's historic houses and monuments, bestowed on the city by aristocratic patrons, "required the illusion of permanence." By contrast, Woolf delights in the ephemerality of the city's tacky, cacophonous, ostentatious retail industry and the throngs of bargain hunters it attracts with ever more lavish displays. Modern London is thus a disposable city being made and remade to fit contemporary whims, fancies, and needs: "We knock down and rebuild as we expect to be knocked down and rebuilt. It is an impulse that makes for creation and fertility" (*London Scene* 19–20). London's unique vitality is a result of continual, premeditated destruction and renewal; striving for solidity or permanence is antithetical to the city's modern ethos.

Mrs. Dalloway (1925), like the city in which it is set, works by combining seemingly irreconcilable processes—creation and destruction foremost among them. The novel begins, of course, with images of rising and falling. "What a lark! What a plunge!," thinks Clarissa Dalloway as she steps out to buy her famous flowers, the narrative transporting readers through her mind's eye to a scene from her gay adolescence, a moment from her past to which she returns often throughout the course of the day (1). A few hours later, Septimus Warren Smith, Clarissa's troubled "twin," commits suicide by throwing himself out a window, an actual plunge that punctuates his symbolic connection with the title character.

The text's narrative economy circulates pairs of oppositional categories as forms of symbolic currency: life and death, decay and renewal, happiness and despair, love and hatred, isolation and connection, freedom and control, women and men, sensuality and frigidity, wealth and poverty, past and present, memory and repression, sanity and insanity, war and peace, combatant and civilian, urban and pastoral.[1] Following Alex Zwerdling, whose influential book *Virginia Woolf and the Real World* first explained the extent to which the author conceived the novel as radical social critique, scholars in recent years have been more attuned to Woolf's stinging attacks on English patriarchy, militarism, imperialism, and the country's loathsome class system. Yet we should also acknowledge that the novel celebrates, in many ways, the sheer vivacity of London. Although Clarissa has her share of flaws—Woolf herself feared that the character would come across as too "tinselly" and unsympathetic—the London we traverse with her is filled with wonder and energy. Given Woolf's well-documented love for the city, it would be unwise to completely discount the text's moments of exultation in London's vibrant atmospherics. The novel is a study of contrasts, most of them documenting the complexity and diversity of life in the modern metropolis.

Mrs. Dalloway's insistent juxtaposition of oppositional images, terms, and ideas is an important aspect of the novel's assembly of modernist techniques. The narrative offers, with its fluid motion in and between the minds of many characters, highly dissonant impressions of urban space. The text regularly contrasts the perceptions of Clarissa, who enjoys her jaunts, with those of Septimus, who feels isolated in and oppressed by his surroundings. This pattern is at the crux of the novel's quintessentially modernist style, suggested by the narrative's lambent shifts between the minds of different characters. Clarissa and Septimus never meet one another, running instead along parallel tracks. Their complementary reactions to London are contrasted through a series of narrative collisions. Often shifting the node of focalization when multiple characters perceive the same external event—Big Ben sounding the hour, a car puncturing a tire, an airplane writing a message in the sky, or a girl bumping into a woman's legs—the novel samples the broad social diversity of the modernist city. These technical innovations provide jarring, contradictory impressions of the urban environment as individual subjects provide incompatible readings of urban space. Such displays of modernist narrative virtuosity converge with Woolf's plan to offer a subtext of social critique: the novel imagines how a diverse range of people see and feel the city, showing perceptive readers how social inequities are inscribed onto the urban landscape and lived through the quotidian practices of metropolitan subjects.

Woolf's novel marks an important junction in literary depictions of city life, especially London. As I discuss in the latter sections of this chapter, postcolonial writers, such as Sam Selvon, both borrowed from and revised the kinds of conflicted representations of England's urban culture epitomized by *Mrs. Dalloway* and other modernist texts. Woolf's distinctly ambivalent portrayal of the city—characterized by these particular combinations of life and death, rising and falling, amity and loathing—captures a range of contradictory attitudes about London and its special place in English society. London represents simultaneously all that is best and worst about national space. For Woolf, it epitomizes an imperial, patriarchal, class-bound England—"butlers, tawny chow dogs, . . . [and] girls in their security," as Peter Walsh, Clarissa's former suitor, ironically describes the signs of upper-middle-class London society (58). Yet London also stands for intellectual energy, social vitality, and personal freedom. By commingling the most exhilarating and most depressing aspects of metropolitan life, the novel consists of equal parts celebration and critique. It constitutes an attempt to disentangle what is wonderful about London from an imperialist, hierarchical, patriarchal Britain, salvaging the useful fragments of metropolitan culture and slating the rest for demolition. Woolf's endorsement of a transitory, ephemeral city pits the energy of modern London against the suffocating weight of imperial history. Monuments to a bygone aristocracy and its legacy of war, imperial conquest, and domestic oppression should be swept away in a comprehensive program of urban renewal. *Mrs. Dalloway*'s representation of metropolitan space is thus quite different from T. S. Eliot's in *The Waste Land* (1922), the other major London text from the high modernist canon. For the Woolf of *Mrs. Dalloway*, London is problematic but worth saving, a city of great potential overburdened with implicit markers of violence and overt forms of inequality.

Readers of *Mrs. Dalloway* spend a great deal of time simply strolling through London's "Imperial Quarter," a narrative strategy by which Woolf makes apparent the ideological parameters of metropolitan space. The text's critique of England's imperialist, hierarchical structures be comes obvious through ironic portrayals of London's monumental districts. Fictional representations of the city's royal parks, in particular, become provocative settings in which Woolf—and later, Sam Selvon—consider the attractions and limitations of metropolitan culture. The heterogeneity of park visitors gives Woolf and Selvon the perfect social laboratory for exulting in the vitality of class differences while condemning the persistence of class oppression. Similarly, central London's parks, littered with monuments to British imperialism, provide ideal settings in which to reflect on the ideological and material impact of imperialism on London itself. In literal and figurative ways, parks in modern London are places where the urban and rural converge, where the dead greet the living as a matter of course: through monuments and other material celebrations of imperial conquest, living Londoners regularly confront the empire's dead soldiers. In the words of Lewis Mumford, one of urban modernity's most influential theorists, monuments are part of an ancient "cult of permanence" in which the dead attempt to secure immortality through myths and superstition organized around sacred memorials (435). The modern city, in contrast, ought to be "oriented to the cycle of life," engaged in a "never-ending process of birth and growth and renewal and death: a process we can neither halt nor limit by ideological fixations or cunning inventions" (438). For Mumford, like Woolf, death in the modern city is simply another aspect of life, even part of a process that leads to rejuvenation of the living. The city's parks allow Woolf and Selvon to capture the full range of urban experience in a compact physical and narrative space, imagining how the decline of London's imperial culture could facilitate the birth of new forms of metropolitan society. Both are eager to demolish the imperial pretensions of metropolitan architecture yet are reluctant to consign London to oblivion. The aleatory motion in these texts, broadly representative of modernist narrative techniques, is here put in service of a specific political agenda, that of simultaneously criticizing and celebrating different aspects of metropolitan culture. These forms of schematic, highly structured ambivalence, embedded in such figurative couplings of death and rebirth, permanence and transience, or affluence and poverty, represent an attempt to envision a more equitable and less imperial version of London.

STAGING THE IMPERIAL CITY

The London we encounter in *Mrs. Dalloway* is, above all else, an imperial capital, littered with testaments to England's waning imperial grandeur, a city still suffering the effects of a debilitating world war. As the novel demonstrates, London's material geography was designed to produce imperial subjects, actively encouraging men, especially, to participate imaginatively in overseas conquest. When Peter Walsh wanders out into the city, we immediately notice that he is surrounded by metropolitan tributes to empire. Temporarily back in London after an absence of five years—he works as a colonial administrator in India, overseeing agriculture in "a district twice as big as Ireland"—he takes particular delight in reacquainting himself with his favorite city (51). Ambling along Whitehall in the direction of Regent's Park, he is overtaken by a group of boys "in uniform, carrying guns," marching in lockstep.[2] Collectively, he notices, their faces wear "an expression like . . . a statue praising duty, gratitude, fidelity, love of England," as if they have borrowed their countenances from one of the city's memorials to dead heroes. Peter comically adjusts his gait to keep step with the teenage boys, thinking their exercises "a very fine training," but he soon loses ground, content to watch them parade past "all the exalted statues, Nelson, Gordon, Havelock, the black, spectacular images of great soldiers." Standing underneath the tribute to Gordon, "whom as a boy he had worshipped," Peter is compelled by the enthusiasm exhibited by the young men; "one might laugh; but one had to respect it, he thought" (54–55).

In these passages, the text deftly explores the connection between London's imperial architecture and its ability to inform metropolitan social traffic. It is not simply that the boys mimic the statues they see before them; they are actively engaged in the project of making London an imperial city and turning themselves into imperial subjects. Similarly, the "bronze heroes" come to life before their eyes, calling out to London's inhabitants as they parade across the city; Peter himself emulates the statue's "marble stare," the dead reaching beyond the grave to guide the actions of the living (19, 54). Peter and the boys in uniform understand their position as imperial subjects both cognitively and physically: their identity as Londoners and Englishmen is embedded in their eagerness to mark and train their bodies for potential imperial service. In Peter's case, temporarily returning to the metropole helps him replenish his flagging self-esteem. During his unhappy stint as a colonial administrator, he had "come a cropper; made a mess of things," but returning to London and its "secure shores" helps Peter regain his fragile self-confidence (115–16). This particular scene wonderfully illustrates how the urban environment recruits individuals and produces subjects by encouraging them to respond in kind. At his post in India, Peter remains acutely aware of not only his own shortcomings but also the general flaws of the colonial administration. By contrast, in London, buoyed by its architecture of conquest, he lays full claim to his imperial identity. The environment does not deceive him or coerce him, nor is it an oppressive apparatus to which he submits unwillingly. Peter is fully conscious of his choice to follow the path of the young men, yet he remains cynical of the project as a whole ("one might laugh," he thinks). The city's ideological appeal, through this counterintuitive operation, repairs Peter's sense of political agency: he feels lost and depressed when he openly questions and resists the logic of imperial domination, but the act of freely submitting to a higher authority reassures him of his autonomy.

Peter's conflicted response—he is both enthusiastic and cynical—is a typical function of ideological structures, which are most potent and visible in our reactions to mundane events. What seems to happen "outside ideology (to be precise, in the street), in reality takes place in ideology" ("Ideology" 175). By this, Althusser means that Peter's superior attitude is a way of placing the marching boys "in" ideology and himself "outside" it—but this intellectual response is itself characteristic of ideological operations. The self, the individual political actor, routinely discounts the extent of his or her own interpellation when acting within or in relation to ideological structures—it is always someone else who is duped by ideology, while the subject remains alienated and tactically self-aware. In other words, it is relatively easy to accuse others of ideological naïveté, but we find it difficult to estimate our own participation in ideological systems. This has the practical effect of "denegation": individual subjects apply ideologically informed arguments to identify someone else's subjection to ideology, thereby positioning themselves outside it, but Althusser insists that this negation is the most ideological of maneuvers. The proposition that only others are deceived by ideology is itself constituted out of the hail-response system of interpellation: we imagine our own responses to ideological systems as free—not only free responses, but free of ideological implications—and therefore nonideological. In literary terms, we might argue that the process of identifying ideology is predicated on ironic interpretive strategies in which reading subjects are quick to identify another's ideological illusions while remaining unable to recognize the ideological parameters of their own subjectivity as it is constructed in the act of reading.

I am particularly interested in how *Mrs. Dalloway* makes extensive use of social traffic in public spaces to articulate a modernist theory of urban phenomenology. Ideologically speaking, London's imperial architecture may have served a didactic function, the text showing how the environment "teaches" subjects by actively recruiting or hailing its targets as part of its program of interpellation. As a system of spatial discipline, it does not inculcate subjects by force, coercion, or other overtly repressive measures—it produces subjects by offering physical and mental stimulation, even pleasure. The targets of hailing become subjects, in effect, by responding to the call of the city. The characters in the novel do not express their subjectivity by mentally insulating themselves from the trappings of urban life (like the *flâneur,* for instance, and other haughty, high modernist urban spectators) but by embracing and reacting to the opportunities of the city. Subjectivity does not arise in the act of being subjected to coercive elements of the urban environment (simple repression or subjugation) or in the struggle for self-assertion against the social life of the city (alienation), but in the constant negotiation between these two extremes. Peter, for instance, simultaneously thinks London's imperial architecture a "splendid achievement" and "ridiculous" (58). This reaction, though overtly contradictory, marks the hesitancy of subjectivity as an ideological condition. *Mrs. Dalloway* shows how urban pleasures can function as a method of moral and bodily instruction, producing subjects by allowing them to paradoxically enhance their individuality by immersing themselves in the social geography of the city.

Despite his reluctance to take the marching teens altogether seriously, the spectacle makes Peter feel younger than he had in years, reminding him of his own boyhood dreams of becoming a decorated general or celebrated explorer. Directly on cue, an attractive young woman catches his eye as her skirts whisk past Gordon's statue, mesmerizing the now middle-aged man. She compares favorably, in his estimation, to Clarissa, but was she, "he wondered as she moved, respectable?" On Regent's Street, crowds of pedestrians obstruct his view of her, but he responds by becoming more dogged in his pursuit. He imagines himself, like the marching scouts, "an adventurer, reckless . . . swift, daring, indeed (landed as he was last night from India) a romantic buccaneer, careless of all these damned proprieties" that inhibit open expressions of sexuality in England (56–57). In this brief encounter, his experiences as a civil servant in India, his fantasy life as a youngster, and London's imperial architecture all combine to inform Peter's understanding of his own sexual subjectivity. London's imperial monuments are not a backdrop, a static reminder of empire, English military superiority, or moral authority, but a framing device that actively shapes everyday metropolitan practices such as sexuality and street life. For Peter, these imperial fantasies become a way to temporarily assuage anxieties regarding his professional shortcomings and sexual troubles (he was jilted by Clarissa years earlier and has come to England to sort out another troubled love affair). Most importantly, this manner of negotiating his sexuality later strikes Peter as particularly remarkable because he actively *dislikes* "India, empire, and the army" (58). In other words, when he consciously positions himself "outside" ideology, England's imperial propaganda has little hold on him. It is not that he is temporarily deceived by his surroundings, momentarily forcing him into a kind of false consciousness as an apologist for empire. Instead, it makes more sense to read this as an instance of interpellation, of the way that London's ideological architecture informs all kinds of social activity. His fantasy, including the anonymity of the woman and the crowded street, becomes a setting *through* which (rather than *in* which) Peter stages his subjectivity within gender-specific circuits of sexual desire. The manner in which he thinks about his subjectivity is both entirely personal and completely dependent on his interaction with the metropolitan environment. Ironically, for a colonial officer who loathes the tedium of his job when in India, the exotic imagination of imperial and sexual conquest becomes available only when he returns to London, where such imagery forms an integral component of metropolitan space. The common pleasures of urban life, including Peter's sexual fantasies, are themselves part of a sophisticated regime of masculine bodily discipline. Through this code of call and response, the city's social geography frames everyday street encounters within a highly nuanced system of imperial subjectivity.

At this particular moment, Peter very much resembles the *flâneur* of Baudelaire and Benjamin, which has become a standard way to read his function in the novel.[3] He is cynical and self-possessed, taking what he will from the urban environment. Like the prototypical urban walker in modernist literature, he offers a distinctively sexualized view of the city, defining his own subjectivity through his ability to invest others with amorous significance. But it is impossible not to notice how London's identity as an imperial city molds Peter's practice of *flânerie*. He is not, in other words, simply the haughty, self-possessed voyeur of Baudelaire's poetry—his fantasy life is both enhanced by and subject to the imperial geography of the metropole. As Peter walks through the city, he actively incorporates London's imperial geography into his sexual self-fashioning. Peter's subjectivity is not defined by his bodily and psychological self-possession but by his eagerness to allow the urban environment to frame and enhance his enactment of masculine rituals. As Henri Lefebvre suggests, monumental space engages both the affective/bodily and political/ideological axes of subjectivity. Such forms of monumental or representational space thus perform the work of interpellation, or participate in subject formation, at several different levels simultaneously—"some at a first level, the level of affective, bodily, lived experience . . . some at a second level, that of the perceived, sociopolitical signification; and some at a third level, the level of the conceived, where the dissemination of the written word and of knowledge welds the members of society into a 'consensus,' and in doing so confers upon them the status of 'subjects'" (*Production* 224). Peter's subjectivity shuttles between and across these different axes of interpellation (affective, political, and social). In the novel's strikingly evocative collisions of dead history and the living, fleeting present, we can see how London's imperial architecture catalyzes a convergence of Peter's death and sexual drives, as if metropolitan space were specially designed to concoct perverse combinations of monumental death and sexual renewal. The text's back-and-forth movement between representational space and representations of subjectivity in space exposes both the ideology effect of imperial monumentality and the specific forms of ironic pleasure offered therein.

After his escapade with the unknown woman, Peter wanders into Regent's Park to idle and enjoy the fine weather. He settles down on a bench across the Broad Walk from Septimus, the troubled veteran of the Great War, and his wife, Lucrezia, who are passing time before a doctor's visit. As Septimus hallucinates about his war experiences and Lucrezia paces between her husband and the Readymoney fountain, Peter naps on a nearby bench (see figs. 4 and 5). This precise spot, adjacent to the London Zoo, is an appropriate place for Peter to enlarge his imperial fantasies: the park (the zoo in particular) was one of the city's most popular and elaborate manifestations of London's identity as the metropolitan center.[4] Thousands of animal specimens, and the descriptive explanations attached to their cages, paid tribute to the ingenuity of British science and the bravery of the country's explorers and armed forces. The collection of animals emphasized not only the breadth of British power but also the technical sophistication required to reproduce the native habitats suitable for its different residents. Londoners could vicariously participate in the pleasures of empire by viewing and

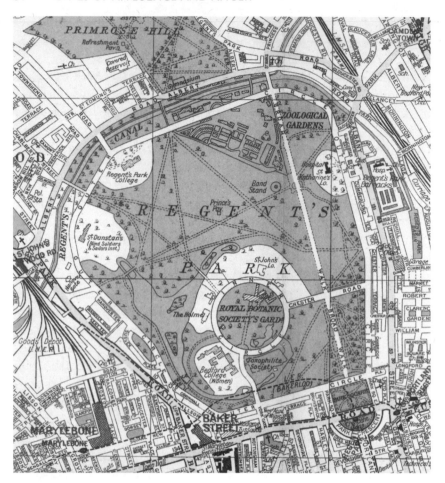

Figure 4. Map of Regent's Park, 1923. (Courtesy of the Map Collection, Yale University Library)

sometimes touching the subjugated animals (which were often likened, in appearance and disposition, to subject peoples). And if animals were not sufficient to fuel the imperial imagination, London's parks housed exotic plants to remind Londoners of their metropolitan position.[5] Until 1932 the Royal Botanic Society had a garden in Regent's Park specializing in many rare species.[6] A carefully manicured park could serve as an instrument of education because it demonstrated the triumph of planning and diligence over unruly, wild behavior. Given the park's carefully managed appearance, it is hardly surprising that Peter thinks he has never seen the metropolis "look so enchanting—the softness of

Figure 5. Readymoney Fountain, Regent's Park, 1930s. In 1869 Cowasjee Jehangir Ready-Money, a wealthy Parsi, donated the fountain in recognition of British efforts to protect Parsi rights in India.

the distances; the richness; the greenness; the civilization, after India, he thought, strolling across the grass" (76). London's parks provided constant reminders of the city's metropolitan character in the form of the zoo, landscaping, or "an absurd statue" (59). Wherever they walked, Londoners saw empire condensed and presented for their enjoyment. Metropolitan subjects imagined themselves as proxy imperialists merely by circulating within the city's imperial quarter. Because a good deal of the novel takes place in Regent's Park—including this crucial meeting of Septimus and Peter—I want to spend a few pages discussing how the material form, ideological content, and political function of central London, especially its parks, evolved during this historical moment.

PARKS FOR THE PEOPLE

The years 1885 to 1914 were the high point of park construction in England. By the turn of the century, London's parks were one of the primary spaces in which the English celebrated their colonial triumphs, articulated their imperial vision, and educated themselves about the gravity of their position as rulers.[7] That this period coincided with Britain's most aggressive pursuit of imperialist policy is no accident: public parks were designed to generate domestic enthusiasm for overseas expansion. Additionally, parks doubled as a means of encouraging physical, intellectual, and moral fitness in the working class, who in the eyes of middle-class reformers desperately needed healthy leisure opportunities. For proponents of empire, however, working-class men became the specific target of this didactic geography because their labor, as soldiers, was urgently required for the maintenance of a colonial army (just as their work in the factory was essential for the continuation of imperial economic exchange). Anxious that poor nutrition, bad housing, and enervating manual labor were leading to physical deterioration and mental degradation, reformers hoped that parks could help restore strength and vigor to urban, working-class families.

Since the middle of the nineteenth century, the reformist elements of the middle class had been championing the cause of park construction in urban areas. As Hazel Conway argues, most historians describe parks as "a prime example of the Victorian 'aptitude for passionate reform' and as an attempt to improve the physical, moral and spiritual condition of the urban dweller" (10). As I have already suggested, the South African War, more so than other colonial campaigns, made transparent the connections between the condition of England's working class, its cities, and Britain's imperial ambitions. Parks became important because many hoped that they could both rehabilitate working-class masculinity and generate enthusiasm for colonial conquest. Not only could parks augment men's physical strength and psychological health by providing space for physical exercise and moral education, but their monuments might allow men to enhance their masculinity by appealing to an imperial narrative of subjectivity.[8] As Jonathan Schneer writes in *London 1900,* the city government managed the return of soldiers from South Africa "in such a way as to create, or to sustain, a mood of imperialist determination among a public" that was otherwise skeptical of the endeavor (28–29). The route of the parade retraced the steps of the Victoria

Jubilee, marching the soldiers through Hyde Park and along the perimeter of Green Park so as to maximize the number of potential attendees. The organizers were similarly eager to create an environment that would fully reflect this commitment to empire, and Queen Victoria's Memorial, commissioned in 1901 and completed in 1911, is perhaps London's most recognizable marker of this trend. The planning committee decided to erect a monument to the recently deceased monarch in front of Buckingham Palace (sitting at the juncture of Green and St. James's parks). The vista from the street was not grand enough, however, so the plans included provisions for a complete overhaul of the Mall, the boulevard leading to the palace from the east. For Richard Dalloway, who strolls by the statue some dozen years after its completion, the memorial testifies to England's glory and instantly reaffirms his belief that it "was a great age in which to have lived" (127). As Tori Smith suggests, the committee and its supporters proposed such an ambitious plan because the city lacked impressive imperial monuments that reflected England's overseas possessions. Smith reads the allegorical figure as a potent symbol, reminding both men and women of their different responsibilities as imperial subjects for the maintenance of empire. The statue's clear message is that women were needed to maintain the home and produce healthy offspring, while the empire required dedicated, selfless Englishmen to stock the armed forces.[9]

Two important considerations emerge from this brief discussion of London and its displays of imperial prowess. First, parks were altered to meet the growing demand for public reminders of empire within metropolitan space. Imperialism was not a project played out simply on the battlefields of South Africa—"over there"—but also on the material and social geography of the metropolis. Parks were useful tools in the struggle to create fit imperial subjects in England and were in fact particularly valuable because they could reach such a diverse population. It would be reductive to suggest that these metropolitan districts, as an overtly ideological architectural project, constitute a repressive disciplinary apparatus. Such architectural forms interpellate subjects by appealing to intellectual and physical desires, recruiting subjects and encouraging them to become active agents in their own subjection. It is not simply that subjects need to internalize these messages for ideology to have an effect: the urban environment always-already produces subjects by framing and informing subjective experiences. Second, the designers of parks and imperial monuments were heavily invested in the project of shaping and directing social and individual bodies by manipulating urban space. Parks, in their very plan and execution, were engaged in the process of creating morally and physically fit people by channeling and regulating human traffic. London's parks were designed expressly for the purpose of attracting, gathering, and circulating bodies within a bounded area. If imperialism created a logic of governance in the colonies themselves, it also necessitated a system of bodily traffic built into the material environment of the metropole.

MAKING MEN

Public parks were more than spaces for leisure and instruction about empire. Throughout England, parks were engaged in the process of "making men." In the wake of the Boer War and the high rate of potential recruits deemed unfit for service, parks were designed to address fears about the degeneration of working-class male bodies. *Mrs. Dalloway* demonstrates how the twin threats of imperial decline and class conflict were played out on men's bodies and how the geography of parks linked these two social problems to the same dynamic of metropolitan space. Through the figure of Septimus, the novel shows how this imperial vision, by the 1920s, had reached a point of insuperable contradictions. London's imperial architecture was largely a prewar relic, and the ostensibly unnecessary death of Septimus reminds the audience how poorly English military ambitions had served most young men. In fact, much of *Mrs. Dalloway*'s irony comes from the dissonance between the novel's largely prewar, imperial geography and a decidedly interwar sensibility, which reflects growing suspicions about England's role in global politics. Septimus, in the narrative's most scathing critique of the city's imperial geography, is the character whose body and mind have been marked most clearly by the effects of English military ambitions.

Since the 1830s reformers had been arguing that park construction ought to be part of a public health campaign to improve the physical fitness of the working class.[10] Almost a century later, Richard Dalloway, walking through Green Park on his way home, suggests that this reformist philosophy still had many adherents: "[H]e was of the opinion that every park, and every square, during the summer months should be open to children" (126). Aside from offering a place of relative peace and clean air within the congested metropolis, parks provided a venue for sporting competition, whose social importance in English culture should not be underestimated. For the middle class in particular, organized sporting activities, especially team games such as cricket, represented an essential component of physical, mental, and moral education. As many cultural historians have noted, the English middle class had an obsessive relationship with cricket, "exporting" it enthusiastically to the colonies as well as to England's working class.[11] Team sports encouraged discipline and cooperation over individualism. Peter, unsurprisingly, is passionate about the institution: "But cricket was no mere game. Cricket was important. He could never help reading about cricket" (177). By subordinating the aspirations of a single player to collective goals, cricket resembled "real life" in war and capitalism, where "group" success might require individual sacrifice. Parks helped the middle class consolidate its position as the arbiters of sporting culture, thereby attempting to assert control over the disposition of men's bodies. Sporting activities were part of ideological training, preparing men to accept the basic premises of social inequity under capitalist modes of production as well as mimicking military life during armed conflict. When Dr. Bradshaw, one of Septimus's doctors, recommends his patient find some kind of diversionary hobby such as cricket, he merely prescribes the culturally accepted cure for male depression (99). Cricket, Bradshaw argues, promises to take his mind off his troubles and "make him take notice of the real things" in life (25). Mr. Brewer, Septimus's employer, also recommends the sporting cure, which he insists would "make a man" out of his young employee. Ironically, as the novel reminds us a few moments later, it was only "in the trenches," not in sporting competition, that Septimus "developed manliness" to a sufficient degree (93). The text's caustic aside reminds us that sports are a grotesque parody of his wartime experiences.

Septimus is the locus of *Mrs. Dalloway*'s social critique. His experience of class difference and the trauma of war forms the basis of the text's narrative irony: his disturbing reactions to the urban environment even haunt Clarissa and Peter as they circulate throughout London, reminding the audience that interpellation can have dire material consequences for individual subjects. His relationship to urban space is quite distinct from Peter's, for example, partly owing to his different class background. He is, like Leonard Bast before him, the self-improving type from the lower-middle class. The scenes in the park, for instance, make it abundantly clear that a man of his means didn't know what to do with himself in central London during regular business hours. His "shabby overcoat" and simple "brown boots" make him difficult to place with any certainty, but the narrator puts him down for "a clerk, but of the better sort" (13, 90). All things considered, he is "a border case . . . might end with a house in Purley and a motor car, or continue renting apartments in back streets all his life." He struggles hopelessly to educate himself by absorbing "books borrowed from public libraries, read in the evening after the day's work" (90). Despite their class differences, however, the novel's stream-of-consciousness technique makes it clear that Peter, Clarissa, and Septimus occupy the same urban environment. They see, hear, and touch the same things, fashioning their subjectivity out of the same basic context. But their distinct social positions give them entirely different hermeneutic strategies for decoding the heterogeneity of the city. While Peter feels comfortable using the city to enhance his masculinity and bolster his self-confidence, Septimus remains cowed by the pace of urban life. In short, he understands himself as subject to, rather than a subject in, the city. Although the novel's characters circulate through the city in similar ways, their very different relationship to the city's ideological architecture leads to highly individualized, dissonant experiences of urban life.

Septimus's feelings of estrangement and otherness are a result not only of his sense of class difference but also of his participation in the war. Although he served with distinction, the psychological traumas of the conflict manifest themselves long after the last gun has been fired. He and Lucrezia spend most of the novel soliciting the advice of doctors in hope of alleviating his shell shock. The narrative repeatedly frames its portrayal of urban life by juxtaposing Septimus's paranoia with Clarissa's exultant strolls and Peter's easy, self-assured spectatorship. The text frequently reminds us that interpellation happens under shared material and ideological conditions but operates on the principle of individuation. Whereas Peter thinks of London and the park as the pinnacle of the civilized world, Septimus's hallucinations lead him to visualize his dead friends moving among the trees. The park taunts the young veteran; the sound of the zoo's baying animals, which temporarily reaffirms Peter's belief in the righteousness of the imperial mission, mutates into an elegy for fallen comrades in Septimus's ears. When he stumbles across statues of military heroes and other tributes to armed conflict, they do not inspire feelings of national pride or patriotism but instead remind him of his comrades who perished during the war. London's imperial architecture gives Peter the space to amplify his sexuality, but those same symbols mock Septimus. The novel consistently relies on the ideological contradictions inherent in London's geography to manufacture this style of narrative irony. The novel's critique of imperialism and military aggression is so effective because it is also a critique of London's built environment. For this technique to work, it is essential that Peter and Septimus occupy the same space and observe the same things but offer radically incompatible readings of the urban condition.

URBAN CONTINGENCIES AS NATIONAL PARTICULARITY

The scene in the park is crucial because it provides the physical and symbolic link between Septimus and Peter, who remain unknown to one another throughout the novel. Peter watches Septimus and Lucrezia arguing, mistakenly thinking they are engaged in a harmless lovers' tiff. Waking up from a dream about Clarissa, he watches a child run into a woman's legs and fall to the ground, causing the young girl to break into tears and Peter to burst out in laughter. The woman, though untroubled by the collision, appears to be in the midst of "an awful scene" with her companion, a man sitting on a nearby bench. As he gets up to leave the park, Peter wonders what the strange man might have been "saying to her to make her look like that," but in the end puts it down to a harmless domestic row, just the "family life of the parks" (76). It makes Peter reminisce fondly on his own youth and his unsuccessful courtship with Clarissa, when he enjoyed the sudden flare of passion caused by an unexpected lovers' quarrel. But Lucrezia and Septimus, the distressed couple Peter observes, are at wit's end. Unlike Peter, who dozes in the middle of Regent's Park, Lucrezia feels horribly "exposed" in "this awful city . . . surrounded by the enormous trees" but no friendly faces (70–71). She and Septimus wait anxiously for an appointment with a Harley Street specialist. Septimus suffers from hallucinations and talks of suicide, a delayed psychological reaction to his experience as a soldier (the novel is set in 1923). The park's foliage, which Peter thinks so beautiful after his stint abroad, tortures Septimus, who imagines his dead friend, Evans, moving among the branches. The doctor's visit only compounds the couple's agony, with Septimus taking his own life a few hours later.

The novel hinges on these kinds of misunderstandings, accidents, and chance encounters. Previous readings of *Mrs. Dalloway* have explored either the novel's investment in technical experimentation or its articulation of political critique, but few have emphasized the mutually constitutive relationship between the two. Most structuralist interpretations of the novel, for instance, focus on the problem of social time (epitomized by the repeated striking of Big Ben) or memory as examples of the text's commitment to principles of aesthetic experimentation. Arguing in this vein, Paul Ricoeur suggests that the narrator's ability "*to move* from one stream of consciousness [i.e., one character's mind] to another" is determined by the novel's manipulation of memory and subjective consciousness. Here is how Ricoeur analyzes the crucial scene on the park bench: "It is in this way that the story of Septimus, completely foreign to the Dalloway's circle, is incorporated for the first time into the narrative field. . . . The unity of place, the face-to-face discussion on the bench in the same park, is equivalent to the unity of a single instant onto which the narrator grafts the extension of a span of memory" (2:104). For Ricoeur, the form of the novel is radical because it allows Woolf to rethink the relationship between memory, modernist subjectivity, and the practice of reading. As Ricoeur insists, the point of the text is to "*refigure time itself in our reading*" by contrasting subjective and objective experiences of temporality, juxtaposing personalized (subjective) memories with shared (objective) experiences, like the sounding of the hour or the backfiring of an automobile (105). In order to see time as a subjective marker—how the text refigures time as discontinuous, multiple, and highly individualized ("onto which the narrator grafts the extension of a span of memory")—Ricoeur must ascribe a temporary "unity of place" to this moment. In contrast, I have tried to show how moments of shared experiences create the effect of radical spatial discontinuity. In other words, my analysis does not proceed by assuming a contradictory relationship between the subjective and the objective; I read subjective experiences in competition with one another rather than with an objective (or narrative) reality. By showing how social space produces and is produced by the individual subject, I have tried to describe how the text theorizes subjectivity and the environment as mutually constitutive. Because the space of the park, to work with the example at hand, is the material articulation of ideological conflicts, it participates in the production of discrete subjects—subjects who may share a space and a time, for that matter, but experience an entirely different place.

The narrative's symbolic economy connects these characters by having them circulate in the same spaces and observe the same events. Peter comes to "know," and grossly misread, Septimus through the narrative manipulation of the urban environment (Septimus returns the favor when he mistakes Peter for a corpse propped up on a bench).[12] The ironic distance between the two men reaches its zenith when Septimus commits suicide. Walking to Clarissa's party, Peter hears the siren of the ambulance that collects the soldier's remains. To Peter, the siren's wail signifies "the efficiency, the organization, the communal spirit of London" (164). He, Septimus, and Clarissa have particularly dissonant ways of moving through the city; their different readings are the grinding gears of the narrative motor, reluctantly meshing and unhappily jerking the novel forward. The narrative uses the social diversity of the city both to critique the ideological character of urban space and to establish its claim to a modernist aesthetics. Through these types of random encounters, which depend on the compact physical space and manifold diversity of London's traffic, the text establishes both structural bonds and ironic distance between its main characters. While the narrative form purports to fashion connections between people, it continually reminds us that those links remain largely symbolic, the product of narrative manipulations and urban contingencies.[13] Such chance encounters, forged through the text's use of stream of consciousness and other modernist techniques, merely underscore the deep ideological contradictions inherent in metropolitan space.

Although Peter's comically misinformed interpretation of the ambulance is perhaps the most biting instance of dysfunctional reading strategies, the text's structural economy as a whole operates through these kinds of ironic narrative conjunctions. In one of the novel's most brilliant scenes, the skywriting incident,[14] the inability of scattered subjects to locate compatible understandings in the urban environment takes a very literal form. Although multiple characters simultaneously see an airplane writing letters overhead, none can decipher the script with any confidence: each character reads an advertisement for an entirely different product. While concentrations of people in urban centers might logically lead to a kind of group consciousness or communal spirit, the novel repeatedly demonstrates that such connections remain more fantasy than reality. A few pages earlier, when the text contrasts Clarissa's easy enjoyment of the crowded city with Septimus's paranoid delusions, this kind of satiric joking assumes a more pointed form. The first dozen pages of the novel describe Clarissa's euphoria as she walks the streets near her home of more than twenty years. She revels triumphantly "in the bellow and uproar" of London's traffic; "she loved" all the chaos, the unpredictability and vitality of walking, of "life" at "this moment in June" (2–3). A backfiring automobile, however, instantly transfers the node of focalization to her doppelgänger, Septimus.[15] By contrast, he feels terrified and exposed in the crowded street, mistakenly thinking, "It is I who am blocking the way" (14). Septimus's paranoia and anxiety serve as an immediate rejoinder to Clarissa's carefree enjoyment of the urban environment. Although they simultaneously experience the same innocuous, random event—a moment that helps the novel fashion a symbolic link between the two characters—their understandings of that event contrast sharply, creating an economy of dissonance even as it promises a formal connection between them.

Mrs. Dalloway's narrative tension between the urban monad and the possibilities of collective consciousness is itself a representation of ideological processes articulated through spatial systems. Interpellation proceeds on the basis of individuation. Ideology hails or recruits subjects by identifying them as discrete subjects and appealing to their sense of or desire for uniqueness as individuals: *"Ideology has the function (which defines it) of 'constituting' concrete individuals as subjects"* (Althusser, "Ideology" 171). If ideology is a discursive system that creates a kind of social narrative that seeks to explain the lived relations between the individual and material conditions, it begins with the premise that the subject, by virtue of consciousness, is discrete and relatively autonomous. Ideological structures, therefore, simultaneously affect and are affected by subjective experience. *Mrs. Dalloway's* narrative system, by allowing subjective interpretations of the city to confront one another, repeatedly stages the articulation of subjectivity as a function of irreducible individuality. Although ideology may be a general system—in this case, embedded in the built environment—it operates by virtue of its ability to parse subjects through the mechanism of interpellation. And this creation of unique subjectivity is not simply an ideological myth but instead the systematic product of interpellation, which recruits subjects as discrete social actors.

The novel's elaboration of urban subjectivity, however, should not be read as a wholesale rejection of corporate sensibilities. Clarissa, for instance, imagines the city itself as a complex organism that will help her recuperate some kind of lost social unity. Despite the vast social, material, and political differences between herself and her urban counterparts, she posits a strong spiritual bond with her fellow metropolitan subjects. Her lone metaphysical "gift," she proclaims, "was knowing people almost by instinct" (7). Using vaguely religious terminology, she calls it a "transcendental theory" that connects her to "people she had never spoken to, some woman in the street, some man behind a counter" (166). Clarissa's quest for metaphysical connection provides a subjective analogue to the novel's narrative theory, which creates symbolic links between otherwise unconnected characters.

The novel concludes with Clarissa's party, through which she seeks to resolve the divisions of the city by assembling people for a celebration, a somewhat misguided attempt to make something coherent out of London's fragments. In the final pages, this promise of social unity culminates as Clarissa imagines herself "somehow very like" Septimus. The most optimistic readings of the novel claim that the text's fluid narrative technique "crests finally in a triumph of discord and martial destruction," establishing an epiphanic moment of "understanding" and deep sympathy between Clarissa, Peter, and Septimus.[16] Although the novel as a whole is fairly sympathetic toward Clarissa, the final pages highlight the shortcomings of her desire to connect with strangers: by withdrawing from her guests and musing on death, even she acknowledges some of the inherent limitations of her "offering." If anything, the novel's continual juxtaposition of contradictory voices makes Clarissa's claim to "feel somehow very like" Septimus read like the well-intentioned but naive fantasy of a privileged metropolitan subject. The novel remains suspicious of Clarissa's desire to empathize with her less fortunate counterpart. Even though the narrative's formal arrangement promises to manufacture allegiances between a disparate cast of characters, its ironic tone and modernist joking belie any straightforward attempts at social reconciliation. In this sense, the novel documents the effects of individual subjectivity, but it also critiques ideology as a discursive system that promises to eradicate social contradictions by organizing material relationships hierarchically. The novel's modernist narrative style—particularly its deployment of stream of consciousness to fabricate ironic juxtapositions—doubles as a form of political dissent, scrutinizing the divisive ideological messages of the city by staging the contradictions embedded in the articulation of individual subjectivity.

I emphasize this point throughout this chapter because previous readings of *Mrs. Dalloway* have not adequately explained the connections between the novel's use of modernist narrative techniques, its depiction of the urban environment, and this subtext of ideological critique. Although many critics have offered sophisticated readings of the novel's aesthetics (Ricoeur) or its oppositional politics (Zwerdling), there are few satisfactory discussions that attempt to bridge the gap between the novel's pursuit of a modernist aesthetic practice and its commitment to social critique. In other words, critics have found it difficult to explain the compatibility of the text's political skepticism and its use of modernist narrative strategies. J. Hillis Miller, for example, provides one of the most sophisticated readings of the text's narrative form, but his reading fails to systematically interrogate the political implications of what he calls the novel's "narrative voice." Because the characters in the novel are largely unaware of one another, he argues, they are dependent on the narrator to turn their experiences into a coherent, collective narrative. Although the text makes use of external events (i.e., events witnessed by multiple characters) to facilitate transitions between characters, Miller argues that the work of the narrator accomplishes this task. In this way, the narrative forges links between individual characters (and by extension, he argues, between the novel and other texts in the English tradition). The novel's collective consciousness, organized by the omniscient narrator, allows the text to function as a fictional All Souls' Day, calling up from the grave the ghosts of the past. This technique loosens the bonds of time and space, permitting Clarissa's adolescent recollections to bracket Peter's sexual fantasies or Septimus's memories of the war.

Miller strengthens the connection between *Mrs. Dalloway*'s webbed narrative structure and this spectral symbolism by demonstrating that the novel quotes directly and indirectly from "Aller Seelen," a Richard Strauss song about All Souls' Day. As Peter leaves the park, he hears a ragged homeless woman outside Regent's Park tube station singing fragments of the tune. Peter gives the woman a shilling as he gets into the taxi; the scene shifts immediately to Lucrezia, who also registers the woman's voice. The narrative achieves continuity between characters because these seemingly random, external events point to a common history as well as a shared present. Miller argues that although individual characters, especially Clarissa, are eager to "take possession of these continuities," it is the organizing consciousness of the narrator "which gathers together disparate elements, pieces them into a unity, and lifts them up into the daylight world in a gesture of ecstatic delight" (117). Similarly, when this moment of unity proves incomplete and illusory toward the end of the novel, this becomes known "only to the agile and ubiquitous mind of the narrator. [These fragments] exist only within the embrace of that reconciling spirit" (125).

In short, Miller's argument puts too much stock in the unnamed narrator and does not pay enough attention to the social and material environment that supports the text's symbolic structure. Miller's argument naturalizes, or ascribes subjectivity to, the narrator, but it fails to fully recognize the cultural and ideological work that the narrator accomplishes. My goal is to connect the novel's aesthetics—what Miller calls its "narrative voice"—with its subtext of political critique. I am not arguing that the narrator performs no organizational function—it arranges all the seamless transitions so essential to the text's creation of a social, intersubjective consciousness—but that we need to know more about the ideological underpinnings of the urban environment, particularly its intermingling of symbolic death and frenetic life, in order to recognize the ironic slant of these narrative conjunctions. What matters is not so much the text's ability to move, neutrally, between different points of view, but its ability to show how each of the characters performs a different kind of interpretive activity on the event in question. In other words, individuals provide radically dissimilar readings of the same event because the social position of each (rather than their narrative positions, as Miller argues) differs so drastically. Lucrezia and Peter do not read the homeless woman differently because the narrator positions them relative to one another, but because they do not move around the park and city in comparable ways. To follow the transition between Peter and Lucrezia through the singing vagrant, we need to have knowledge of social space more so than of narrative techniques: we need to realize that a homeless woman leads the two characters to highly dissonant conclusions because they understand and circulate within the space of the park differently. The novel creates meaning through the contrasting interpretations provided by its characters, and these are as dependent on their relative social positions as they are on the techniques of the narrative itself. Most importantly, this type of narrative irony functions as a system of critique, demonstrating how the ideological function of the built environment informs individual subjectivity. These regular conjunctions show the unique combinations of pleasure and oppression that characterize life in the modernist city.

Miller's argument, however, makes a convincing case that fragments of the past, especially Clarissa's and Peter's memories of their courtship, figure prominently in *Mrs. Dalloway*'s narrative construction. As we wander through London, the text periodically returns us to Bourton, the country home of Clarissa's family. Miller reads these moments as running commentary on the history of English fiction: such references to Bourton allude to the pastoral tradition and the condition-of-England

novel I discussed in the previous chapter. Although many critics emphasize Woolf's innovative style and the text's affinity with cosmopolitan
modernism, Miller shows that it is possible to read her work as the "fulfillment" of the English tradition rather than a definitive break from it
(100). But reading the novel this way also encourages us to consider how
it regards itself in relation to this literary heritage. Peter, still smitten
with Clarissa, remembers her "ravishing, romantic, recalling some field
or English harvest. He saw her most often in the country, not in London"
(167). Despite these fantasies, other passages make it clear that, however
pleasant those days at Bourton were, they are definitely over: Clarissa
remains a steadfast Londoner, though the countryside might be better
for her health, and Sally Seaton wistfully reminds Peter that those golden
summers are "a thing of the past—all over now" (205). The shuttling
back and forth between Bourton of the 1880s and London of 1923, in
fact, forces us to reflect on England's plight in the intervening years. The
theme of shattered innocence, like so many texts of the World War I era,
infuses these sporadic recollections. Though Clarissa regularly harkens
back to her country retreat, thinking of it also makes her realize "how
sheltered the life at Bourton was" (34). Peter, likewise, remembers fondly
the heated political discussions he and Sally, self-appointed radicals,
would initiate. Their dreams of social and political reform seem quaint
and distant when compared with the failures of the intervening years.
The ensuing violence has made other forms of social oppression much
more difficult to ignore. The war may have compromised such forms of
pastoral naïveté, but they remain embedded in the novel's memorial to
national literary culture. It is as if the novel drags the misty greensward
of Bourton kicking and screaming into urban modernity, not so much
to repudiate the past as to consciously connect readers with that bygone moment. The shifts between Bourton and London, like the novel's
interest in metropolitan imperial architecture, highlight the difference
between pre- and interwar sensibilities (as well as the difference between
pastoral and urban literary sensibilities) of which Woolf was so acutely
conscious.

   Mrs. Dalloway's regular references to a collective pastoral memory,
which Miller persuasively reads as an attempt to plant the novel firmly
in the soil of the English canon, speak to the particular forms of ambivalence rooted in the text's contrary pairs. The novel's use of high
modernist narrative techniques to render the political ironies of metropolitan life functions as way to imagine a specifically English form

of experimental writing. Woolf's vexed attitude toward her European, overtly avant-garde contemporaries is well documented. As the broad outlines of her fictional oeuvre suggest, Woolf was eager to soak modernist aesthetics in the social realities of metropolitan culture and national literary traditions.[17] *Mrs. Dalloway* chronicles, with measured proportions of love and frustration, the subjective conditions of metropolitan life in the years following World War I. The novel's commitment to formal innovation—its desire to "make it new," to cite Ezra Pound's now-famous dictum—does not merely fulfill an abstract need for aesthetic experimentation but also facilitates the expression of political dissent by capturing the delicate ironies of metropolitan space. The text's social critiques, particularly of England's urban class system and London's imperialist architecture, are not only a way to make it new but a way to make it *English*—a way to domesticate continental modernism's pursuit of novelty by translating the aesthetics of the avant-garde into the political idiom and geographical space of England. The novel's reformist impulses, much like Forster's in *Howards End,* work on the basis of political dissent and recuperation: though much of London's imperialist and patriarchal culture ought to be destroyed, the text suggests that there is much worth preserving, too. The narrative uses modernist techniques to juxtapose contrary ideas, allowing the novel to capture both the delightful and depressing sides of metropolitan culture. *Mrs. Dalloway* offers, in other words, a culturally specific modernism, or a practice that engages the emerging techniques of global modernism while articulating the geographical particularities of metropolitan life. The novel's unique narrative system, so dependent on the conjunction of London's material and representational geography, effectively anglicizes modernist narrative techniques, situating the quest for aesthetic experimentation in the discourse of English exceptionalism.

FOR THERE SHE WAS

If the first half of the novel wanders London's streets, squares, and parks to establish symbolic connections between its main characters, the second half of *Mrs. Dalloway* orients itself around Clarissa's exclusive social world and the Dalloways' domestic realm. But as the novel shows, a strict division between public and private space in the modernist city is impossible to maintain.[18] Continuing its politically motivated representation of metropolitan geography, the text is unwilling to let Clarissa

retreat peacefully to the sanctuary of her home, family, and social inti-
mates. In a concrete effort to mold the disparate, isolated subjects of the
city into a harmonious social organism, Clarissa defends her investment
in the party by describing it as a simple "offering," an attempt "to combine, to create" something new out of the fragments of modern, urban
existence (132). Though the novel is far from dismissive of Clarissa's
party or her domestic affairs, the final passages suggest that even she becomes somewhat disillusioned with the contours of her social life. The
text continually reminds us that spaces of bourgeois sociability, like the
Dalloways' party, are constantly under threat of disruption in the form
of imperial anxieties and class resentments, such as those embodied by
Septimus and Miss Kilman, who competes with Clarissa for the affection of Elizabeth Dalloway, the couple's adolescent daughter. If Clarissa's
party represents an attempt to establish the kinds of direct connections
promised by the narrative's symbolic economy, the text's political ambivalence and commitment to ideological critique underscore the exclusivity of her plans.

The intrusions of Peter, Septimus, and Miss Kilman into the Dalloways' social world suggest that repressed anxieties—colonial and
domestic—tend to return at inauspicious moments. Peter, for his part,
simply refuses to respect the informal rule that guests refrain from raising contentious political issues at these kinds of functions. He goes to the
party, against his better judgment, "because he wanted to ask Richard
what they were doing in India—the conservative duffers. . . . What did
the government mean—Richard Dalloway would know—to do about
India?" (175). In spite of Clarissa's thorough planning, she cannot exclude from her party the social contradictions on which metropolitan
subjectivity is constructed. Peter, with his political ambivalences and
personal jealousies, completely unnerves Clarissa, threatening to throw
the whole affair into disarray. Clarissa immediately intuits his unsaid
reproaches: "She could see Peter out of the tail of her eye, criticising
her. . . . It was extraordinary how Peter put her into these states just by
coming and standing in a corner" (182–83). Troubled by the instabilities
that put his own future in doubt, Peter has the potential to disrupt the
party and expose the hypocrisies of Britain's imperial project.

The introduction of Septimus, through casual conversation, further
clouds the party's horizons. Bradshaw, the attending physician who has
witnessed Septimus's suicide, brings the shocking news of his patient's
death to the collective life of the party. Clarissa, already nervous about

the gathering, reacts shrilly to the revelation: "Oh, thought Clarissa, in the middle of my party, here's death. . . . What business had the Bradshaws to talk of death at her party? A young man had killed himself. And they talked of it at her party—the Bradshaws, talked of death. . . . But why had he done it? And the Bradshaws talked of it at her party!" (200–201). The hostess recoils at the mention of such unseemly topics. Unable to comprehend the Bradshaws' ignorance of proper decorum, Clarissa frets over the unnecessary disclosure, as if death had no place in the temporary world of celebration she has created. The cynical reader, of course, will immediately recognize that it is only through a messy suicide that an nameless, lower-middle-class war veteran could insinuate himself into and potentially contaminate the secure space of the party. This moment gestures, in parody, toward the kind of deep social bond Clarissa envisions throughout the novel. She continually imagines her subjectivity organically connected with strangers of all kinds, and his unwelcome interruption offers a technical analogue to her imaginative intersubjectivity, providing highly symbolic connections between Clarissa and other characters in the novel.

Clarissa's resentment of the Bradshaws is short-lived, however, for she begins to contemplate more seriously the plight of this unknown man. Guided by her instinctive dislike for Bradshaw, she reads the suicide as a stark act of "defiance" and also "an attempt to communicate. . . . There was an embrace in death" (201). Like many modernist novels, the text culminates with a scene of private contemplation, making its thin plot seem particularly inconsequential in the context of this narrative crescendo. During a moment of introspective clarity, Clarissa feels "somehow very like him—the young man who had killed himself. She felt glad that he had done it; thrown it away. . . . He made her feel the beauty; made her feel the fun. But she must go back [to the party]. She must assemble" (203). Revisiting the novel's theme of unlikely metaphysical connections between strangers, affirming the continuity of life for the final time against the finality of death, Clarissa imagines herself as "somehow very like" Septimus. In her mind, death not only gives way to life but actually reinvigorates it, making life's beauty more palpable. But how is she like him—or more important, why might she wish to project her subjectivity in such terms?

Clarissa's desire to recuperate the suicide of Septimus, to read the desperate act of an anonymous soldier as an event that confirms the immanence of life, reflects the novel's general system of contraries.

Subjectivity, the text suggests, emerges in the push and pull of competing forces, life and death in particular. Though Clarissa is the character we most associate with vitality and energy in the novel, she contemplates her own demise on several occasions, believing that the individual survives beyond life's corporeal end in "the ebb and flow of things, here, there . . . she being part, she was positive, of the trees at home; of the house there, ugly, rambling all to bits and pieces as it was; part of people she had never met" (8). Death assimilates the subject into the materiality of the modern city; monuments to the dead are oppressive because we all melt, democratically as it were, into the nooks and crannies of the urban environment. The modern metropolis is thus an inimitable monument to its dead and a crucible of renewed life at the same time. Septimus, likewise, is the character we most associate with death, yet even he experiences the beauty and passion of life as vividly as anyone in the novel. As his wife paces anxiously in Regent's Park, Septimus feels earth's beauty speaking to him alone: "We welcome, the world seemed to say; we accept; we create. Beauty, the world seemed to say . . . beauty sprang instantly. To watch a leaf quivering in the rush of air was an exquisite joy. Up in the sky the swallows swooping, swerving, flinging themselves in and out, round and round . . . all of this, calm and reasonable as it was, made out of ordinary things as it was, was the truth now; beauty, that was the truth now. Beauty was everywhere" (74). This unqualified assertion of life's beauty by Septimus, relying once again on images of rising and falling, and fertility amid decay, underscores the contradictory function of metropolitan subjectivity in the novel. Being a Londoner means experiencing this unexpectedly intense convergence of pleasure and pain. The novel shows every major character oscillating between blissful crests and harrowing troughs. This regular alternation of emotional peaks and valleys works toward the text's larger project of debunking London's oppressive structures, imagining a metropolis divested of its imperial architecture and class hierarchies. Yet even these forms of political oppression, the novel concedes, create their own forms of enjoyment. It is a narrative caught in two minds, exposing the hypocrisies of imperialism and the English class system while reclaiming the special attractions of a vibrant, diverse city. The metaphorical end of life—understood here as the death of an imperial, hierarchical city—becomes an occasion for its social rebirth.

Clarissa's interest in Septimus, or at least his suicide, would be more straightforward and less politically complicated were it not for the

presence of Miss Kilman in the novel. If Septimus allows Clarissa to find
hope in death, Miss Kilman forces her to confront jealousy and hatred
as an integral part of life. Miss Kilman, with a university degree and a
grasp of history that impresses Richard Dalloway, works as a tutor for
Elizabeth after being sacked from her job as a teacher during the war (for
her German heritage and sympathies). Poor, educated, evangelical, and
self-righteous, Miss Kilman can't be in the room for a moment without
making Clarissa ashamed of her wealth and lack of serious, intellectual
interests (10–11). Worse, her visceral hatred of Miss Kilman eats away at
the very foundations of Clarissa's happiness:

> It rasped through her, to have stirring about in her this brutal mon-
> ster! . . . this hatred, which, since her illness, had power to make her
> feel scraped, hurt in her spine; gave her physical pain, and made all
> pleasure in beauty, in friendship, in being well, in being loved and
> making her home delightful rock, quiver, and bend as if indeed there
> were a monster grubbing at the roots, as if the whole panoply of con-
> tent were nothing but self love! this hatred! (11)

Coming as it does in the middle of her morning stroll, this passage invites us to compare Clarissa's embrace of London's vitality with this sear-
ing hatred that infests her friendships, family, and home. Her loathing
of Miss Kilman is so powerful that it goes beyond simple, fleeting emotions, becoming a physical condition that wracks her fragile body with
pain, momentarily effacing all knowledge of beauty or contentedness.
Merely thinking of Miss Kilman makes Clarissa experience emotions
with more physical immediacy than the flights of fancy inspired by her
delightful walks in the city.

Yet Clarissa is emotionally astute enough to realize that her revulsion
comes less from hatred of Miss Kilman, the actual person, than "the idea
of her, which undoubtedly had gathered in to itself a great deal that was
not Miss Kilman." Although walking through London's crowded streets
allows Clarissa to experience all that is right with the world, Miss Kilman
brings Clarissa face to face with her own vanity and privilege. Furthermore, despite the depth of her loathing, Clarissa also recognizes that
things easily could have been different, "for no doubt with another throw
of the dice . . . she would have loved Miss Kilman! But not in this world.
No" (11). One's wealth and the other's poverty, Clarissa's blissful ignorance and Miss Kilman's moral indignation, turn the pair into natural

enemies. But their mutual hatred, such passages imply, is so intense that it approaches love itself. For her part, Miss Kilman competes with Clarissa for the affection of Elizabeth, while Clarissa's feelings are so strong that they resemble nothing so much as desire: "[T]he gilt rim of the Sir Joshua picture of the little girl with a muff brought back Kilman with a rush; Kilman her enemy. That was satisfying; that was real. Ah, how she hated her—hot, hypocritical, corrupt; with all that power; Elizabeth's seducer; the woman who had crept in to steal and defile (Richard would say, What nonsense!). She hated her: she loved her. It was enemies one wanted, not friends" (190). As this passage suggests, the fine distinctions between desire and revulsion become difficult to draw in the rush of emotions. Like her earlier reflections about Miss Kilman, which come in the midst of her exultant morning stroll, these thoughts occur to Clarissa at the height her party, just after the prime minister makes a grand entrance. It is, Clarissa acknowledges, an appearance that guarantees the unqualified success of her party, yet the awareness of this gives her no lasting pleasure. Instead, it is the thought of Miss Kilman that consumes her. When she sees her guests filled with admiration and a touch of envy, Clarissa is briefly cognizant of the "intoxication of the moment," but then concludes that "these triumphs" had a certain "hollowness; at arm's length they were, not in the heart," whereupon her thoughts veer again toward her enemy (190). Even as she parades her star guest past an approving audience, the pinnacle of achievement for a London hostess, she is drawn to the intense emotional matrix of Miss Kilman, rival for her daughter's loyalty.

Together, the figures of Miss Kilman and Septimus amplify the convoluted emotional parameters of Clarissa's class position. Clarissa's ability to experience pleasure is always counterbalanced by her heightened awareness of pain and insecurity, an ambivalence that becomes most apparent in her unstable relations with these two lower-middle class figures. The novel describes her class position through these affective conditions: class relationships frame her understanding of personal relationships, organizing her feelings of longing and disgust. Miss Kilman's relative indigence threatens her employer, particularly because she does not mask her spite with social graces. More intellectually accomplished but less refined than the typical society matron, Miss Kilman makes no secret of her contempt for and envy of Clarissa. Septimus, in contrast, fits more easily into the position of a nonthreatening victim. Clarissa can read his act of refusal as an embrace of life partly because she does not know him, partly because his act of violence is directed inward, not outward. The novel's frequent depictions of such drastic emotional swings produce two different but related effects: they offer a sustained discourse of ideological critique, showing in great detail the affective conditions and consequences of London's imperial and hierarchical culture, but they also suggest that ideological structures can operate so effectively because they are embedded in sites of real pleasure. The project of making metropolitan culture more equitable and less imperial is so challenging precisely because systems of injustice have been thoroughly enmeshed in tangible forms of emotional, mental, and physical stimulation.

The novel's coupling of emotional contraries shows the underlying ideological function of metropolitan space. As *Mrs. Dalloway* demonstrates, the ideology of class difference becomes operational through the contradictory play of affect, through exasperating combinations of corporeal, bodily, and intellectual pleasures, hesitations, and agonies. Woolf's London becomes coextensive with English culture, simultaneously representing everything admirable and despicable about metropolitan society. The modern city functions as the ideological occasion and physical location of social decay and spiritual renewal. This particular trope of literary London gathers momentum as the century continues; such bipolar portrayals of the capital become progressively more pervasive in descriptions of English exceptionalism. Being a Londoner is part curse, part blessing, and there seems little chance of escaping this sentence, though the particular forms of angst and joy may ultimately depend on one's social position. This form of tortured ambivalence announces the possibility, but also the difficulty, of imaginatively reclaiming London as a postimperial, socially progressive city.

For scholars grown accustomed to feminist readings of Woolf's fiction, what may be most surprising about *Mrs. Dalloway* is that it provides a detailed map of how the twin crises of imperialism and class conflict were played out through male subjectivity in metropolitan space. Interestingly enough, it was the threat of imperial contraction that encouraged the English to think more deeply about the potential costs of domestic social inequity. Because of London's position within the nation and the empire, its inhabitants had a unique vantage point from which to observe the close connection between imperialism and domestic class politics. As the novel shows, public parks were at the forefront of political efforts to organize social traffic within metropolitan space and therein produce an imperial brand of male subjectivity. Through sites of urban pleasure, such as sports and sexual fantasies, parks actively informed the bodily practices of metropolitan men in an attempt to shape masculine subjectivity. Septimus's suicide is only the most drastic example of resistance to this system of physical and psychic discipline, but we can read the whole novel as a subtle assessment of London's material and representational geography.

POSTIMPERIAL PARKS

Briefly discussing *The Lonely Londoners* (1956) will allow me to anticipate the later chapters of this book because the novel offers an opportunity to consider the afterlife of modernism in the context of an emerging postimperial metropolis. Selvon's novel is apposite to this discussion of urban modernism, incorporating many thematic concerns and formal properties of *Mrs. Dalloway* and other texts of the modernist canon. As I mentioned in my first chapter, *The Lonely Londoners,* which documents the experiences of first-generation Caribbean immigrants, counts familiarity with and possession of the imperial capital among the meager dividends of emigration. Although the characters are fully cognizant of the hardships they endure in London, they remain determined to claim their rightful share of metropolitan space.

Most critics, following the lead of another West Indian expatriate, George Lamming, situate this underrated novel in the oral/folk/peasant tradition, citing its extensive, though not exclusive, deployment of a modified West Indian dialect.[19] Such a reading, however, tends to downplay the extent to which the text is invested in metropolitan space and modernist techniques. Emulating Woolf's novel, the text relies on an omniscient, even intrusive, narrator, haunting the novel's large cast of characters as they drift along London's backstreets and byways. The fragmented, lonely Londoners yearn for deeper connections, a possibility explored through the text's restless, constantly shifting narrative. The central character, Moses, is based partially on the itinerant, foreknowing, foresuffering Tiresias, a transcendental homage to English modernism's other great urban text, *The Waste Land.* Selvon's adaptation of high modernism's urban aesthetics speaks to the longer trajectory I am outlining in this book: metropolitan postcolonial literature abandons neither modernism nor its engagement with urban space but instead uses and transforms them to participate in debates about English national culture. In this respect, I read modernism less as a high point, after which there is only decline and dispersal, and more as a transitional, exploratory moment. Postcolonial literature seizes the aesthetic territories and material spaces charted by metropolitan modernism. *The Lonely Londoners* is just as fascinated by, and just as ambivalent about, London and Englishness as its forerunner *Mrs. Dalloway.*

The imperial capital is indeed quite hard on "the boys," as the novel's West Indian men refer to themselves. Racism, explicit and covert, affects nearly all facets of their lives, with the text cataloging the various instances of discrimination they encounter in search of housing, employment, and personal relationships. They even debate whether the situation is more desperate in America or England; most conclude that in America, at the very least, people don't hide their racism, whereas in England they maintain "the old diplomacy," an ironic phrase for the polite but unequivocal rebuff mastered by the local population. Without ignoring the novel's descriptions of xenophobic attitudes, it is difficult not to notice its incorporation of distinctively modernist imagery to convey the effects of metropolitan living. As several of the characters complain, the city is so anonymous and alienating that most Londoners "don't know what happening in the room next to them, far more the street, or how other people living. London is a place like that. It divide up in little worlds, and you stay in the world you belong to and you don't know anything about what happening in the other ones except what you read in the papers" (74). Like many modernist depictions of the modern urban environment, Selvon's London separates its inhabitants from one another. Although it masses large numbers of people in the same space, this same process enforces a degree of anonymity and encourages psychological detachment. Reminiscent of Georg Simmel's diagnosis of the metropolitan experience, the text charts the fractured, overstimulated, hypersensitive mentality endemic to large cities. Selvon's main characters, like Clarissa Dalloway, constantly seek some form of emotional connection with their urban counterparts, hoping to mitigate the isolation they endure. As a coping strategy, many of the characters, including Moses, adopt a jaded, haughty attitude toward the city and their fellow urbanites, encouraging still more critics to cite the *flâneur* in an attempt to unravel the text's aesthetics of urban space.[20]

It is no coincidence when we discover that Selvon saves his most identifiably modernist section of the novel for a scene in London's Hyde Park during the summer. The episode, which spans about ten pages, serves up breathless, stream-of-consciousness prose, eschewing punctuation of any kind. The summer provides a brief respite from the cold as the city dwellers shed their overcoats and uninviting scowls: "everywhere you turn the English people smiling isn't it a lovely day as if the sun burn away all the tightness and strain that was in their faces for the winter." Echoing Peter Walsh's urban frivolities, many of the characters visit the parks simply to "coast a lime" and "see all them pretty pieces of skin" (102). If Peter's sexual subjectivity depends on his ability to play the voyeur by remaining invisible, characters in *The Lonely Londoners,* most of whom are not white, have a paradoxically visible anonymity. Although their racial difference is something of which they and their fellow Londoners are acutely aware, it is a difference that effaces their individuality in the eyes of most white subjects. Many of Selvon's characters have no problem attracting interest from white women, however, as long as they are willing to sleep with partners who ask them to play to exotic stereotypes. Such cross-racial sexual liaisons, though, become less and less gratifying for Selvon's characters, tending on the whole to reinforce the types of bias they face elsewhere. Apart from the sexual opportunities enclosed therein, London's parks also provide a venue for relaxation and unusually diverse social traffic. It is the only space in London where black men can freely interact with "all sorts of fellars from all walks of life don't ever be surprised at who you meet up cruising and reclining in the park it might be your boss or it might be some big professional fellar because it ain't have no discrimination when it come to that in the park in the summer" (104). For a novel in which many of the characters suffer the effects of discrimination on a daily basis, even this temporary relief is welcome. The park's unimpeded social intercourse makes it an ideal space in which Moses and his fellow West Indians can explore the meaning of their metropolitan journey. The park is one of the few venues in which recent immigrants and white Londoners meet on relatively equal terms. Ironically, for the ex-colonials the paltry fringe benefits of life in London coalesce in its monumental districts, which remain so important to England's lingering imperial identity.

Overall, the novel's attitude toward London and England is conflicted. Following metropolitan modernists, the characters have deeply ambivalent responses toward their adopted home. Whereas Galahad, a more recent arrival, proclaims that "when the sweetness of summer get in him he say he would never leave the old Brit'n as long as he live," the more world-weary Moses, too condescending to reply out loud, simply "sigh a long sigh like a man who live life and see nothing at all in it and who frighten as the years go by wondering what it is all about" (109–10).

Selvon's London represents neither a promised land nor a new form of colonial hell, but a purgatorial cycle of draining work and changing seasons, punctuated by brief interludes of enjoyment. Though most of Selvon's characters quickly lose the starry-eyed tourist gaze of the new immigrant, usually replaced by the hungry look of men short of regular employment, the grim realities of life are not enough to send them scuttling back to the Caribbean:

> What it is that a city have . . . that you get so much to like it you wouldn't leave it for anywhere else? What it is that would keep men although by and large, in truth and in fact, they catching their royal to make a living, staying in a cramp-up room where you have to do everything—sleep, eat, dress, wash, cook, live. Why it is, that although they grumble about it all the time, curse the people, curse the government, say all kind of thing about this and that, why it is, that in the end, everyone cagey about saying outright that if the chance come they will go back to them green islands in the sun? (137–38)

There is no clear answer to the narrator's rhetorical questions. *The Lonely Londoners* never achieves, even in parody, the kind of metaphysical connection/delusion implied by *Mrs. Dalloway*'s concluding moments. Moses and his fellow West Indians remain equally fascinated with and frustrated by English culture to the very end, coping with hardships by striking a pose of haughty indifference. The endless supply of new, ingenuous arrivals only heightens Moses's aloofness. He regularly boasts that he is a hardened veteran of the metropolitan scene. Having been one of the first to emigrate after the war, he chides newcomers that he has forgotten more about London than they are ever likely to know. Moses's cynicism is itself a kind of intellectual triumph: in his detachment, he offers a reading of the city that complements, and even goes beyond, that of his modernist predecessors. Yet even he acknowledges that there is a tangible pleasure in staying on, in trudging home after a hard day of work and still being able "to write a casual letter home beginning: 'Last night, in Trafalgar Square . . .'" (137). His conflicted position, as both insider and outsider, Londoner and West Indian, affords him a special perspective from which to survey metropolitan space and the anticipated effects of decolonization. In many ways, his embrace of emotional detachment allows him to become exactly the kind of urban reader metropolitan modernism helped imagine.

The novel's only definitive gesture toward reconciliation and mutual sympathy between white and black Londoners comes in passing references to the white working class, with whom Selvon's characters express a provisional, sometimes strained, common cause. "It have a kind of communal feeling with the Working Class and the spades," muses the narrator, "because when you poor things does level out, it don't have much up and down" (75). As several readers have pointed out, the novel's growing West Indian population establishes beachheads in London's working-class areas, convincing landlords and merchants to cater to their specific needs. The grocers begin carrying saltfish and other Caribbean staples, while the tailors and barbers learn to cut clothes and hair the way their new customers expect. The merchants who adapt first thrive, while some of the more recalcitrant businesspeople are unceremoniously shoved out of the way. Selvon's recent arrivals understand England, and their place within it, by figuring out—and ultimately participating in—the trappings of local class difference. It is not simply that the immigrants transform the areas into which they settle; they learn to live, shop, and labor alongside their white, working-class neighbors. If Conrad and other writers of the urban jungle could confidently judge London and its slums as spaces of cultural negation, Selvon, only fifty years later, had no trouble describing black and working-class districts as pockets of vitality and cultural richness. As these brief reflections suggest, the arrival of postwar immigrants may have changed the ethnic composition, but not the fundamental reality, of class difference in England. Yet class here also functions as a legitimate, if hopelessly frustrating, category of belonging—these West Indian men understand themselves as Londoners partly through guarded expressions of solidarity with working-class whites. In no small measure, it was the modernist urban turn that enabled this reconsideration of English cities. Calling this heterogeneous collection of immigrants genuine Londoners is one way that the novel engages debates about the changing meaning and function of Englishness. But Selvon also participates in debates about national culture by adapting the ambivalent urban textualities of his metropolitan predecessors.

Curiously, the novel concludes with yet another hint of solidarity between black and white working classes. Moses, standing on the banks of the Thames, thinks for the last time on the plight of the few "black faces bobbing up and down in the millions of white, strained faces." On the surface, things "don't look so bad," yet he knows that a more penetrating gaze would reveal "a kind of misery and pathos and a frightening." Like

Woolf, Selvon imagines London as a space of irreconcilable contraries jostling against one another. Moses yearns to find concrete images for his London experience, but a few sentences seem inadequate to articulate the complicated dynamics and conflicted responses he endures. Suddenly, he recalls a friend who had been explaining to him

> how over in France all kinds of fellars writing books what turning out to be best-sellers. Taxi-driver, porter, road-sweeper—it didn't matter. One day you sweating in the factory and the next day all the newspapers have your name and photo, saying how you are a new literary giant.
>
> He watch a tugboat on the Thames, wondering if he could ever write a book like that, what everybody would buy. (141–42)

The Lonely Londoners, we guess, is the eventual product of Moses's final ruminations. Adapting the premises of working-class fiction, which apparently flourishes across the channel, Moses speculates on whether its form might suit the needs of immigrant narratives. The synergy between black immigrants and the white working class, as these concluding reflections indicate, may extend to fictional paradigms as well. To borrow a phrase from Ian Baucom, Moses here imagines the working class and new immigrants as collaborators in a project to redeem both English literature and culture.

Writers like Selvon, as these final passages suggest, are the inheritors, protectors, and transformers of the modernist legacy. Selvon, however, was not the only Englishman working with this model of literary production in which unknown, less privileged writers could become the next generation of celebrated novelists. As I discuss in the next chapter, a group of white writers known as the Angry Young Men—whose lightning rod text, *Look Back in Anger,* appeared in the same year as Selvon's novel—were also using the everyman narrative to explore their place in English society. Approaching the problem of the urban class system by triangulating modernist, first-generation postcolonial and 1950s white English writers may allow us to reassess the dividing line of World War II—and the radical break implied by the transition from modernism to postcolonial literature—in our conventional models of literary and cultural history.

4. CITIES OF AFFLUENCE
DOMESTICITY, CLASS, AND
THE ANGRY YOUNG MEN

In 1956 *Look Back in Anger* opened at the Royal Court Theatre, enjoying an extraordinary run before moving to Broadway, where it won the Drama Critics Award for Best New Play in 1957. A short two years later, John Osborne's play debuted as a successful film with a young Richard Burton in the lead role. In the words of one enthusiastic reviewer, it had such wide appeal because "it is intense, angry, feverish, undisciplined. It is even crazy. But it is young, young, young."[1] Though it borrows some of its techniques and themes from Strindberg and Beckett, the play must have appeared fresh and unconstrained by the relatively polite conventions of British theater at the time.[2] Soon thereafter, critics began using the phrase "Angry Young Men" to refer to a whole group of authors emerging during the 1950s. The popular novelists Alan Sillitoe, John Braine, David Storey, and John Wain, whose texts were also adapted for the cinema, as well as more established writers, like Kingsley Amis and Philip Larkin, were fitted under the umbrella term. The group's name continued to circulate in the theatrical world, too, where John Arden, Arnold Wesker, and other "kitchen sink" or "New Wave" dramatists were linked to the movement. Even a few women, such as Shelagh Delaney and Doris Lessing, could claim honorary Angry membership.

Critics have typically described the Angry Young Men as leftist dissidents who use social realism as a means of protesting against the affectations of the experimental, high modernist literature that flourished between the wars. As one review of *Look Back* overconfidently asserts, we all know that Osborne, and by extension, Jimmy Porter, are outspoken opponents of "Apartheid, the H-bomb, the British class system: and they see in Socialism the ethical standard by which these things can be judged and condemned."[3] Social realism, in one form or another, was the dominant style because it offered an explicit rejection of inter-war modernism.[4] For playwrights Wesker and Arden, as well as novel-ists Wain and Sillitoe, this translated into the abrupt, sometimes crude speech thought characteristic of working-class existence.

Yet most Angry texts were not written by working-class writers, nor did many depict the actual conditions of working-class life in England. The most well known Angry protagonists, including Jimmy Porter, Joe Lampton of *Room at the Top,* and Jim Dixon of *Lucky Jim,* are disgrun-tled members of a lower-middle class literary constituency for whom postwar prosperity had fueled social aspirations but failed to deliver real opportunities. It would be more accurate to say that most Angry texts display a sense of acutely conflicted, highly ambivalent class conscious-ness. *Look Back*'s first audiences, for instance, must have been struck by Jimmy Porter's regular rants against an ineffectual government and En-gland's rigid social barriers. While some may have associated the play's tone with a radical working-class agenda, there is little evidence of this in the dialogue itself. At times, Jimmy casts his lot with a groundswell of disaffected youth, frustrated by the inherent limits of welfare state progressivism. He berates his wife because she comes from an upper-class family, rhetorically positioning himself with a legion of dispos-sessed Britons. Elsewhere, however, this university-educated jazz aficio-nado is all too eager to distance himself from the uncritical, unthinking masses by asserting his intellectual superiority. He is proudly elitist and freely acknowledges the gains he has made out of welfare state reforms. This contradictory set of positions, which rely on a heightened, but ex-tremely flexible, sense of class politics, typifies Angry displays of class affect. Cagey ambivalence best describes Jimmy's tactical deployment of political rhetoric: though he incessantly utilizes the language of class difference to vest himself with moral authority, he regularly shifts terms of inclusion and exclusion to fit his needs at any particular moment. It makes little sense to read his character, or the play as a whole, as un-equivocally "radical" or "reactionary." His ambivalence constitutes an astute but unsympathetic manipulation of available social and political positions.

The rise of an extremely class-conscious literary movement, however confused, represents a minor historical anomaly. By the late 1950s, most people in England took it for granted that class differences were rapidly, ineluctably disintegrating. As I discussed in my introductory chapter, the myths of "working-class affluence" and "deproletarianisation" were

so strong during this period that even members of the British New Left /
cultural studies movement—themselves committed to a progressive
politics of class—by and large accepted the premise that full employment, mass consumption, and relative material security were erasing
the most visible markers of working-class difference. Yet the persistence
of class inequity and anxieties about minute social injustices continue
to trouble so many Angry protagonists, even if the political sympathies
of individual characters tend to be fuzzy and unstable. The multivalent
deployment of class difference by Angry protagonists reflects the tension between the material and ideological axes of class politics in the
context of the British welfare state. As a general rule, Angry texts continually pose the *fact* of relative material security against the *affect* of class
anger. This range of discursive hesitations and inconsistencies should
be set in the context of prevailing economic and political conditions,
where lingering feelings of class anger could be explained less force-
fully by sheer material deprivation or massive income inequality (as was
common during the interwar years). In contrast, the rhetoric of anger so
characteristic of this literary moment depends on the apparent disjuncture between the material and ideological operations of class politics.
Even as the material bases for class difference were, according to popular
opinion, on the wane, Angry protagonists regularly mobilize the rhetoric of class tension to articulate highly individualized manifestations
of collective grievances. In this chapter I examine *Look Back in Anger*
and Sillitoe's first novel, *Saturday Night and Sunday Morning* (1958), to
think more about the cultural politics of class, anger, and masculinity
as they relate to welfare state reforms of the postwar period, England's
particular position in postwar Europe, and the effects of decolonization
on Britain itself. The availability of class to mark provisional conditions
of both belonging and exclusion—especially among those who use it
so flexibly and self-consciously, as do the Angry protagonists I discuss
here—speaks to the often confusing and contradictory strategies for
representing class difference I have been considering in this book.

Beyond a mutual interest in class as a means of working through ambivalences about the welfare state project, Angry texts display an unusual
degree of formal symmetry. Most surprising, perhaps, is their consistent
use of domestic melodrama, a set of generic protocols that seems so
incompatible with the class and gender politics on offer.[5] Following the
lead of Larkin, in *Jill*, and William Cooper, in *Scenes from Provincial*

Life, Angry writers continually adapted and reworked domestic literary forms to meet their diverse aesthetic and political commitments. *Look Back* offers a typical example of its kind. The play's setting, a modest flat Jimmy shares with his wife, provides concrete physical parameters for the dramatic content. More importantly, the dramatic action, including Jimmy's vituperative diatribes, consists of the protagonist's vacillation between two love interests, his wife and her friend Helena. Though he rails against the narrow sexual and emotional confines of monogamy and marriage, we gradually realize that Jimmy relies heavily on the support and love of a heterosexual partner: his flashes of misogyny conceal deep feelings of social, sexual, and emotional dependence. In the end, like most Angry protagonists, Jimmy looks forward to settling down with his wife and caring for the children to come, gleefully exchanging the pleasures of sexual license for the security and responsibilities of family life.

Though domestic forms have a long history in English literature, their use by the Angries may seem a little strange. The irony was not lost on Osborne, who later described *Look Back* as a "rather old-fashioned play," especially in its cultivation of a simple, domestic plot.[6] As Nancy Armstrong argues, domestic fiction played an important role in the articulation of modern feminine, bourgeois forms of political consciousness during the eighteenth and nineteenth centuries. Many Angry texts, in contrast, combine exaggerated heterosexuality with a simple rhetorical style and domestic plotline to fashion a rough-and-ready version of masculinity that had great cross-class appeal. This peculiar resurrection and transformation of domestic literature negotiates the competing and complementary pressures of class difference, masculinity, and national identity under the auspices of welfare state reform.

With this in mind, it would be difficult to overstate the importance of the family home as a trope for capturing the social atmosphere of the 1950s. Accounts of the period regularly perform ethnographic surveys of domestic space to rehearse the peculiar salience of class in postwar social life. A wide array of texts preoccupied with the social conditions of the decade—academic, popular, and literary—represent the family home as a space of both remarkable continuity and pronounced change. In other words, domesticity became a site of commentary on both newfound prosperity and the subtle persistence of class boundaries. The dominant symbols of widespread affluence were domestic, including the construction of single-family homes for lower-middle and working-class people. As a consequence, the domestic became a physical and affective space in which forms of class difference were paradoxically most stable—drawing on long traditions of marriage, gendered divisions of labor, and distinct patterns of family life—and also most susceptible to outside pressures. This chapter reads the Angry reliance on domesticity in the context of England's postwar reconstruction and alongside contemporary accounts of the home. I draw on vernacular architecture of the period and the welfare state's urban planning initiatives to sketch the parameters of class and masculinity in literary accounts of family life. The particular forms of class affect so prominent in Angry texts—a vague sense of social/political injustice combined with vexed attitudes toward women and marriage—make visible the latent tensions inherent in postwar urban England.

The Angry emphasis on domesticity can also be read as a metaphor for national culture and the "repatriation" of English literature with the assistance of the welfare state, which itself represented a political attempt to foster self-reliance. Many Angry writers, including Amis, Osborne, and Lessing, made conscious attempts to rescue English literature from its association with French letters, commonly seen as pretentious, abstract, and overly intellectual. In his contribution to *Declaration,* a collection of manifestos by young writers of the 1950s edited by Tom Maschler, Kenneth Tynan reads Angry literature as the first step toward resuscitating the dramatic arts in England. Tynan, one of the Angries' earliest and most eloquent apologists, argues that the Angry emphasis on the straightforwardness of the English, as opposed to the ethereality of the French, would energize domestic stagecraft. Osborne, in his contribution to the collection, insists that the audience must feel and react first; thinking and abstract contemplation could come later. The crude, sometimes violent themes found in Angry literature thus imply a dubious rejection of "foreign" materials. This effort to nationalize the practice of literature also reflects the curious position of England after a debilitating war. The national mood in the late 1940s was rather dour. Signs of national decay abounded, including the imminent end of empire and prolonged rationing of basic necessities. The Angries' defiant attitude approximates a perverse pride in English insularity and resilience in the face of adversity. It was in this context that Angry writers insisted on the value of more uncomplicated, parochial themes thought suitable for the English constitution.

ANGER AND ART

Although many literary critics of the 1950s associated the Angry Young Men with some form of proletarian or leftist art, the politics of the group, in retrospect, seem far less stable or consistent. If these protagonists share anything beyond ritualized displays of masculine truculence, it is their rhetorical appropriation of cultural and political dissidence. While Angry protagonists do not consistently ascribe to any clearly articulated political system, they liberally mobilize disaffection to position themselves as morally indignant citizens standing up for the rights of the underprivileged in the face of widespread indifference or hostility. Rather than investing seriously in a coherent ideological platform, however, most Angry protagonists conveniently slide in and out of these positions as a way of emphasizing their intellectual prowess and skepticism. Jimmy Porter, for example, displays all the markers of class antagonisms and failed aspirations. He continually reminds anyone within earshot that he "learnt at an early age what it was to be angry—angry and helpless" (58). His misogynistic behavior, no doubt exciting but unpalatable to predominantly middle-class audiences, clearly supplements his deployment of class anger. His wife, Alison, absorbs most of his vitriol; he mocks her "Mummy and Daddy" and her privileged background, bragging that her parents had threatened him when learning of their marriage (52). Between his abusive diatribes, Jimmy bemoans "the injustice of it. . . . The wrong people going hungry, the wrong people being loved, the wrong people dying" (94). Jimmy's father died a broken man, neglected by Jimmy's mother, whose "posh" family unceremoniously distanced themselves from him after he volunteered to fight for the Republican side in the Spanish Civil War.

Given these biographical details and Jimmy's self-appointed role as a champion of "the wrong people," it would be relatively easy to interpret the protagonist's anger as a deeply personal, if highly problematic, form of working-class politics. A more nuanced reading of the play, however, might account for the deeper ambivalences in the drama's class character and its allusions to political dissent. Jimmy alternates between styling himself as a brilliant, uncompromising individualist and as a neurotic, persecuted malcontent. Though he empathizes with the working class, he has no desire to become working class himself. His high educational achievement, sophisticated command of the language, and bohemian cultural preferences mark him as part of the postwar generation of new, lower-middle-class university graduates excited by the promises, and subsequently disappointed by the failures, of the welfare state. His viru-lent critiques of the leisure classes can be read as a way to articulate a form of moral and intellectual superiority. In this, he claims both the en-titlements of the time—such as increased educational opportunities— yet reserves the right to declare independence from any larger collective bodies, political or otherwise. His self-inflicted isolation gives him the authority to criticize without agitating for progressive change or relin-quishing any privileges.

Jimmy's anger is neither a defense of nor an attack on the class com-promise managed by the welfare state, but instead a more complex re-action to his social conditions. Kenneth Allsop suggests that the typical Angry Young Man defines himself "against the class he replaces: against a blend of homosexual sensibility, upper-class aloofness, liberal poli-tics, and avant-garde literary devices" (18). Although Allsop, a sympa-thetic reader, interprets Angry protests as a form of political dissidence, it becomes apparent that Angry writers saw the issue in primarily lit-erary terms. Caricaturing an effete, dandy artist figure, epitomized by Bloomsbury of the interwar period, enabled 1950s writers to differentiate themselves from the previous generation without forgoing the privileges associated with creative genius. As Alan Sinfield shows in a brilliant read-ing of "Movement" and Angry writers, the central component of their aesthetic philosophy is a conscious objection to high modernism, which leads to the demonization of women, homosexuals, the leisure class, and the "effete" aspects of highbrow cultural production.[7] In *The Uses of Literacy,* Richard Hoggart echoes this general sentiment, suggesting that "highbrow-hating" was a popular pastime for working-class people. "Modern art" features in conversation only as a pejorative term, and the Arts Council "is a 'fiddle' by a lot of 'cissies' who despise the amuse-ments of the plain Englishman" (138). Most Angry texts appropriate the language of class difference—invoking the preferences of the plain Englishman—to mark aesthetic, rather than strictly political, distinctions between themselves and the more finicky modernist artists.

But characters such as Jimmy Porter did not abjure elite culture al-together: they were jazz enthusiasts, which allowed them to repudiate leisure-class (i.e., effete) art, yet retain a sense a cultural accomplishment that distinguished them from the working class, who tended to prefer more popular art forms, as Hoggart's characterizations suggest.[8] This maneuver, argues James English, enables the Angry writer, through his protagonist, to steer clear of the "cissie camp . . . without relinquishing any of the prerogatives of the 'serious' writer. . . . Such an operation . . . casts the Movement writer as a paradoxically privileged outsider and underdog" (143–44). Angry texts thus mix together and blur the distinctions between a vast collection of real and imagined antagonists: the wealthy (especially those from the southeast of England), homosexuals, artists, and "soft," overeducated liberals. Jimmy positions himself as an outsider—sometimes by choice, sometimes by involuntary exclusion—a figure for whom the welfare state opened doors but failed to create real opportunities. As we learn from the opening scenes of the play, Jimmy knows he is "an enormous cultural snob," yet casts himself as a "self-flagellating solitary in self-inflicted exile from the world, drawing strength from his own weakness and joy from his own misery" (Taylor, *Anger* 41). This cultural snobbery hints at the play's complicated relationship with the welfare state.

Despite offering protests against and satiric representations of the metropolitan world of high art, many Angry writers had strong connections with London's arts community and the fledgling world of subsidized theater. As Dan Rebellato points out in *1956 and All That: The Making of Modern British Drama,* pitting the Angry Young Men against the literary establishment ignores the role of the Arts Council and the function of state-subsidized theater in postwar Britain.[9] In 1946 John Maynard Keynes transformed the temporary Council for the Encouragement of Music and the Arts (CEMA) into a permanent, publicly funded organization. The Arts Council's authority came directly from the Treasury, allowing it to distribute its funds without much interference from Parliament (no doubt Keynes used his influence there). Its charter states the explicit goal of developing "a greater knowledge, understanding and practice of the fine arts exclusively, and in particular to increase the accessibility of the fine arts to the public." [10] Despite this lofty aim, Sinfield argues, it essentially functioned as a middle-class subsidy, catering to the needs and desires of a very specific audience (52–53). Not surprisingly, many writers of less commercial appeal turned to the Arts Council for support. *Look Back,* for instance, was produced by the English Stage Company and staged at the Royal Court Theatre with the help of a sizable Arts Council grant.[11] Arden, Wesker, and Pinter also wrote for the English Stage Company, and it is fair to say that the support of the Arts Council was pivotal to London's postwar theatrical revolution.

This apparent contradiction—we can observe in the Angry corpus overt signs of antagonism toward the government, the Arts Council, and

its milieu of elite art, yet there remains a direct material connection between these writers and such institutions—typifies the politics of anger
within the larger social arena of the 1950s. It does not follow that Jimmy's
anger can be comprehended as a simple expression of class antagonisms
or allegiances any more than we can characterize *Look Back* as "for" or
"against" the welfare state. It therefore becomes difficult to neatly characterize Angry attitudes toward either the state or the world of elite culture. Instead, it makes more sense to read Angry texts as ambivalent participants in broader discussions about the changing relationship among
the government, the arts, and the public. At a moment when the means
of literary production were being transferred to the state, many Angry
texts show signs of resentment about and anticipation of the terms and
conditions of this transition.

Comparing *Look Back* with Sillitoe's *Saturday Night* shows how the
rhetorical strategy of the disaffected misanthrope not only cuts across
but actually reinforces the differences between lower-middle and markedly working-class characters. Jimmy's anger stems from a typical lower-
middle-class predicament of the 1950s: increased access to education had
fostered a sense of entitlement and fueled aspirations, but real material
gains and opportunities for social advancement were less forthcoming
(by comparison with the 1930s and in contrast to other social classes).[12]
In this way, Jimmy's lower-middle-class *ressentiment* resembles, rhetorically and thematically, the working-class anger with which it was often
confused in Angry literature. Structurally, however, the sources of his
dissatisfaction run quite contrary to the dissatisfactions of working-class
Angry protagonists, as I discuss below. Though the figure of the mal-
contented protagonist appears in most Angry texts, it has the effect of
inflecting, rather than masking, subtle class differences. More than their
obvious class character or political sympathies, Angry texts share and
explore, to very different ends, the figure of the masculine outsider.

"THE ABOLITION OF WANT": POLITICAL CONSENSUS
AND THE NARRATIVE OF AFFLUENCE

Before turning to Sillitoe's more identifiably working-class text, I want
to spend a few pages sketching a basic outline of the welfare state and its
urban policy because they formed the political environment in which
the Angry Young Men articulated both their heterosexual masculinity
and forms of political ambivalence. Although the fundamental tenets of

the welfare state—general improvements in employment, housing, diet, health care, and education—were not implemented until the close of World War II, the idea began as a wartime pledge to the working class.[13] With the publication of the Beveridge Report (1942), the government made an explicit commitment to full employment and a broad social security network in exchange for acceptance of and participation in the war.[14] The premises of the welfare state became the foundation of a comprehensive mainstream political consensus for the next thirty-five years; until the late 1970s, all three major political parties endorsed the ideology of "welfare capitalism" and Keynesian economic policies. Sinfield describes the program as "an unprecedentedly ambitious project of state legitimation" (16). In an effort to secure the political quiescence of the general population, the state and Britain's ruling classes made large concessions to the working class by implementing a broad social services plan.

Part and parcel of this social security package was the popular narrative of postwar affluence. In contrast to the dark interwar years, the late 1950s were a moment of confidence: full employment, low inflation, and a robust market for consumer goods lent credence to the myth of universal prosperity. Proportionally, it was the working class, about 70 percent of the population, who benefited most from welfare state reforms (given the conditions of the 1930s, however, this achievement should be taken with a grain of salt).[15] At the time, many on the left feared (and many conservatives self-righteously proclaimed) that basic material security would lead to the deproletarianization of the working class, signaling an end to political militancy.[16] Opponents of the welfare state—few in number—were relegated to the political margins. In chapter 2 I discussed how Evelyn Waugh's antagonism to land reform and more egalitarian class politics allowed him to depict the aristocracy as a marginalized, persecuted class fraction. In a curious parallel, many Angry protagonists, frustrated by the climate of political conformity and the inherent limits of welfare state reform, vociferously denounce the state and its agents without advocating any clear political alternative.

An aggressive postwar housing policy, which called for about 300,000 new homes a year designed specifically for low-income families, was perhaps the most tangible effect of welfare state reforms.[17] "New Towns" and other suburban developments, theoretically based on Ebenezer Howard's Garden City principles, sprang up all over the country in the twenty years after the war, providing relatively spacious, affordable housing for thousands of young working-class families: "A generation ago, the English suburban house—and garden—still belonged to a middle class way of life beyond the reach of the mass of workers. Today the whole nation feels entitled to this privilege: hence you have the sprawling suburban housing estates." [18] By subsidizing the cost of construction, the government helped make home ownership, uncommon before the war, feasible for many less affluent families. From the very beginning, improving the material conditions of the family home ranked high on the welfare state agenda. The Beveridge Report, for example, insists that married women, in particular, have "vital work to do in ensuring the adequate continuance of the British race" by bearing children, remaining loyal to their husbands, and anchoring domestic space (qtd. in Sinfield 14). While the eugenic overtones of such statements take us back to earlier discussions about modernism, imperialism, and the city, the terrain had shifted dramatically by the 1950s. In contrast to the engineers of London's imperial quarter, who designed ostentatious public monuments, the welfare state focused on the family home as an important site of cultural rehabilitation after the war.

During the period in question, the single-family home became the undisputed archetype for domestic living arrangements. The welfare state did not invent the nuclear family, but it certainly supported its dominance in the popular imagination through the narrative of postwar affluence and the reconstruction of urban space. Frederic Osborn, vocal advocate of state planning initiatives and influential director of the Town and Country Planning Association (an outgrowth of Ebenezer Howard's Garden Cities Association), argued that reformers needed to consider first and foremost "the end-product for which the whole complex apparatus of civilization exists—satisfaction in the personal life . . . especially the family life" (Osborn and Whittick 121). Postwar urban planners used the template of the single-family home to the near-total exclusion of other building types, erecting modest residences designed to accommodate small families rather than larger or smaller groups. Moreover, government benefits—in the form of housing subsidies and unemployment insurance—were allocated on the basis of the nuclear family. The state tracked economic progress by measuring the growth of men's jobs with sufficient wages to support a family.[19] Organized labor, likewise, participated actively in creating this gendered division of labor, advocating a platform based on the so-called family wage for male employees.

Similarly, the commodities most often cited as markers of increasing affluence were domestic accoutrements. It is important to recognize that the kinds of urban planning regimes dominant in European welfare states were integrated into a much more complex process of social and political change.[20] In many ways, Britain's commitment to social justice was also a way to reinvigorate the national economy during a period of imperial contraction by organizing both commodity production and consumption on a large scale. It is no accident that the most widely cited indicators of material affluence during the postwar period—products such as televisions, domestic appliances, and even automobiles—were first marketed on a mass scale when possession of a single-family home became possible for most residents of Britain. These markers of material security contributed directly to anxieties about (or celebrations of) the erosion of working-class coherence and political solidarity.

Some version of deproletarianization, or even socialism, was neither the objective nor the outcome of welfare state policies, in which the state typically acted as a mediator between labor and capital interests with the aim of creating a "New Jerusalem." The state's fairly progressive agenda, as Sinfield points out, was a last-ditch effort to manufacture political stability, ushering in "a phase unique in history and in the modern world, where the social order was secured—more or less—by consent, rather than force" (16). But it is important to recognize that these concessions were not designed to undermine the country's commitment to a capitalist economy. It ultimately protected the medium-term interests of business by creating stability—hence the name welfare capitalism, the term favored by theorists such as Sinfield, Manuel Castells, and David Harvey. Moreover, the high period of welfare capitalism coincided with a period of imperial contraction, in which political consensus helped manage Britain's transition to postimperial governance. Such efforts were an attempt to salvage the functional utility of a nation-state that still included Scotland, Wales, and Northern Ireland but was losing its overseas colonies. Welfare state policies were a deliberate attempt to coordinate both consumption and production with the aim of securing cultural and economic self-sufficiency. Rather than rely on a vast overseas empire to maintain the competitiveness of British industry, the welfare state attempted to reinvigorate a national economy by creating a stable labor force and expanding the domestic market for consumer goods.

Given this context, Angry ambivalence can be read as a more logical, if conflicted, reaction to the contradictions inherent in welfare capitalist politics. With the memories of prewar indigence still fresh in the minds of many, the reality of full employment and material security held obvious appeal. Most Angry protagonists are fully aware of and enthusiastic about this newfound prosperity, enjoying a run of steady employment and participating eagerly in the world of consumer goods. If they have any reservations about the politics of the welfare state, they arise from the recognition that basic material security has come at the cost of more systemic political and social reform. The welfare state consensus, rather than providing an impetus for radical change, actually reinforced the latent conservatism of mainstream society by foreclosing the need for more contentious debate. Their conflicted sense of class politics is a reaction against the narrow range of options available in the postwar consensus. Moreover, forms of Angry protest also invoke the prerogatives of a regional form of national culture. The literary phenomenon was specifically English and frequently draws on the unique qualities of provincial class differences. Whereas the welfare state was an attempt to assert the primacy of the British state in managing the national economy, the appeals to class anger in such texts also function as a regional, decidedly English protest against the national coalition envisioned by Britain's leaders. Angry literature picks at the class and cultural seams of the welfare state consensus, exposing the limits of both social reform and the attempt to maintain the integrity of Britain during a moment of imperial disintegration.

GOOD TIMES

In *Key to the Door,* Sillitoe's autobiographical novel set in Nottingham during the 1930s, Harold Seaton takes his young son, Brian, to watch the demolition of their erstwhile home, which has succumbed to the escalating slum clearances of the interwar years. The previous evening, the family had moved surreptitiously to another building, also condemned, to evade the rent collectors. "You'd think the Jerries was after us," a family friend jokes as they shift their meager possessions under the cover of darkness. "The rent man is, and that's worse," replies a hapless Seaton (14). But in *Saturday Night,* Sillitoe's commercially successful novel about postwar working-class life, the fortunes of the Seaton family have improved considerably. Arthur, Brian's younger brother, has only vague memories of the family's lean years. Now a young man, he thinks himself lucky "to see the TV standing in the corner" of their modest home. "The old man was happy at last," Arthur mumbles to himself as he watches his father propped in front of the television for hours at a time: "a sit-down job at the factory, all the Woodbines he could smoke, money for a pint if he wanted one, though he didn't as a rule drink" (22). For the thousands of employees at the local bicycle factory where Arthur and his father work, there was "no more short-time like before the war," everyone "took home good wages," and no one feared "getting the sack if you stood ten minutes in the lavatory reading your *Football Post*" (23). The times of supplementing one's midday meal with "a penny bag of chips to eat with your bread" were over because "you got fair wages if you worked your backbone to a string of conkers." With this newfound prosperity, "you could save up for a motor-bike or even an old car, or you could go on a ten-day binge and get rid of all you'd saved" (23). The postwar years, marked by steady employment and readily available commodities, represent a life of welcome but unexpected comfort.

For the Seatons, this change has a clear, material impact on the way they experience, and tell narratives about, the urban class system. No longer relying on the trope of deprivation to articulate either a group identity or a sense of political disenfranchisement, Arthur freely appropriates popular narratives of affluence to describe his family's condition. Unlike lower-middle-class Angry protagonists, he has no anxieties about or pretensions toward social advancement: he despises snobbishness, and the novel's incorporation of a salty, working-class dialect reflects a conscious reaction against both highbrow modernism and the more polished registers of other Angry texts. Arthur's expressions of anger do not emanate from the same kinds of social limitations experienced by the new wave of university graduates, such as Jim Dixon and Jimmy Porter. Moreover, his experience of relative affluence must have seemed remarkable when measured against his Angry peers: his £14 weekly wages were comparable to the salaries drawn by many lower-middle-class professionals such as educators or clerks.[21] Considering the importance of the troubled 1930s in the collective memory of working-class communities, it is easy to see why their greater incorporation in the consumer marketplace generated such enthusiasm. If working-class Angry protagonists such as Arthur retain any sense of deep-seated political or social resentment, it does not begin with a complaint about regular employment or the infiltration of commodities into working-class domestic space.

Through his periodic venting of anger, Arthur not only clears a symbolic space for his political frustrations but also performs a specific style of masculinity. Like most Angry texts, this novel stages masculinity primarily through the protagonist's vexed attitude toward heterosexuality and marriage. At times, Arthur seems to consolidate his gender position only through multiple sexual conquests and resistance to a conventional marriage and the "snares" of femininity. But here, too, a closer reading reveals deep ambivalences in Arthur's gender-coded deployment of emotion. At other points in the novel, he complicates his resistance to more "conventional" sex-gender roles by eagerly anticipating his eventual identity as a husband and primary wage earner, even adding this role to his sexual fantasies. In short, he articulates his masculinity by simultaneously resisting and inhabiting the role of husband and family provider. This highly ambivalent portrayal of masculine sexuality becomes possible only within the context of the welfare state, when homes, jobs, and commodities all became more readily available to England's urban working class. As this text demonstrates, Arthur fashions his masculinity both by flaunting his sexual prowess (and thereby resisting the straits of monogamy and marriage) and by imagining himself as an enthusiastic husband and steady provider. New understandings and uses of domestic space, along with a rehabilitated form of the domestic narrative, provide the material and imaginative geography of this specific trope of postwar, working-class masculinity.[22] Ambivalence best characterizes the Angry performance of heterosexual masculinity: women and monogamy are the objects of both censure and desire.

FOUR ROOMS

The family's four-roomed terrace home in one of Nottingham's "respectable" neighborhoods represents a typical domestic arrangement in the postwar era. In comparison with the late 1940s, when the country was crippled by an acute housing shortage—war damage and returning soldiers left many young couples without accommodation—the government's aggressive building programs of the 1950s had eased the crisis considerably, even making home ownership, rare before the war, quite common by the end of the decade. In England, two-story single-family homes were long considered the "ideal" architectural form, but the welfare state made the realization of this goal on a wide scale possible for the first time.[23] In most areas, the state utilized an inexpensive, highly flexible architectural form known as the "two-up, two-down." With a pair of rooms upstairs (usually bedrooms) and a pair downstairs (typically a parlor/living room and a kitchen/dining area), the two-up, two-down proved a remarkably popular architectural model (see fig. 6). A modified version of older domestic forms, it had the advantage of enormous adaptability. The basic type could be built in rows (terraces), most common in urban areas; as semidetached dwellings, like the units shown in figure 6 (two connected edifices, side-by-side); or, less frequently, as stand-alone homes.[24]

In "Domestic Space and Society: A Cross-Cultural Study," Roderick Lawrence offers a fascinating ethnographic survey of the two-up, two-down, considering the relationship between vernacular architecture and changing social practices. As he points out, this specific style of home is not unique to the postwar building boom. As early as the mid-nineteenth century, this distinct arrangement of domestic space was already common in urban areas: "This historical study . . . has revealed a pattern of domestic space which has been consistent since the Industrial Revolution. The family has usually been housed in an independent dwelling for domestic life . . . the dwelling sometimes had a parlour . . . with a living room or kitchen behind [on the ground floor]. . . . There were two or three bedrooms [upstairs]. . . . Irrespective of the size of the floor area of the house, the organization of space followed the

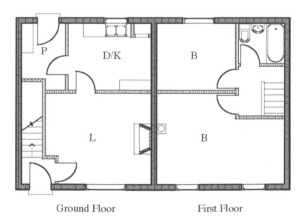

Ground Floor   First Floor

Key: L=Living Room, D/K=Dining/Kitchen, P=Pantry, B=Bedroom

Figure 6. Floor plan of a typical "two-up, two-down." This drawing shows adjacent houses, designed as semidetached units. (Courtesy of E+D Architecture and Design)

same pattern" (110). With some improvements (size and inclusion of interior bathrooms), this model was used throughout the 1950s and 1960s for New Towns and government-built homes all across the country. Its dominance, with its emphasis on "independent" spatial dimensions, played an important role in defining the parameters of the modern nuclear family. Capacious enough for a small family but too cramped to house lodgers or accommodate extended family members (and difficult to expand or rearrange for that purpose), this built form helped establish specific patterns of domestic life for the postwar generation.

Lawrence's project demonstrates the normative power of the nuclear family in the popular imagination. Restricting his study to one "typical" government-built working-class housing estate, he found that the "predominant household structure was the nuclear family" and that *every* respondent to the questionnaire was the "housewife" (105–6). In the entire sample, there were only four single mothers (there were children in every household), two of whom were widows, while the husband or father was or had been the primary (and usually only) source of income for the family. Such studies suggest that, with the help of this particular architectural style, working-class masculinity became strongly linked with supporting a family—both in reality and in fantasy, as we shall see in the case of Arthur Seaton. Lawrence argues that such attitudes about domesticity may incorporate older habits, but he goes out of his way to demonstrate that the built environment of postwar housing estates added a sense of stability to these social arrangements. England's domestic geography was not solely responsible for this dominant narrative of family life, but it was a necessary (and often overlooked) condition of its existence.

Early in the novel, *Saturday Night* sketches the basic typology of a working-class patriarch, charged with providing for a family. Arthur's father, if not a kindly middle-aged man, was "happy at last" by the late 1950s. With a steady job and a stable home, the elder Seaton could finally derive some enjoyment from his daily toils. Arthur muses that his father "deserved to be happy, after all those years before the war on the dole, five kids, and the big miserying that went with no money and no way of getting any." The six years of war represent a kind of dividing line for the family, resulting in something few could have anticipated: relative domestic security, even prosperity. Solid employment transforms the young, bitter Harold Seaton into the kind of patriarch with which we are now familiar. "The difference between before the war and after the war didn't bear thinking about" (22), Arthur notes, observing the drastic change in his father and his family's situation. The husband and father of the 1930s had been less of a man, unable to care adequately for his wife and his children.

Saturday Night was far from unique in its placement of this familial narrative at the heart of working-class experience. Sillitoe's novel clearly draws on the same fount of ethnographic data as *The Uses of Literacy*, Hoggart's scholarly treatment of urban, working-class domesticity: "The more we look at working-class life, the more we try to reach the core of working-class attitudes, the more surely does it appear that the core is a sense of the personal, the concrete, the local: it is embodied in the idea of, first, the family" (18). After a highly romanticized portrait of "Mother," the pivot of domestic life, Hoggart turns to "Father," calling him an "almost physically recognizable" type, a kind of immutable physiological category. Hoggart describes him as sallow, dark, somewhat unhealthy, with a particular bone structure about the face and neck. Because of these characteristic physical limitations, perhaps, Hoggart argues, "The point of departure for an understanding of the position of the working-class father in his home is that he is the boss there, the 'master in his own house.' This he is by tradition, and neither he nor his wife would want the tradition changed" (34). Hoggart alludes to the specific "position" of the father within the home. In order to appreciate his masculinity, we ought to observe his behavior in the context of domestic power relations. The father sustains this mastery not only by tradition and the mutual consent of his spouse but also by economic means: his ownership of the physical structure is both real and metaphorical. Not surprisingly, the "home as a man's castle" trope runs throughout this passage and all Hoggart's descriptions of working-class social life.

Hoggart posits a direct relationship between codified displays of heterosexuality and the types of labor practiced by men. The male head of household affirms his status by acting as "the main breadwinner and heavy worker" and asserting his sexual prerogatives. Though the home is "his" in fact and by tradition, a father would never be asked by his wife to "help about the house": things of that nature "are woman's work." Hoggart even suggests that most women would not want their spouses to participate in domestic chores, "for fear he is thought womanish" by prying neighbors. As children begin to accept some domestic responsibilities, working-class boys soon acquire the sense that "it's different for men" and consequently contribute less to household chores than their sisters do. Though a cause for concern, these "rough boys are often admired; the head-shaking over them is as proud as it is rueful—''e's a real *lad*,' people say." Later in life, after marriage, this hardiness often evolves into "a kind of roughness in his manner which a middle-class wife would find insupportable." He may occasionally yell at his wife if unhappy about trivial things, or even hit her if he has had a few drinks after work and finds something amiss. We should not, however, confuse this crudeness with a lack of affection for his wife or fecklessness where family matters are concerned: "The man who is able to growl is also able to defend; he has something of the cock about him" (34–36).

Hoggart attributes very specific qualities to the working-class father, blending the domestic performance of masculinity with an acute aware-ness of popular habits to sketch a broad outline of working-class fa-therhood. But his story is not without its tensions, making it clear that the home is a contested space. Hoggart's father asserts social and sexual prerogatives, but these can only be supported by his status as "bread-winner" and active involvement in "the real world of work [paid em-ployment] and men's pleasures" (36). Men must be married in order to fully achieve their masculinity, but must constantly assert their virility and heterosexuality against and within the demands of marriage. A man who is "too" sympathetic to his wife might be charged with effeminacy, but a man who neglects his family, especially financially, also compro-mises his symbolic position in the household. Men's heterosexuality can even be threatened by excessive sympathy: "Emotionally, his best con-tribution is to be, without being soft or 'womanish,' ready to agree, to live according to the idea that happy married life is 'a matter of give and take'" (37).

It would be easy to neglect the centrality of the physical geography of this domestic arrangement, but it too plays an important role in the staging of working-class masculinity. This narrative about marriage, work, and the family—and the man's proper role in it—is not pos-sible without the existence of specific architectural spaces. In Hoggart's story, sexual identity and class meet in a discrete and well-known physi-cal and social location: the family home. He never questions the logic of the nuclear family and its need for domestic space. While the extended family may figure prominently in the neighborhood and even provide a valuable support network for married women, Hoggart's family consists of two parents and their children. He might add that the working-class father would find intolerable the presence of lodgers or even extended family members in his home, for they might undermine his authority. For many of the urban working class, this narrative became possible only after the war and the welfare state's housing programs.

How does this domestic typology relate to Arthur Seaton, the novel's young, unmarried protagonist, or indeed the conventions of Angry texts in general? A close examination of the generic protocols in any of these texts reveals a fairly typical marriage plot. Each unmarried protagonist has at least one affair, often with a married woman, but usually rejects that attachment in favor of a conventional marriage to a young, virginal bride. Despite their renunciations of monogamy and their suspicions about marriage, most Angry protagonists never abandon the idea altogether. Although they repeatedly cast aspersions on the idea of a permanent domestic union, characters such as Arthur also yearn for the social and sexual privileges implied therein. As *Saturday Night* demonstrates, the powerful trope of domesticity structures the scope of the narrative precisely when it is being challenged, when characters such as Arthur seem to resist or ignore the importance of the family. Early in the novel, for instance, we learn that Arthur has become entangled with Brenda, the spouse of one of his coworkers. Splitting married men into distinct groups, "Arthur classified husbands into two main categories: those that looked after their wives, and those that were slow." Jack, the cuckolded husband, unfortunately falls into "the latter class" (41). "Looking after" a woman implies all sorts of emotional, financial, and sexual responsibilities. Describing his affection for Brenda, Arthur muses that married women were the best kind to know, for finding pleasure in their attention was not simply a matter of self-gratification: "For Arthur, in his more tolerant moments, said that women were . . . warm wonderful creatures that needed and deserved to be looked after, requiring all the attention a man could give, certainly more than the man's work and a man's own pleasure. A man gets a lot of pleasure anyway from being nice to a woman. . . . Make a woman enjoy being in bed with you—that's a big part of the battle—then you were well on your way to keeping her with you for good" (41–42). Slow men, on the other hand, have no idea how to please women, and therefore no business getting married in the first place. Arthur, though he likes Jack personally, neither respects nor pities "slow" husbands. They are somehow less masculine, deficient in fulfilling their duties as a husband and a man: "There was something lacking in them, not like a man with one leg that could in no way be put right, but something that they, the slow husbands, could easily rectify if they became less selfish, brightened up their ideas, and looked after their wives a bit better" (41). By Arthur's reasoning, the less masculine husband is the one who is less attentive to his wife's emotional needs, not in a "womanish" way, but rather as a virile, responsive lover. But looking after one's wife involves more than satisfying her material and sexual needs. As Arthur later points out, it is important to keep vigilant for signs of infidelity or disloyalty.

Even as he rationalizes his affair with a married woman, Arthur regularly fantasizes about married life. While Brenda sits with Arthur at his club, sharing a pint of ale, Arthur cannot help thinking she "should be at home looking after her two kids" (155). Despite the genuine love he feels for her—he expresses such sentiments regularly throughout the novel—he continually reminds himself that she is someone else's wife. Ironically, he often thinks how lucky Brenda's husband is, being able to return to her every day after work, having children by her, and being able to take care of her. By the same token, if he ever discovered his wife—speaking hypothetically, for he is not yet married—"carrying on" with another man, Arthur vows that retribution would follow in due course: "If I ever get married, he thought, and have a wife that carries on like Brenda and Winnie carry on, I'll give her the biggest pasting any woman ever had. I'd kill her. My wife'll have to look after any kids I fill her with, keep the house spotless. And if she's good at that I might let her go to the pictures now and again and take her out for a drink on Saturday" (155). As this passage illustrates, Arthur continually transforms his illicit love affairs into more "idealized" domestic relationships, creating an anxious and unconventional fantasy life in the process. Arthur longs to play the patriarch, with a bit of Hoggart's "cock" in his swagger, but as we can see, this role, at least in his fantasy, will be protected not only by mutual agreement but also by threats of violence. In his imagination, at least, Arthur plans to maintain his domestic position by supplementing financial and emotional support of his spouse with careful policing of her social and sexual life. His characteristic rage betrays his own sense of inadequacy and dependence, asserting his masculinity through proposals and promises of violence.

On the surface, Arthur's sexual behavior seems to undermine the centrality and sanctity of the family.[25] As he expresses anger at and resistance to the idea of marriage, however, the protagonist slowly reveals that his anxiety stems in part from his unstable relationship to a normative trope of domesticity, suggesting that his resistance becomes overdetermined by a compensatory fantasy life. Arthur even works such longings, stronger than mere velleities, into his programs of sexual conquest. For example, when he later seduces Winnie, Brenda's sister, he relies directly on popular narratives of domestic security. Approaching Winnie while her husband is away on military duty, he contrasts her solitude with the promise of a more attentive partner:

> "No," he said, "it's no life for a woman. Nobody to look after her and take her out when she feels like a good time. It must be miserable for you. A woman wants a bloke to look after her, not to be stuck in Germany. I can't understand a bloke as signs on for the army, especially when he's married, and never could. And when he's got a nice sweet little woman like you I reckon he's even barmier. . . . No, duck, the sooner he's home the better, then he can look after you as a bloke should. He can get a job and settle down, and bring a regular pay-packet into the house every Friday. There's nowt like it." (99)

This seduction speech makes apparent his ambiguous performance of masculinity by appealing to competing and complementary codes of sexual behavior. As the unwed seducer, the protagonist asserts his masculinity by flaunting the conventions of marriage and resisting monogamy. Arthur forges an identity through sexual prowess and demonstrations of unbounded heterosexual virility. At the same time, however, he freely acknowledges the implicit and explicit inappropriateness of his suit. When he receives a beating at the hands of Winnie's husband, who gets wind of the affair, Arthur bears no grudges: the man had a right to protect his position as husband. Even as Arthur competes with Winnie's spouse through his rhetorical performance, he underscores the symbolic significance of marriage and domestic tranquility, supplementing the power of that trope even as he seeks to circumvent its parameters. As unusual as it may seem, his speech borrows directly from the myth of domestic harmony. Rather than interpreting his exaggerated displays of heterosexual masculinity as simple rejections of monogamy and marriage, his rhetorical performance underscores distinct ambivalences about domestic ideals. As the novel continues, marriage appeals more and more to Arthur, promising a stable refuge from the trials of everyday existence. In the end, the happy protagonist gets engaged to a local girl, and he anticipates the comforts of domestic life as the novel concludes.

A THIN MAN

As these passages illustrate, Arthur's fantasies about married life imply much more than masculine sexual prerogatives and material security. These features of domesticity complement a much grander vision as the head of a household, of "taking care" of one's wife: possessing one's own home, working outside it, and supplying it with material goods. Like Hoggart and Sillitoe, Carolyn Steedman, in her autobiographical study of gender in postwar England, *Landscape for a Good Woman,* organizes her life "as a point between two worlds: an older 'during the War,' 'before the War,' 'in the Depression,' 'then'; and the place we inhabit now" (29). She remembers the wartime cityscape with "bomb-sites everywhere" and "prefabs [factory-made, temporary homes] on waste land," while the 1950s were notable for the "growth of real income and the proliferation of consumer goods" (29, 36). Many of these new commodities entered the Steedman home as gifts to the children. Although the "clothes and shoes" her mother presented at birthdays were "conventional gifts for all post-War children," Carolyn was also given a number of consumer durables, such as a vacuum cleaner. A phonograph "also came into the house this way," and Steedman takes pleasure in relating the story of a young neighbor who was given a refrigerator as a gift—"the last thing an eight-year-old wants," she wryly observes (36).

Although material goods feature prominently in Steedman's narrative, she mentions them primarily to undermine the position of her father, thereby complicating Hoggart's and Sillitoe's accounts of working-class sex-gender systems. From an early age, Steedman's mother taught her children that any "extras" came solely from the sweat of her brow, leaving the girl to think that the family relied entirely on her mother for its financial well-being (37). While the rest of the world seemed to attain a life of affluence with unaccountable speed, the "new consumer goods came into the house slowly," her mother voicing her discontent audibly and teaching her children "to understand that [their] material deprivations were due entirely to [her] father's meanness" (36). Later, we learn that her father's stinginess undercut his position as the head of household, even his masculinity. In "A Thin Man," the book's chapter about her father, Steedman offers his physical attributes as a kind of metaphor for his effeminacy. Unlike Hoggart's working-class father, who, though modest in size, cuts a robust figure, Steedman's dad seems wasted and hen-pecked. First, she relates a story about her overmatched father losing an argument with a park ranger—tellingly, a man vested with state authority. She recalls her father as "quite vulnerable . . . a thin man," his physical attenuation a visible manifestation of hidden emotional deficiencies. His antagonist, "very solid and powerful, was made to appear taller than him," while her father's loose clothes made him appear emaciated and impotent. She wonders if this impression comes from the fact that in this confrontation "he was the loser, feminized, outdone," remembering the glowering look of the park official as they scurried away (50). Even in his strongest moments, she insists, he could offer only "passive resistance" to unwelcome situations both at home and outside (59–60).

Although Steedman's book presents a formidable reply to popular narratives about domestic life in the 1950s—working-class men did not necessarily adhere to any prescribed category of manhood—her narrative simultaneously reinforces the normative appeal of that version of masculinity. Steedman's father fails to live up to his material responsibilities: though he works, he does not provide adequately for his family, nor does he "take care" of his wife and children. This leads to several other intractable problems. Aside from his inability to defend his family with the necessary vigor, her father cannot assume his rightful position within the physical geography of the house. Relegated to an increasingly peripheral role as time wears on, he is virtually banished from the house by her mother. During the middle of the decade, he began to live in the attic, assuming his place among the lodgers that the family took in periodically (58). Later, her mother stopped making or buying him food, though he was permitted to brew his own tea in the kitchen. After his death, Steedman learns that her father and mother had never wed. He had been married to another woman all along, and the adult Steedman retroactively interprets their struggles as a battle over his reluctance to sanction their relationship through matrimony. Their two daughters were an attempt to broker a marriage; his refusal was a conflicted attempt to assert autonomy yet retain the privileges of domestic life. Though complicating tropes of postwar masculinity, Steedman clearly suggests that her father was an anomaly: he was effeminate, deficient, a failure. Despite her desire to challenge established models of working-class autobiography, Steedman does not suggest that her father offers a viable alternative to the portraits of working-class masculinity offered by Sillitoe and Hoggart.

Steedman's father's inadequacies are multiple and specific, each introduced as evidence of his effeminacy. In his sexual failure, he embodies

Arthur's foil. The particular relationship between sexual behavior and the other dominant feature of working-class masculinity, the provision of material goods to the family, became possible during the postwar period because it was supported by a physical geography—the single-family home and its attendant commodities—that became realistic for the majority of working-class families only during the 1950s, when houses and commodities reached a mass market as part of welfare state planning. In retrospect, it is clear that the state played an active part in the changing function of gender and class relations through an aggressive reform policy that affected the material conditions of domestic practices. But this does not imply that the state was a monolithic force, unilaterally determining the way working-class men and women used domesticity in narratives about themselves. As my discussion of masculinity and marriage demonstrates, working-class men asserted their masculinity both within and against the contours of marriage and family responsibilities. The discursive manifestation of this paradox is the systematic articulation of political ambivalence through vacillating emotional expressions of contentment and rage.

BUYING POWER

The prevalence of the two-up, two-down both provided the setting for and enabled these attitudes about gender. Nowhere was this change more visible than in the family's function as a unit of consumption. Manuel Castells uses the idea of "collective consumption" to describe the complicated distribution of resources typical in western European welfare states. In addition to the more familiar consumption of commodities, Castells reminds us that we spend much of our income on necessities such as housing, power, travel, education, and health care. After World War II, many wealthy countries began to organize these types of consumption on a mass scale through public programs: the building of homes, the nationalization of key industries, and the guarantee of basic social security. In addition to ensuring certain levels of consumption, often at higher and higher levels, collective consumption works to create new material needs, thereby supporting domestic commodity markets.[26] In Britain, for instance, it is hardly surprising that the proliferation of material goods such as vacuum cleaners, refrigerators, televisions, and cars coincides with the massive housing projects of the 1950s.[27] A 1961 government-commissioned study on the relationship between these commodities and

Britain's domestic geography uses the word "revolutionary" to describe the changes of the postwar period. By 1962 over 80 percent of households owned a television, greater than 70 percent a vacuum cleaner, and almost 50 percent a washing machine; more surprising, these figures did not depreciate considerably in poorer areas.[28] Functioning as a manager of labor relations and a distributor of resources, the state became increasingly more involved in regulating the country's economy. Through collective consumption, the state participated in the creation of new domestic forms: not only did it help working-class families find homes, it helped determine how those homes would be used, with what objects they would be filled, and how the country paid for them.

As Castells argues, welfare states use collective consumption to try to resolve the economic contradictions of mature capitalist economies. Thus we ought to theorize social class by considering not only a person's relationship to the means of production but also access to resources in planned economies. In postwar Britain, for instance, the welfare state attempted to resolve several contradictions—including working-class political intransigence and the decline of international commodity markets for British industrial products due, in part, to imperial contraction—by building housing for workers and reorganizing urban space. The state hoped to alleviate the shortage of housing while also making it more affordable; by the 1940s, both housing prices and rents were putting accommodation out of reach for many Britons. At a more general level, the welfare state attempted to secure long-term capital growth without perpetuating the widespread economic hardships of the 1930s.

Like many working-class people who remembered the difficulties of the 1930s even as they enjoyed the more comfortable 1950s, Sillitoe's protagonist divides his world into two temporal categories. For Arthur, the postwar years come with a reliable, well-paid job in the local bicycle factory and the security those wages afford. He elects to spend spare money on clothes. After returning from work on a typical Friday evening, he would wash up, then cast his overalls aside and select "a suit from a line of hangers. Brown paper protected them from dust, and he stood for some minutes in the cold, digging his hands into pockets and turning back lapels, sampling the good hundred pounds' worth of property hanging from an iron-bar. These were his riches, and he told himself that money paid-out on clothes was a sensible investment because it made him feel good as well as look good" (66). Almost in disbelief, Arthur realizes how lucky he has been. The war, and the changes it set in motion, has altered the family and the country's fortunes to an almost incomprehensible extent: "War was a marvelous thing in some ways, when you thought about how happy it had made so many people in England. No flies on me, Arthur thought" (22).

However, we should not believe that material comfort had transformed the young man into a docile political subject. "What did they take us for?" he asks of the government, the factory managers, the police, tax collectors, party officials, and other representatives of the state. "They think they've settled our hashes with their insurance cards and television sets, but I'll be one of them to turn round on them and let them see how wrong they are" (140–41). Though the welfare state, with its postwar consensus, attempted to mitigate some of the fundamental inequities of unmanaged capitalism, we should not imagine that material security had fully pacified—or even incorporated—working-class constituents. Arthur uses Hoggart's "Us" and "Them"—"Us" representing everything local and familiar, "Them" meaning anything foreign, official, or bureaucratic—to articulate his personal understanding of political dissidence.[29] "One day," he muses, "they" will bark like sheep dogs, telling "us" where to go, but "we" won't do as were told, refusing to "run into a pen like sheep." An unexpected return to the bad days, with starvation and lack of jobs, may not be needed to incite people like Arthur: some will simply tire of being told how to behave. The "fat-bellied union ponce," "Chief Inspector Popcorn," and "Harold Bladdertab" (Harold Macmillan, the prime minister) will ask "us" not to "muck things up" by refusing to abide by the terms of the welfare state consensus. "They" will be unable to comprehend the source of Arthur's dissatisfaction, thinking that the working class now have "television sets, enough to live on, council houses, beer, and pools—some have even got cars. We've made them happy. What's wrong?" (221).

Arthur repeatedly poses this central question—a general sense of injustice is the source of his incessant angry tirades, his ultimate and total dissatisfaction with the existing world—but leaves it unanswered. Making use of "Them" and "Us," Arthur's utterances display the ambiguous outlines of class as it takes shape in welfare state England. He is at once part of "Us," a working class defined by its opposition to authority, yet he also refers to "Us" as a body of third persons, "They" when he feels inclined to rescind his membership. The "Us" formation is temporary and contingent. At times, he gladly thinks about the "qualities" of war, steady work, and newfound material security, but elsewhere he excoriates the "mindless masses" for their uncritical participation in the world of commodities. Like his understanding of masculinity, in which he both resists and fantasizes about the virtues of marriage, Arthur defines his political relationships through wild oscillations, both lauding the state for the stability and material comfort it has effected and deriding it in visions of violent revolution that reflect his individual commitment to dissident politics. As the novel demonstrates, his conflicted expressions of masculinity are closely related to this convoluted understanding of class politics. The protagonist inflects his gender identity through a complicated set of domestic relationships in which sexual attitudes, positions of domestic authority, and financial responsibilities converge. He freely acknowledges the role of the state in the postwar economy of relative affluence, yet he thinks himself an outsider, one for whom violent, disorganized opposition to "the system" constitutes the basis of political action.

Nowhere does Arthur voice those contradictions more succinctly than when he speaks of his wages. He guards them jealously, exploding into furious tirades when anyone mentions taxes, little more than legalized theft in his mind. His wages not only enable his masculinity—they ensure his entry into a world of consumption and his ability to maintain a family—but also facilitate his sense of individuality, providing him with the one thing that he can unequivocally call his own. Recycling one of the many war metaphors that run throughout the novel, Arthur thinks to himself that he will keep "fighting every day until I die." Refusing to cede ground to anyone, he vows to continue battling "with mothers and wives, landlords and gaffers, coppers, army, government. If it's not one thing it's another," he laments, philosophically, "apart from the work we have to do and the way we spend our wages" (238–39). Money and work, it seems, float above life's other petty injustices, both enabling those struggles yet operating at a different register. As he puts it, Friday afternoons, when wages are disbursed, allow for a temporary "truce" between workers and management. While the foreman, "the enemy's scout," passes out the brown envelopes filled with cash, tensions gradually weaken. Arthur even condescends to trade some friendly banter with his supervisor. We learn that the label of "enemy" comes from a "policy passed on by his father." Although these new, affluent times have dissipated any "strong cause for open belligerence," feelings of antipathy "persisted for more subtle reasons that could hardly be understood but were nevertheless felt" (61). Unlike the "cat-and-dog" days when such attitudes were widespread, the value placed on the men's labor has increased considerably. Although this helps ease tensions at the level of open discourse, Arthur reminds us that many working-class men remain intransigent political subjects.

At the most obvious level, we can see how these statements help clarify Arthur's understanding of class politics. Material circumstances have changed dramatically. Being working class does not mean leading a life of deprivation. On the contrary, it means working hard and entering the world as a consumer of goods. The protagonist's anger, however, reminds us that he remains, at least on the inside, an uncompromising dissident. Though the reasons for his belligerence remain difficult to identify, they nevertheless survive and even multiply. The persistence of his anger and his inability to coherently identify its source betray both the state's centrality and the ambiguity of class relations: we cannot say that the state is either for or against the working class in any simple or meaningful way. Instead, it makes much more sense to understand Arthur's conflicted reaction to welfare state politics as a way of asserting independence by being working class and a man. Arthur freely acknowledges and even appreciates the material circumstances of his existence, eagerly participating in a new world of readily available commodities, but at the same time he realizes that this does not correspond with more equitable access to or distribution of power. He lives a working-class position by negotiating this complicated, contradictory nexus of social relationships and performing gender through elaborate codes of masculine affect.

His enjoyment of higher wages and consumer goods has done little to mitigate his sense of political disillusion, which traditionally went hand in hand with the narrative of working-class poverty during the interwar period. In the context of social reform and political consensus, his volatility exposes a trenchant gap between the material experience and imaginative expression of working-class positionality. If, historically speaking, material deprivation and formal political marginality were complementary aspects of working-class life, the immediate postwar period represents a moment during which there were clear contradictions between the way working-class men lived on a daily basis and how they, both collectively and individually, narrated the persistence of political frustrations in a climate of material stability. In other words, these sentiments reflect a pronounced split between the real and imaginary components of the group dynamic; there are irreconcilable differences between the quotidian experience of working-class life and the imaginative, or ideological, structures of class consciousness. Materially, we might say, characters such as Arthur become some of the most vocal advocates of welfare capitalism. Ideologically, however, he tenaciously clings to a political dissidence that seems relatively autonomous from, even diametrically opposed to, his earnest appreciation of relative financial comfort. The novel outlines a distinct contrast between his easy appreciation of improved material circumstances and his ideological complaints about the marginality of radical working-class constituencies in the postwar consensus.

This split between the real and the imaginary is manifested in the novel's discursive patterns and narrative structures, or what Althusser calls the symbolic order. Arthur's rhetorical performance of masculine rage along with his belief in the narrative of postwar affluence—which, together, are structured by deeply ambivalent understandings of heterosexuality and politics—encode the tension between his experience of material realities and his ideological commitment to revolutionary politics. What I have called Angry ambivalence, often articulated through the elaborate staging of masculine affect and a proclivity for exaggerated displays of heterosexuality, is precisely this symbolic rendering of the tension between class as an everyday experience and class as an ideological predisposition. To use the terminology of the time, a concept like "deproletarianization" is not sufficiently complex to theorize the polyvocal symbolic registers of class politics during the high period of welfare capitalism. Such reductive terms mask the range of social and individual responses to contradictory conditions: if material prosperity had become close to universal (and widely appreciated), the welfare state consensus had not yet fully incorporated the range of ideological objections to the massive expansion of the state apparatus. I also want to suggest that this contradiction is not a reproduction of the split between the personal and the collective, or private and public discourse: as we can see in the case of the Angry protagonists, the "personal" or individual experience of class politics freely draws on widespread narratives of affluence, while their understanding of dissident politics is often a way to mark their individuality rather than to express any kind of class solidarity. Instead, it makes sense to read the tensions in Arthur's narrative representations as indicative of more fundamental discontinuities between the material experience and ideological intransigence of working-class masculinity. It is in the symbolic order, characterized by startling combinations of carefree enjoyment and bitter enmity, that we see the manifestations of this particular set of contradictions.

The protagonist's participation in the rituals of affluence, combined with his articulation of political dissatisfaction, results in a cleft system of representation. The retooling of domestic narrative space reflects this discursive tension and ambivalence, creating a symbolic structure that is itself a sophisticated accommodation of paradoxical emotional and cognitive processes. His specific reliance on political anger should not be analytically separated from his appreciation of material security, nor should his exaggerated heterosexual virility be parsed out from his enthusiasm for monogamy and domestic partnership. This particular model of working-class masculinity shows how messy, contradictory, and provisional the project of theorizing representations of class can be, or should be. In this example, my model of working-class masculinity demonstrates not only an attempt to recognize the potential for incompatibility between ideological structures and material conditions but also an effort to set those categories in motion against one another, showing how they complement and counteract one another on the symbolic or discursive plane. That the rehabilitation of domestic melodrama combines these competing pressures is far from incidental to the Angry project but rather reflects an effort to adapt and transform existing narrative paradigms to respond to new historical conditions and political attitudes.

We can immediately recognize that Arthur's violent disaffection also adds heft to the novel's portrayal of working-class masculinity. He calls attention to his masculine attributes by affirming an oppositional politics as well as by emphasizing the physical strength required for his work. Experiencing this class position, however, requires a complex negotiation of a specific and contingent gender position. We can only gain access to Arthur's understanding of class through his demonstrative displays of masculinity. Similarly, his working-class politics only become legible once we understand how he annunciates them through masculine prerogatives: Arthur understands his class position through his roles as consumer and family provider, sexually free bachelor and potential family man. Furthermore, he articulates both political relations and gender identities through the metaphorical and physical space of the home. Ironically, he can only solidify his claims of masculinity by accepting marriage. By beginning to map the domestic geography of postwar England, I have also tried to initiate a discussion about the provisional connections between class and gender in texts such as *Saturday Night*. In its representational form, then, the existence of class difference can be fully explained neither by accounting for prevailing economic conditions nor by mapping divergent political interests. Depictions of class difference and solidarity, as the work of the Angry Young Men suggests, constantly negotiate between the political and material axes of class politics. As a result, I have tried to demonstrate how such narratives work within and against larger social, and theoretical, categories.

The Angry use of domestic literature also participates in a running argument about national space in postwar England. Set almost exclusively outside London and saturated with the social conventions of provincial life, such texts represent a momentary protest against both the hegemony of London in the literary imagination and the welfare state's attempt to manufacture a unified postimperial Britain. The Angry repudiation of elite modernist writing, which Sinfield insightfully reads as an attempt to demonize homosexuals and the dandy artist figure, can also be understood as a reaction against the consolidation of cultural production in London during the modernist period. This rejection of London as the cultural center of a decolonizing Britain anticipates Tom Nairn's famous "breakup of Britain," the final installment in a long narrative of imperial decline. For Nairn, of course, the inevitability of regional autonomy for Scotland, Wales, and Northern Ireland became evident just as the welfare state consensus was falling apart during the 1970s. Yet the Angry interest in a literary form of home anthropology as a means of articulating political dissidence bears all the markers of regional protest—in this case the region being provincial England, in contradistinction to the pan-British welfare state and its administrative center, London. In this respect, the rhetorical flexibility and widespread availability of class affect in Angry literature is embedded in a larger discourse of English cultural exceptionalism peaking during welfare state reforms. The cultural distinctiveness of England's urban class system is at once problematic and vital, enraging and fascinating to its witnesses and chroniclers. The emergence and popularity of a full-blooded, class-conscious domestic literature at this moment, prefigured by Orwell and shadowed by British cultural studies, contain all the frustrations and pleasures of a culture struggling to define itself anew.

As I discuss in the next chapter, this ambivalent investment in the urban class system as a repository of authentic Englishness also became an intellectual paradigm for postcolonial writers who came to live in and write about metropolitan space. For novelists such as Doris Lessing, who began caricaturing England alongside her Angry counterparts, coming to terms with their new environs meant diving headlong into the waters of an increasingly local, insular culture. Despite having little in common with the Angry writers or protagonists I have considered here—raised in colonial Rhodesia, she is more educated, self-consciously literary, and politically informed—Lessing shares a common interest in domesticity and the urban class system as the defining features of English cultural particularity. This unexpected convergence reflects the cultural logic of an incipient postimperial England in which both old hands and new-comers felt authorized to plot the literary boundaries of national space.

5. THE ELUSIVE ENGLISHMAN
DORIS LESSING GOES TO
LONDON TOWN

The ability to imagine Englishness as a repository of class affect is not the exclusive property of writers born and bred in England itself. *In Pursuit of the English* (1960), Doris Lessing's autobiographical account of her first years in London, is obsessed with the location, meaning, and function of English culture, finding its essence in the convoluted folds of a class society. After living in the metropole for two years, the semifictional narrator, Doris, complains that she has yet to stumble upon any genuine, bona fide Englishmen. "I don't think I've met any," she moans to a friend, explaining, "London is full of foreigners." The English, she concludes, have become a skittish, endangered species, vanishing under deep cover whenever strangers begin sniffing around. Once she thought she had met the real thing in a pub, the ideal context in which to observe local customs: "[M]y friend and I laid delighted hands on him. At last, we said, we are meeting the English." Their specimen, however, quickly corrects their misapprehension: "'I am not,' he said, with a blunt but basically forgiving hauteur, 'English. I have a Welsh grandmother'" (3). Though her search for the elusive Englishman proves exasperating, the narrator refuses to give up the hunt easily. After taking up lodgings with an English family, she begins to look for evidence of Englishness in their complicated domestic rituals. While gathering material, she meets a fellow tenant who offers a promising lead by commenting on the landlady's idiosyncratic behavior, but her new informant excuses the woman because she doesn't understand English standards of decorum: "It's because she's a foreigner, it's not her fault." When Doris asks her informant about the landlady's place of birth, we discover "she was born here. But her grandmother was Italian, see?" The landlady's husband, whom her new acquaintance thinks a bad influence, only exacerbates the problem: he, after all, hails from

Newcastle, and "[t]hey're different from us, up in places like that. Oh no, he's not English, not properly speaking." Naturally, Doris turns the question on her local guide, who fails to grasp the point of the query: "Me, dear? But I've lived in London all my life. Oh, I see what you mean—I wouldn't say I was English so much as a Londoner, see? It's different" (56–57).

In spite, or perhaps because, of the resistance she encounters, this anthropological mission becomes an all-consuming passion. National customs obsess the young writer, who hopes that solving the riddle of Englishness will help her unravel the "quintessential eccentricity" of her father, a bizarre man who "would merge into the local scene without so much as a surprised snarl from anyone" (1–2). Through her narrator, Lessing implies that she could not write effectively—her emigration from Rhodesia was motivated by a desire to become a novelist—until she had learned something definitive about English culture. Presciently, she reckons that her identity as a former colonial subject will enhance her chances of success. "For real perception into the side-channels of British culture," Lessing surmises in one of her more contemplative moments, "one has to go to a university in Australia or South Africa. The definitive thesis on Virginia Woolf will come, not from Cambridge, but from Cape Town" (30). Being a writer, for Lessing, means becoming an undercover anthropologist charged with the task of explaining the enigma of Englishness to the English themselves.

Lessing's reverse ethnographic narratives offer a delicately balanced critique of and investment in the discourse of English exceptionalism, complicating her status as a post-/anticolonial writer. By laying bare the peculiarities of English culture in such texts as *In Pursuit* and *The Golden Notebook* (1962), Lessing suggests that the idea of Englishness could be an effective tool in the hands of thinkers eager to demystify British hegemony. Her interest in exposing the hollow core of Englishness—a culture, we might say, being stripped of its imperial vocation—represents more than the cleverness of an emphatically anti-imperial writer. Lessing's work demythologizes Englishness by relativizing it, making it appear less robust and comfortable with itself, more vulnerable and parochial instead. Yet this desire to map the eccentric character of Englishness in the service of an anti-imperial politics represents a strange convergence with writers less immediately concerned with imperial expansion or contraction, such as the Angry Young Men. Lessing's depiction of a quirky, dysfunctional, "splendidly pathological" society paradoxically remystifies England as a culture virtually unconnected with and untouched by imperialism (*In Pursuit* 2). By echoing descriptions of England as a cold, unimportant, insular island, her work draws a surprising line of continuity between writers interested in fictionally deconstructing Englishness, like Lessing and her postcolonial colleagues, and those invested in the project of retrieving national customs for use in a progressive political agenda, such as Forster, Woolf, or Orwell.

Like the English, whom Lessing pursues with comical zeal, the "real" working class captivates the young, politically committed writer. As a young Communist in Rhodesia, Lessing's mentors insist that she "could never write a word that made sense until [she] had become pervaded by the cultural values of the working-class." After timidly suggesting that she had already acquired some of the requisite cultural knowledge by living for a quarter century among Rhodesian blacks, who, after all, worked quite a bit, her tutors reply, "Africans in this country are not working-class *in the true sense*. They are semi-urbanized peasants." Figuring that working-class subjects might be easier to find in England, Lessing travels there with the hope of finding the "correct" Marxist perspective from which to begin her career as a writer. She hopes that a year of living "in a household crammed to the roof with people who worked with their hands" might have rectified her political innocence, but a member of her local committee informs her that her housemates "are not the real working-class. They are the lumpen proletariat, tainted by petty bourgeois ideology." Her fellow party activists, likewise, are "obviously *not typical*" representatives of the working class. Stubbornly, Lessing departs for a mining village, where she learns that "[m]iners, like dockworkers, are members of a very specialized, traditionalized trade. . . . The modes of being, mores, and manners of a mining community have nothing whatsoever to do with the working-class as a whole." She also visits a New Town, described to her as a hub of working-class activity, but she meets disappointment there, too. Only then does she give up the chase and reveal the punch line: "If you really want to understand the militant working-class," one of her comrades advises, "you have to live in a community in France, let's say near the Renault works, or better still, why don't you take a trip to Africa where the black masses are not yet corrupted by industrialism" (7–8). As these circuitous jokes demonstrate, the location, meaning, and relevance of the working class, like those of the English, can be endlessly displaced. They can even be substituted for one another under the right circumstances. The writer/ethnographer is overeager but outflanked by the ineluctable advance of capitalism. The

European working class has been corrupted, while indigenous Africans have yet to encounter a mature industrial capitalism that may bring political credentials with it.

The Golden Notebook, published two years after *In Pursuit,* explores this narrative of atypical Being and insufficient Becoming in the wake of 1956, a devastating time for European leftists. For Lessing, a workable politics of class, like a workable definition of Englishness, becomes a circular and self-defeating proposition. Deploying a variety of postmodernist techniques—including extensive use of pastiche, experimentation with madness and paranoia, and dizzying metafiction—the novel offers a reluctant, ambivalent disavowal of the Communist Party, suggesting its culture of deceit and insecurity is incompatible with the urgent need for praxis. The text's reluctant repudiation of radical leftist parties implies that a formal politics of class cannot successfully navigate the straits of English culture. But if the novel's formal politics of class get short-circuited by party dysfunction, it uses postmodernist narrative methods to reinscribe class as a cultural object. Lessing uses class, unreliable or misleading in political terms, to get a handle on England's oddball culture. *The Golden Notebook* effectively captures the profound sense of disillusionment on the left during the 1950s by satirizing of the inner workings of Britain's Communist Party. In so doing, however, the novel mitigates the political significance of class politics, instead transforming it into a sometimes humorous, sometimes disturbing site of ethnographic fieldwork. The existence of class difference becomes tangential to understanding political conflict, but essential to rendering the irritating uniqueness of English culture, which Lessing figures as the paradigmatic class society. Anticipating relativist, postmodernist critiques of Marxism, Lessing strips class of its "master narrative" status by using it to provincialize Englishness. In this deft maneuver, we can observe how the project of reclaiming a more bounded, coherent national space could be requisitioned by postcolonial writers eager to attack a culture embedded in imperial power.

A KIND OF DARKNESS HERE

Because a good deal of the following discussion attempts to work through the bewildering narrative structure of *The Golden Notebook* by situating it within contemporaneous accounts of class and Englishness, readers might find a short description of the novel helpful. At times, it reads like a fairly straightforward realist narrative, the kind with which Lessing's admirers would have been familiar in the early 1960s. These realist sections make up the narrative "frame," which Lessing describes as a "conventional short novel, about 60,000 words long." It has five sections, collectively entitled "Free Women." Elsewhere, however, the novel swirls to intimidating heights of autoreferentiality: the protagonist, Anna Wulf, writes a novel, in the form of a journal, about a woman writing a novel. In her notorious 1971 introduction, Lessing herself hoped to clarify some of the basic premises of the novel. Between each section of "Free Women," we read fragments of "The Notebooks," the four diaries kept by Anna. Anna keeps multiple diaries—black, red, yellow, and blue—rather than one because, "as she recognizes, she has to separate things off from each other, out of fear of chaos, of formlessness—of breakdown." Between the last selection of the Notebooks and "Free Women: 5," we encounter the "inner" Golden Notebook, a fresh diary Anna begins in an effort to bring her experiences together, creating "something new," a space in which "things have come together, the divisions have broken down" (23). As I suggest in the following pages, Lessing figures English society as an intricate piece of class machinery in desperate need of repair. *The Golden Notebook*'s complicated narrative form—its postmodern form—can be read as a paradoxical attempt to both obliterate and reconstruct Englishness and class politics in postwar London. London, the seat of imperial culture, is the obvious place in which to erase and then redraw the outlines of postimperial Englishness.

Lessing uses Joseph Conrad's *Heart of Darkness* as a narrative template for writing about uncharted territories, inscrutable customs, and feelings of alienation caused by hostile environments. Turning around Conrad's depiction of the Congo, Lessing figures metropolitan geography and culture as unknown and virtually unknowable. She, like Conrad, also suggests that knowledge of space is an exercise in power. Being baffled by London makes her feel vulnerable, but describing the fine details of metropolitan space in her work restores the balance of power to a degree. As Edward Said and many others have argued, Britain administered a vast empire through "the coincidence between geography, knowledge, and power" (*Orientalism* 215). Marlow, Conrad's oft-quoted character-cum-narrator, likewise describes cartography as an economy of power: "Now when I was a little chap I had a passion for maps. . . . At that time there were many blank spaces on the earth, and when I saw one that looked particularly inviting on a map (but they all look that)

I would put my finger on it and say, 'When I grow up I will go there.' . . .
But there was one yet—the biggest, most blank, so to speak—that I had
a hankering after" (216). Although this passage implies that the ensuing
tale will shed some light on the Congo, the biggest blank space of them
all, his story does nothing of the sort. If many Victorian novels paint
the picture of a "knowable community," Conrad's short novel does the
opposite: the further we travel up the river, the less our narrator seems
to be able to convince us of the material reality of his experiences. The
landscape becomes fantastic, in Marlow's words, as if we were going
back "to the earliest beginnings of the world," severed from "the comprehension of our surroundings" and "leaving hardly a sign—and no
memories" (244–46). Toward the end of his journey, of course, the intrepid narrator locates a transmogrified Kurtz, a physical incarnation of
the atavism Marlow sees swirling around him. At the center of Conrad's
early modernist novella, then, we do not encounter the geographical
exercise we have been promised, but a void, a parody of the sort of mapping a colonial administrator might find useful.[1] If Marlow's narrative
were truly a cartographic exercise, we might call the method "unsound,"
or really "no method at all" (275). The text's highly subjective mapping
of the Congo offers a narratological and psychological space instead:
Marlow captivates his audience by deliberately obscuring the geographical and cultural specificities of the Congo (the people Marlow meets are
as incomprehensible as the landscape), steadfastly refusing to offer any
definitive information about the great blank spaces on the map. His
recitation foils any desire to know more about this mythical landscape:
its absorption with Kurtz's madness effectively monopolizes the reader's imaginative space, leaving little room for the contemplation of the
Congo's material, rather than narrative, reality.[2]

Lessing, in comparison, reverses this modernist trope of colonial romance, writing instead about the adventures and horrors of immigrating
to the metropole from colonial dominions. She arrived in 1949, when the
effects of war were still apparent everywhere. Much as Marlow finds the
African coast so impenetrable, the young writer has a difficult time getting oriented in the labyrinth of blitzed London thoroughfares:

My head was, as usual in those early days in London, in a maze. To
my right and left stretched that street which seemed exactly like all the
main streets in London, the same names recurring at regular intervals,

the same patterns of brick and plaster. It seemed to me impossible that the people walking past the decent little shops that were so alike, and the cold stone slabs decorated with pale gleaming fishes and vivid parsley . . . could ever know one part of London from another. (*In Pursuit* 41)

Later, as she travels into working-class areas destroyed by German bombs, it looks "as if the houses had shaken themselves to the ground." A familiar sound among the desolate, war-torn streets reminds the narrator "of a cricket chirping with a quiet persistence from the sun-warmed grasses in the veld," an unlikely reminder of her childhood in Rhodesia (47). Gradually, we realize that it is London, in fact, that has become unfamiliar, unrecognizable, and inhospitable, while the colonies represent what is comfortable and known. As the writer gets lost amid the chaos of London, we only rediscover our bearings by comparing the blankness with something alien but familiar, the sound of crickets in Rhodesia.

Lest her readers misinterpret the political stakes of her narrative geography, Lessing indicates that her representation of London as a confusing mess directly relates to England's political and cultural vulnerability, underlined by postwar austerity and imminent imperial dissolution. Whereas novelists such as Conrad or Woolf, in *The Voyage Out*, fashion a modernist aesthetics through journeys to colonial possessions— following the tide of emigrants and administrators—Lessing seeks to cultivate an artistic practice by mapping the trip in reverse: "Not long ago people set foot for the colonies—the right sort of people, that is—in a spirit of risking everything and damning the cost. These days, a reverse immigration is in progress. The horizon conquerors now set sail or take wing for England, which in this sense means London, determined to conquer it, but on their own terms" (*In Pursuit* 9). If narratives of imperialism, such as Conrad's, helped create what Said calls the social space of narrative, it is equally clear that Lessing imagines a project in which postcolonial subjects could conquer England "on their own terms." Like Selvon's lonely Londoners and Lamming's emigrants, Lessing's characters intend not only to visit but to forcibly occupy metropolitan space. The kinds of cartographic obstacles put in the way of such conquerors also resemble many of the structural features of "postmodern space" identified by the leading theorists of postmodernism (Harvey, Jameson, Soja). Lessing's use of a bewildering, alienating environment calls to mind

Fredric Jameson's crisis in "cognitive mapping," with a subtle twist: this description of postmodern confusion is steeped in the trope of reverse colonization. While most accounts of postmodern culture attribute this sense of bewilderment to internal crises of capitalist production, perhaps postmodern understandings of space owe more than we realize to successive waves of immigration during the postwar period. Lessing's deployment of geographic confusion, I argue, works in service of the broader and more self-conscious political objective of rendering metropolitan culture less formidable and coherent.

In *The Golden Notebook,* London's mystifying illegibility assumes less amusing, far more sinister forms. Like *Heart of Darkness,* the novel suggests that madness tends to afflict enterprising explorers set to conquer London. In the yellow notebook, one of the four journals kept by the novel's main character, Anna, we learn that London has become an absolutely terrifying city. Ella, Anna's fictional alter ego, becomes enraged while moving, "mile after mile, through the weight of ugliness that is London in its faceless peripheral wastes." Occasionally, she forces herself "to face what she hated," walking through the miles of "grey mean little houses that crawled endlessly." Even the pretty light and warmer weather of the summer cannot mitigate "this ugliness, this meanness" that flowed out in all directions, for that "was London—endless streets of such houses." Anna's fictional mouthpiece, Ella, who is confusingly writing a novel herself, often finds the whole situation "hard to bear, the sheer physical weight of the knowledge because—where was the force that could shift the ugliness?" (176). As in Conrad's story, where Marlow's terror increases as he moves further up the river, we can chart *The Golden Notebook*'s uneven progress by watching the steady erosion of Anna's mental capacities as the chaos of London infects her. The city's greatest defense against the incursion of such reverse colonists is its stereotypical Englishness—its inhospitable climate, stultifying ugliness, and the peculiar forms of madness to which local residents have become accustomed.

Although Anna ultimately treats her lapse of sanity as a potential source of regeneration, she does not willingly relinquish her grip on emotional health, using a variety of techniques to maintain her balance. We see evidence of this corrosive process in the novel's first passage from "The Notebooks," introduced by the black notebook.[3] Here are the first few lines, of "THE DARK," Anna's title for the black notebook, whose entries begin in 1951:

black
>   dark, it is so dark
>   it is dark
>   there is a kind of darkness here

[And then, in a changed startled writing:]

>   Every time I sit down to write, and let my mind go easy, the words,
> It is so dark, or something to do with the darkness. Terror. The terror
> of this city. Fear of being alone. Only one thing stops me from jump-
> ing up and screaming . . . it is to deliberately think myself into that
> hot light. (56)

Once merely illegible and foreign, London becomes hostile. As the passage moves on, we gradually learn that the "hot light" refers to her memories of Rhodesia, the "rough pulsing heat of a granite boulder," or the
smell of the dusty warmth on her sunburned cheeks (56). If Conrad's
insistence on "efficiency" and "sound methods" allows him to differentiate the British from the Belgians (214, 275), and, of course, their colonial subjects, Lessing, through Anna, contrasts the robust simplicity of
Rhodesia with the emotional dysfunctionality of the English.

We could explain the textual correspondence between psychological
and geographical instability in several ways. Because the novel also relies
on the theme of "breakdown" as "a way of self-healing" (viii)—in the
inner Golden Notebook, Anna decides to combine the four notebooks
and eradicate arbitrary divisions in her life—we could argue that the text
works as a kind of early dramatization of a *Thousand Plateaus*, where Deleuze and Guattari argue that only through "deterritorialization" of the
ego can humans achieve mental health. Alternatively, we might maintain that the novel provides a typical example of what Jameson would
call the failure to cognitively map our surroundings, known as the postmodern condition for short. Although most of postmodernism's leading
theorists spend little time considering the effects of postcolonial immigration, in Lessing's text, at least, metropolitan-colonial relationships influence, both imaginatively and materially, the novel's experimentation
with postmodern forms. By rewriting Conrad, Lessing's version of madness is embedded in England's historical circumstances, built geography,
and narrative tropes. *The Golden Notebook* may generalize psychological
instability as a condition of postwar England, but in so doing, the text

also circumscribes madness, or at least this particular type of insanity, as a constitutive feature of metropolitan society. The spatial parameters of insanity provide a kind of political structure in the text—who is insane, when, where, under what circumstances, and to what end—because this psychological condition is embedded in the experience of travel and Lessing's practice of reverse ethnography, of what it means to locate England on the cognitive map of postimperial global politics.

For readers of Conrad, the shock of the journey to the colonies contributes to the epistemological crisis we now recognize as an early form of modernist writing. The material reality of the colonies, a collection of traumas that cannot be rendered effectively through the medium of narrative realism, are translated instead by the modernist privileging of aesthetic experimentation: as Marlow repeatedly explains, "you wouldn't believe me if I told you." Colonial space in *Heart of Darkness* represents an imaginative problem rather than a material reality, demanding some kind of aesthetic innovation—in this case, a reference to the impossibility of accurate or stable narrative devices—in order to compensate for the epistemological crisis at the center of the project. Conrad's gesture toward a modernist aesthetics allows *Heart of Darkness* to elide the material conditions of imperial domination by representing them as aesthetic or narrative contradictions to which the narrator has no easy reply. In *The Golden Notebook,* in contrast, this representational problem becomes even more significant because the novel is organized around Anna's writer's block, a postmodern intensification of Marlow's discomfort with the reliability of narrative. Anna copes with her "freezing up," or her waning of affect—which she attributes to a general social condition, "to the times we live in" (574)—by writing in four notebooks instead of one. As she explains to both the audience and other characters in the novel, she must keep four notebooks to ward off the "chaos," to maintain a semblance of order in her life—without an external order, an exterior form, her life and her thoughts would devolve into total disarray. From the very beginning, then, Lessing suggests that the form of the novel is a spatial problematic. Anna wards off insanity by remembering the hot sun of Rhodesia—in other words, geographical space *in* the novel also is transformed into the narrative space *of* the novel, determined by the relationship between the frame of the text and the novel's notebooks. The complex interactions between the text's content and form reflect the narrative desire to represent the anxieties associated with conquering and provincializing London.

Beyond the novel's depiction of reverse colonization, the text's post-coloniality is most tangible in its obverse, its recollections of Anna's life in Rhodesia. Though the warmth of Rhodesia initially serves as a stable point of reference, helping Anna recover her emotional balance when London becomes unbearable, her long stay in the metropolis gradually undermines her ability to visualize, and therefore represent, her memories of Rhodesia. For the most part, she restricts these writings to the black notebook, where she also records the "factual" narratives that serve as source material for her fiction, as well as financial transactions related to the publication of her first novel, *Frontiers of War*.[4] Though her memories of southern Africa help Anna maintain her sanity, the textual recollections of her time there become plagued by emotional blockages and aesthetic instability. For example, she often interrupts the narrative to chastise herself for "falling into the wrong tone," a "self-punishing, cynical" mode of address (65, 90). After she finishes the story of her six years in Rhodesia during the war, Anna complains that her "factual" record of the events is even worse than her novel, which she has come to despise: "It's full of nostalgia, every word loaded with it, although at the time I wrote it I thought I was being 'objective'" (153). In short, Anna's inability to adequately remember and represent her life in the colonies leads to writer's block.

Later, Anna's malfunctioning tonal register begins to corrupt the quality of her fictional writing, too. She and an American writer, James Schaffer,[5] have been having fun with editors by submitting parodies of the more conventional travel essays they had been writing. When, to their amazement, several editors express admiration for their ridiculous stories, their amusement turns to more serious reflection: "James and Anna decided they were defeated; that something had happened in the world which made parody impossible" (440). Like many postmodern texts, *The Golden Notebook* narrates tonal dysfunction, the attenuation of parody into its blanker, less ambitious cousin, pastiche. But before abandoning pastiche entirely—Anna writes that she and Schaffer "wrote no more bits of pastiche" after the incident with the publisher, and she ends the yellow notebook by swearing off it (440, 541)—Anna offers up the story "Blood on the Banana Leaves." Ostensibly, the story is told by a black African man who avenges the rape of his lover by a white colonial. Falling back on the stock tropes of colonial romance, the story begins, "Frrrrrr, frrr, frrr, say the banana trees ghosting the age-tired moon of Africa, sifting the wind." As the importunate Noni explains that her "heart is ebony with uneasiness and the guiltiness of my fate," John, the narrator, implores her, "Be still and sleep . . . the moon is four-horned with menace and I am making my fate and yours, the fate of our people." As John "seek[s] out the white man's lust and kill[s] it," Noni and the unidentified old women of the village chant "Aie, Aie" in chorus with the banana leaves. After the murder, the moon shines crimson on the banana leaves, "singing frrrr, frr, scream, cry and croon, oh red is my pain, crimson my twining pain, oh red and crimson are dripping the moon-echoing leaves of my hate" (440 – 43).

This experimental parody of bad colonialist fiction, which plays with Orientalist tropes, is Anna's final attempt to write "about" Africa. She had begun her literary career with *Frontiers of War,* but since then, her writer's block has precluded subsequent attempts at fiction. We can see that her artistic blockage is related directly to her problems with her colonial experiences. She starts the black notebook as an attempt to keep the chaos of England at bay by remembering the physical sensations associated with her life in Rhodesia. She follows by writing an "objective" narrative of the source material for her novel. After excoriating herself for the results of that experiment, she turns to parody, but in this too she fails to locate a satisfactory register. The problem of finding a language to represent her colonial experiences becomes increasingly intractable; it determines not only the thematics of her fiction but her ability to write at all. That parody is the last stop on her quest for an appropriate form is instructive. Parody requires not only linguistic mastery and subtle manipulation of style and tone but also a striated audience with comparable faculties. There is a putative "object" of the parody, those who employ the style earnestly and might not understand the joke, and also a privileged reader who comprehends the language and the context as well as the writer does. In this particular instance, Anna's parodic dissonance comes from an inability, in both herself and her audience, to master and negotiate the linguistic complexity that her story necessarily employs. Not only must her readers be familiar with the conventions of colonialist stories and know the difference between "good" and "bad" fiction, they must understand the basic historical facts about British domination in Rhodesia.

After this attempt at parody or pastiche of the colonialist short story—it is unclear which, given the context—Anna's entries in the black notebook begin to tail off. She includes excerpts from several literary reviews of *Frontiers of War,* her successful novel about the color bar in Rhodesia, followed by a series of newspaper clippings (which are not "reprinted" in the novel) from the years 1955–57, each referring to "violence, death, rioting, hatred, in some part of Africa" (524). She ends the notebook with one final entry in which she recounts a strange dream about her time in the colonies. The dream, like so many of her stories, goes quite badly, not at all as she remembers it: "I shall close this notebook. If I were asked . . . to 'name' this dream, I would say it was about total sterility" (525). Anna's ability to recall the specifics of her adolescence in Rhodesia has been deteriorating for some time. As early as 1953, two years after her first entry in the black notebook, she tells of spending "all morning trying to remember" herself "sitting under the trees in the vlei near Mashopi. Failed" (57). She later compares the "Anna" of Rhodesia to "an enemy, or like an old friend one has known too well and doesn't want to see" (153). Anna's last attempts to represent her Rhodesian experiences result in a vision of total creative sterility. Crippled by her inability to cognitively and aesthetically process her uneven relationship to imperialism and its effect on her subjectivity, her creative productivity comes to a standstill. Unlike Marlow, who compensates for any discomfort he may feel about his role as a storyteller with sheer loquacity, Anna cannot find an acceptable solution to the formal difficulty of representing colonial space in her work. Instead, she fills her diary with ambiguous satires and unsatisfactory fragments, an inconclusive dramatization of the novel's aesthetic anxieties.

Anna's attempt to cope with her writer's block is one of the central formal properties of the novel. In many ways, the novel is about Anna's creative freezing, though she only admits to the problem near the conclusion (604). We do not, in fact, know for certain whether she eventually overcomes her difficulties. If we read the whole novel as Anna's work, we can only assume that she has resolved her problem and decided to resume her career as a professional novelist.[6] Alternatively, toward the end of "Free Women," *The Golden Notebook*'s narrative frame, Anna declares her intention to become a social worker, abandoning writing, leaving the audience to wonder how the novel gets written and arranged in the first place (665). The gap left by a fading grasp of her colonial experiences accelerates Anna's descent into madness and disrupts her capacity to write fiction. Through this, we can begin to understand Lessing's narrative spatially, as a cartographic exercise: the notebooks, conceived as a process to think through her blockage—itself a cognitive product of her colonial memories and experiences, her desire to map the cultural, political, and geographical relationship between metropole and colony—determine the form of *The Golden Notebook* as a whole. As Anna's ability to write about her life in Rhodesia collapses under the weight of her emotional and aesthetic malfunctioning, she turns to newspaper excerpts, replacing her observations with distant and "objective" records of Africa's facticity. This, too, proves unsatisfactory, leading to the abandonment of the black notebook altogether. Lessing's fiction attempts to accommodate and negotiate the cultural hole left by her frustrated reverse ethnography.

At this point, then, the novel's formal structure—and I will restrict the discussion to the relationship between the novel's black notebooks and "Free Women" sections, or the colonial material and the realist narrative frame—emerges through Lessing's attempt to narrate the problem of finding the proper discursive perspective, the position from which one can imagine and create an aesthetic object. In other words, *The Golden Notebook*'s dizzying, novel-within-a-novel-within-a-novel form attempts to negotiate the disjuncture between the material realities of imperialism and her subjective experience of reverse colonization. Ultimately, in the black notebook, this attempt fails, implying that imperialism "wins" by thwarting Anna's reverse ethnographic impulses. Anna first tries to write an objective narrative of her source material for *Frontiers of War,* but complains that it is saturated with nostalgia. She often falls into the "wrong tone," leading her to parody/pastiche. This, too, she abandons, turning instead to newspaper clippings of the "real" events in Africa of the mid-1950s. We can read this failure, this creative dilemma, as the aesthetic paradox of postmodern form. This representational crisis, instigated by the contemplation of her colonial past, forces her to turn to the other notebooks, then to the inner Golden Notebook, and eventually to combine them all. It is as if the novel stages a struggle between historical conditions and the narrator's ability to recapitulate them. The novel is a narrative assembly of this struggle which culminates in the creation of the novel's unusual structure, the interplay between its several inner narratives.

The novel's aesthetic preoccupations and patterns of narrative innovation resemble, in many ways, the basic thematic and structural problems in modernist texts such as *Heart of Darkness.* Lessing's postmodern reply, however, proceeds by disrupting and reinscribing the kinds of political relationships and imaginative journeys on which such earlier aesthetic experiments were based. The novel's postmodern style becomes discernible, in part, through Lessing's political decision to write the metropole, rather than Rhodesia, as the epicenter of madness. What Jameson might call a crisis of cognitive mapping—a prototypical symptom of postmodernity exhibited clearly by Anna—cannot be attributed simply to the proliferation of mass media and commodity culture or the breakdown of traditional class relationships, but also to the experience of imperial contraction in the postwar era. This period of rapid decolonization demanded an intensive material redrawing and imaginative reordering of England's geographic, political, and cultural boundaries, yet most articulations of postmodern theory—particularly those using "space" as a central metaphor for postmodern culture—have been resistant to theorizing the effects of imperial decline on postwar avant-garde literature in Europe.[7] In a country such as England, especially a city such as London, the center of imperial operations, metropolitan subjects were forced, by independence movements and the arrival of immigrants, to reconsider their position in the world vis-à-vis former colonial subjects. The epistemological crisis of postmodernity becomes salient just as metropolitan culture is subjected to analysis and inspection by postcolonial immigrants. Perhaps this persistent sense of postmodern trauma, which Robert Young and Alistair Pennycook identify as the crisis caused in the West by the realization that it is no longer the center of cultural production, comes from the knowledge that the metropole does not provide a stable vista from which to organize the workings of global space. As I discuss below, understandings of class politics were among the first metropolitan structures to be disrupted by the arrival and assimilation of former colonial subjects. In Lessing's particular case, her interest in a progressive politics of class both supplements and complicates this impulse to provincialize Englishness through such forms of ethnographic writing.

A PARTY TO IRONY

Though Lessing actively participated in the formation of the British New Left, it is in many ways more difficult to situate her political sentiments than those of other postwar leftists.[8] Roberta Rubenstein notes that Lessing had been involved in progressive politics in Rhodesia as early as 1942, where her eclectic reading of canonical Marxist literature and work against the color bar offered her a perspective that most of her contemporaries in England lacked (66 n. 1). Interested in feminist politics and a twice-divorced "free woman," Lessing also occupied an anomalous gender position compared to others in party circles—the New Left's dominant figures, including E. P. Thompson, John Saville, Raymond Williams, Eric Hobsbawm, Christopher Hill, and Stuart Hall, were all men, and only Hall had direct experience with British colonialism overseas. Lessing's status as an autodidact and established novelist by the mid-1950s further emphasized her distance from many university intellectuals as well as party rank and file. Nevertheless, Lessing was an important part of the emerging political movements of the postwar years. She edited *Daylight,* a supplement of *World News,* which encouraged working-class writing, and published articles in *Reasoner,* edited by Thompson (Jenny Taylor 24). In 1956 she returned to Rhodesia as an agent of Tass, the Soviet News Agency, the results of which were published in *Going Home* later that year. Thompson recruited her for the editorial board of the *New Reasoner* with the aim of attracting "new and younger constituencies"; she left the Communist Party in 1957 along with many *New Reasoner* dissidents, serving also on the first board of *New Left Review.*[9]

In this respect, as James English points out, Lessing had an ambivalent relationship with the political movements in which she participated. She was both inside and outside the main currents of British leftist thought, itself on the margins of mainstream politics. If many leftists and orthodox Marxists considered problems such as the color bar in Africa or gender inequities "secondary contradictions," Lessing's fiction makes it clear that she could never accept such simplistic explanations of important political matters. The 1950s offered confusing political options for progressives of all kinds. Although we can read it historically and intellectually as a time of renewal (I am thinking of all the New Left scholars who can trace their lineage to the 1950s), it was also a moment of bitter recriminations and political fragmentation. Lessing's uneven relationship with her political peers—*The Golden Notebook,* for instance, emphasizes her concern with "the sex war" as a major point of contention—could only have been intensified by the demoralizing events of 1956.[10] Thus even if Lessing shared some important experiences and attitudes with her contemporaries, it is important to recognize that she approached the problem of class and its relevance to politics (both national and global) from a more complicated position. Unlike Hoggart or Thompson, who could confidently assert that class was *the* political issue of the moment, Lessing was perhaps less eager to celebrate class politics as the main source of political oppression. In the red notebook, the space in *The Golden Notebook* where Anna reflects on her political life, class is not simply a way to describe political affiliations, conflicts, or material relationships. Gradually, we come to understand that class is a curiosity endemic to metropolitan culture, and therefore a local custom available for anthropological study and postcolonial critique.

From the very beginning, the novel's main character, Anna, is ambivalent about joining the party. She has many doubts, taking mental stock of them as she prepares to meet a party recruiter. As a writer and a self-described solitary, Anna instinctively loathes larger groups, though she also chides herself for this attitude. Of more serious concern is the party's open hostility to artists. More than anything, she faults the organization for its patent incapacity for truthfulness, its unwillingness to admit or confront its manifest problems during the Stalin years. Despite these reservations, Anna finds herself joining almost against her will. Having known many party members over the years, she quickly grasps the intricate social rituals practiced by insiders. Throughout the recruiting interview, she finds herself attracted by the "sardonic" speech patterns of Comrade Bill, her recruiter, who expresses incredulity that an intellectual would want to join the party under the circumstances (by then, stories of party purges in the Soviet Union were difficult to dismiss). As Anna signs on, he resumes his not-so-subtle jibing by predicting that within "five years' time" Anna will be "writing articles in the capitalist press exposing us as monsters, just like all the rest." She intuits that by "all the rest" Bill means intellectuals, and because she knows intellectuals and artists are no more likely to leave the party than other members, she bristles at his humorous barb but continues the joking. "It's lucky that I'm an old hand," she reminds him, because a "raw recruit" might have been "disillusioned by [his] attitude." Comrade Bill rounds off the exchange by giving Anna "a long, cool, shrewd look which said: Well, of course I wouldn't have made that remark if you hadn't been an old hand" (154–55).

Like the bad colonialist fiction Anna tries to parody, the language of the party is a complicated game of technical mastery and political repudiation. Participants create meaning by differentiating levels of knowledge, privilege, and discursive authority. Such linguistic manipulation has the ability to both include and exclude its objects: by astutely reading the situation, Anna feels a measure of satisfaction, an acknowledgment that she is "back in the fold" and "already entitled to the elaborate ironies and complicities of the initiated" (155). At the same time, how-ever, her position allows Bill to criticize her, to make her feel periph-eral to the party's truly committed inner circle. If we read his words "straight," without the irony—and there is nothing in Bill's piercing glance that negates this reading—we can discern the party's suspicious attitude toward intellectuals like Anna. Finally, and most important for my reading, the subtext of this exchange underlines the ultimate dys-functionality of party life. Anna says that she would have been disil-lusioned had she been a raw recruit; by implication, we can see that she comes to the party disillusioned. The party's complex ironies ultimately short-circuit themselves. Though the official political languages Anna records in the red notebook permit limited forms of social analysis and intricate, complicit joking, they cannot create a space in which to carry a sustained politics of class.

Despite the strained, disingenuous language of the party, or perhaps as a way to compensate for it, the organization is full of creative writ-ers. Commercially speaking, Anna has achieved more success than most of her new comrades. After several frustrating years of socializing and studying with various leftist groups, she claims that she has not yet "met one Party member, anywhere, who has not written, half-written, or is planning to write a novel, short stories, or a play" (168). Although such writing, as a general rule, is unspeakably terrible, she finds herself vol-unteering her time as a sort of literary consultant for the party press. She does "welfare work," as she calls it, answering the letters and submissions of those trying to get their work into print. When she starts, she quips, "every member of the Party must be a part-time novelist, but then it stopped being a joke" as old, dog-eared, moldy manuscripts, "some of them obviously hoarded in drawers for years," continue to pour in from all corners of the island (354).

Though most of the stories are "ordinarily incompetent," Anna oc-casionally comes across a story that piques her interest (354). One com-rade from Leeds, for instance, submits a piece of short fiction about a delegation of British teachers visiting the Soviet Union. After the group has been in Moscow for a couple of days, Stalin himself summons the protagonist, Ted, to solicit advice from his English comrade about the USSR's policy regarding Western Europe. Comrade Ted, who has been preparing all his adult life for this moment, challenges the wisdom of the party's misguided foreign policy. Stalin thanks him and then dismisses him with a handshake and a wordless smile. The story is no better than the rest of the prose she has been reading—the narrative switches from first to third person halfway through—but Anna reads it ironically at first, and then as a "very skillful parody of a certain attitude." Quite suddenly, she comes to the realization that the story was written seriously, and does so because she recognizes the fantasy as a variant of her own. It troubles Anna most that it "could be read as parody, irony, or seriously" (302). When she reads it to other members, one calls it "honest basic stuff" but then admits to thinking it was parody at first, producing a spate of uncomfortable laughter (305). The piece's "honesty" is not a function of its ability to reliably, or skillfully, communicate information, attitudes, or sentiments. The honesty of the story is its ability to capture the linguistic and emotive instability of party circles during the crises of the 1950s, circulating meaning at several different, contradictory levels. This observation complicates a common postmodernist reading of pastiche. Pastiche is not always parody, in Jameson's words, "without vocation," the "neutral practice of . . . mimicry, without any of parody's ulterior motives, amputated of the satiric impulse, devoid of laughter and of any conviction" ("Postmodernism" 65). Instead, it would be more useful to think of pastiche as a productive, if confusing, style of mimesis with multivalent levels of signification rather than neutral or blank properties. Lessing's pastiche—we can also think back to Anna's "Blood on the Banana Leaves"—calls attention to the polyvocal channels through which speech, in these times of acute political crises, can signify.

As we delve deeper into the red notebook, Anna's political diary, we begin to recognize this style of bifurcated speech—"doubles talk," as Claire Sprague calls it—as a general condition of party discourse. Political speech is "honest" only when it underscores the subterfuge inherent in the party at this historical moment. Sarcasm, deceit, and explicit affirmations of party doctrine often encode a subtext of fear, shame, and disbelief mixed with genuine, highly personalized commitments to progressive causes. Discussions of Stalin usually expose the duplicity most painfully. Although Anna shares with most members the disturbing, painful knowledge that the rumors of atrocities are likely true, she also shares the impulse to defend the party against public criticism of any kind. While discussing one of Stalin's pamphlets on linguistics with a group of intellectuals, for instance, she becomes less and less comfortable with the trajectory of the conversation. One discussant excuses the pamphlet's crude language by urging the others to remember that the tradition of polemics in Russia is much more "rough and knockabout" than their own. Though Anna gets "discouraged" because the weak apology for the pamphlet's lack of sophistication seems "nonsense" to her, she remains momentarily quiet because she lacks formal training in philosophy and fears making a naive error. When she eventually raises her concerns, she, too, makes excuses. "Perhaps the translation is bad," she suggests. Instantly, in this clear evasion, Anna sees that she has "expressed everyone's feeling that the pamphlet is in fact bad." Her equivocation captures the mood of the meeting exactly, and the group tacitly agrees to cease discussion of the essay. No one has the courage to say that "something is fundamentally wrong," though "the implication" of Anna's words "amounts to that" (300–301).

Like many embattled constituencies, party members have become less willing to incorporate a robust critical language within their rules of discourse. But Anna reckons that the problem runs deeper than that: if members willingly admit that Stalin is a murderer and the party ethically bankrupt, they will also have to concede that their dreams for peace and social justice have been similarly compromised. Ironically, party members have pinned hopes for a better world on the individual least likely to deliver such change within and beyond the party. If members were to face up to the truth that the Communist Party, as constructed in the mid-1950s, offers little scope for change, the "dream" of "democracy, of decency . . . would be dead," even though the party itself is one of the great obstacles to reform (302). As a result, and for a variety of reasons— not least of which is the fear of recriminations from party bureaucracy itself—members speak a very careful, stylized, ambiguous language.

This discursive pattern, related to the problem of parody/pastiche, is a characteristic feature of *The Golden Notebook*'s postmodern form. It would be too simplistic to say that Anna's apologies are unequivocally false. In fact, her dilemma encodes the truth of party life surreptitiously, as it were, in her evasions. Anna's self-deluding statements may not reflect what she feels "inside," but her personal reactions don't tell the whole story either. Rather, she captures the problem with alarming, uncomfortable honesty by speaking to a complex, contradictory situation. Meaning does not exist on a single discursive plane—neither the literal nor the implicit messages of Anna's speech can account for the experience she wants to describe—but in the reality of linguistic flexibility, in the necessity of multiple levels of speech and interpretation. In the three examples of "doubles talk" I have discussed—Anna's party initiation with Comrade Bill, the short story, and the discussion of the party pamphlet—it would be insufficient to read any of these discursive exchanges either straight or ironically. This linguistic trope, of course, resembles the postmodern waning of affect, of pastiche eclipsing parody. In saying this, however, I want to situate this aesthetic condition within the profound political traumas of the 1950s. Whereas Alex Callinicos argues that the evolution of relativist, postmodernist writing can be attributed to post-1968 conservative retrenchment (162–70), I would argue that this form of postmodernist politics has its roots in the more harrowing experiences of the 1950s. Strong critiques of class as a master narrative, an important component of postmodernist discourse, were themselves a product of postwar crises on the left.

Like the black notebook, the red notebook ends with a collection of newspaper clippings, these focusing on the cold war. Overcome by despair, we are led to believe, Anna feels she can no longer put political affect into words, turning instead to the factual, objective record of the press. The notebook then ends abruptly. Before dropping it for good, however, Anna foreshadows how she will overcome her writer's block. During an election campaign, she canvasses door-to-door in an indigent neighborhood. Visiting undecided voters, encouraging them to vote Communist, she meets a string of harried women, worn out by demanding children and unsupportive husbands. She gets detained in one house for nearly three hours by a particularly lonely woman. Her complaints, offered in a "dragging, listless" tone, leave a lasting impression on Anna. When she returns to party headquarters, she relates the story to a more experienced colleague, who admits to seeing similar things: "[W]henever I go canvassing," she concurs, "I get the heeby-jeebies. This country's full of women going mad all by themselves." Anna's confidante also admits to experiencing similar feelings of depression until she "joined the Party and got some purpose in life." Anna's doubts, though, are not so easily assuaged. The party could not produce the same palliative effects in her. After giving it some serious thought, she concludes, "[T]hese women interest me much more than the election campaign" (165–67).

In this brief digression, Anna reveals why she will eventually leave the party: it cannot, or will not, do anything to help cure England's madness, which seems to affect women especially. Neither the black notebook, in which she records her thoughts about Africa and colonialism, nor the red notebook affords Anna the proper perspective from which she can overcome her creative sterility. In the overall structure of the novel, the language of formal class politics and the experience of colonial oppression lack narrative staying power: both close in on themselves, remaining stuck in ironic holding patterns, leaving only unsatisfactory narrative experiments behind.

This is another way of saying that neither class nor an inside knowledge of colonialism allows Lessing to fully satisfy her anthropological imperative. In the red notebook, class politics becomes a useful way to describe the madness of the English, but it ceases to function as a reliable way of organizing political activity. In *The Golden Notebook,* class difference connotes primarily cultural, rather than political, attributes. The kinds of rigorous ideological explanations of class exploitation are the object of gentle satire, gradually becoming a site of political malfunction, and then aesthetic crisis. What begins as a straightforward political issue—from Anna's perspective, the party's refusal to acknowledge or address real political problems, such as those faced by women on a daily basis—is transformed into an aesthetic or representational crisis, culminating in Anna's writer's block. The text's pursuit of class exposes both the delightful and the debilitating sides of metropolitan culture, portraying England as a provincial, unstable nation on the brink of collapse. By describing the insurmountable problems of the Communist Party, Lessing turns class into a useful descriptive tag (even if it also represents a political blind spot). The English obsession with class becomes a distinguishing cultural condition. Class differences, perhaps, are so deeply ingrained in English culture that class itself obstructs, rather than clears the way for, progressive political mobilization. These ethnographic vignettes help Lessing locate and critique Englishness, yet they ultimately close in on themselves, forcing us back to the text's framing mechanism. Like its fantasy of reverse colonization and ethnography, the novel's pursuit of class politics stalls. The inconclusiveness of the notebooks forces readers back to "Free Women," the short, conventional, realist narrative that brackets the novel's other sections. Lessing's ethnographic curiosity, frustrated by her inconclusive pursuit of the English and class politics, leads her to study the rituals of domestic space in "Free Women."

DOMESTIC FICTION AND THE ATTACK ON REALISM

In "The Small Personal Voice," an essay first published in 1957, Lessing implores contemporary novelists to return the art form to its "greatness" of the previous century. Originally included in *Declaration,* a collection of aesthetic policy statements from young writers of the Angry generation, Lessing's piece appeared alongside contributions from John Osborne, Colin Wilson, and John Wain. Like many of her colleagues, deeply suspicious of modernist experimentation, Lessing argues that "the highest point of literature was the novel of the nineteenth century . . . the work of the great realists." Although the great European novelists of the nineteenth century were a diverse group who did not have language, politics, culture, or aesthetic principles in common, they shared "a climate of ethical judgment; they shared certain values." Realist fiction offers the most promising aesthetic method for the pursuit of such goals, and the realist novel or story, she maintains, "is the highest form of prose writing; higher than and out of the reach of any comparison with expressionism, impressionism, symbolism, naturalism, or any other ism" (4). Contemporary fiction, on the other hand, she calls "provincial," limited by the pettiness of postwar English culture and its refusal to take on weightier moral questions. Though she describes the emergence of the Angry Young Men as "an injection of vitality into the withered arm of British literature," they too could not escape Lessing's charge of provincialism (15). Postwar English writers, she surmises, are merely the literary products of a culture sliding backward.

If Lessing's aesthetic and political naïveté seem out of character—her outright rejection of "isms" puts her perilously close to the type of provincialism she abhors—we should remember that Lessing was at least a provisional member of the Angry Young Men, as her inclusion in *Declaration* suggests. The style of her early fiction, in *The Grass Is Singing* and the first two novels of the Children of Violence series, is largely consonant with the indignant realism of an Osborne, Amis, or Wain. Her early work, in effect, resembles the kind of domestic fiction I discussed in the previous chapter. Lessing's unequivocal endorsement of realism is supported by her belief that politics and aesthetics cannot be separated: the form of the novel ought to reflect its political content. By 1962, with the publication of *The Golden Notebook,* Lessing must have revisited her position on the value of strictly realist novels. As Molly Hite points out, it is "her most obvious attack . . . on the coherence that realist fiction demands" (64). But the novel's repudiation can be read as a provocative critique, rather than an outright abandonment, of realist principles. The "Free Women" sections of the novel, for instance, offer a running satire of the domestic forms so popular with the Angry Young Men. Aesthetically, *The Golden Notebook*'s postmodern turn does not, strictly speaking, react against an institutionalized high modernism, but rather against the aesthetically conservative, antimodernist reflux of the postwar realist novel. By reinterpreting the domestic melodrama of Amis, Sillitoe, and even herself, Lessing sought to expose and supersede the provincial conservatism of her Angry counterparts.

The Golden Notebook articulates its political critiques, in part, by subverting the strategies of postwar domestic fiction. In contrast to Angry writers and postwar urban planners, who imagined a domestic sphere in which economic and sexual dominance could be consolidated through a masculine subject position, Lessing's characters resist those tropes by highlighting the political inequities embedded in domestic relations. As in the work of her fellow postwar writers, domestic space functions in this novel as a metaphor for national culture. Forms of oppression found in the home mirror hierarchical relationships in English society. The text's postmodern form, however, does not come from a sense of bewilderment but rather from its direct engagement with, and rejection of, the kinds of social spaces and spatial narratives popular in 1950s England. Instead of describing the postmodern condition as a lack of cultural coordinates—or worse, a sign of political capitulation—*The Golden Notebook*'s postmodern turn can be read as an explicit rejection of dominant cultural narratives and the insertion of subjugated and marginalized voices in their place.

Anna shares a large flat with her daughter. With five rooms—three upstairs, and two down—Anna organizes her space, and her life, to accommodate a nuclear family. Although she and her lover, Michael, split up before she even moves into the flat, Anna retains her original plans for the space, waiting in vain for his return. To keep the rent manageable, she takes in a lodger. At times, Anna muses that "it could be said she was sharing a flat with a young man," but alas "he was a homosexual," an unconvincing surrogate for her estranged lover. After Michael's departure, Anna spurns her bedroom, which had been planned for a domestic partnership, and elects to sleep in the downstairs living room, pouring over her four notebooks. The space of her home, the narrator suggests, "was the framework of Anna's life," though Anna does not feel comfortable unless alone, "in the big room," by herself (54). The frame of her life promises a conventional domesticity only to subvert it later. The actual details of Anna's domestic situation, though tending toward the atypical, are not remarkable in and of themselves. She was not the only single mother living in London in the 1960s, nor is she unique in her choice of lodger. Yet the novel regularly depicts Anna's situation as highly unusual. The frame of her life—indeed, the frame of the novel itself—is a conventional domestic melodrama, but its coordinates are slightly askew. In this short account of Anna's home life, the reader must immediately confront the bleak qualities of the description; her home compares unfavorably to more familiar narratives of domesticity. The deficiency of her domestic life is both socio-spatial (she makes physical and mental space for an absent partner) and sexual (she describes her housemate as a puerile homosexual, someone incapable of fulfilling his domestic responsibilities). Similar to Carolyn Steedman's account of her childhood home, Anna's descriptions exude deficiency rather than alterity: the arrangement does not present a viable, satisfying domestic setting. She regularly finds herself "leaving space," both physical and psychological, for a man she knows will not return (307).

As my discussion of the novel's reverse ethnography suggests, Lessing challenges our assumptions about England's normative social conventions by citing madness as a prominent condition of local culture. To the naked eye, "everything's fine—all quiet and tame and suburban," but just below the surface, hidden behind the facade of domesticity, the country seethes "hatred and envy and people being lonely" (189). Lessing explores this domestic dystopia most directly in "Free Women" and the yellow notebook, in which Anna reflects on her life through Ella, a fictional double. Ella imagines the "hundreds and thousands of people, all over the country," mostly women, "simmering away in misery" (172). Like Anna, Ella performs a kind of "welfare work": she finds employment at a women's magazine, handling the correspondence for a column dispensing medical advice. Ella answers the disturbing letters, usually complaining of loneliness and psychosomatic illnesses, that the regular columnist, a physician, finds unsuitable for publication. In her personal life, too, Ella resembles the notebook's "author," Anna. A recently divorced single mother, Ella also calls herself, ironically and bitterly, a free woman. Despite the label, she and her friend Julia consider themselves "very normal, not to say conventional women. The fact that their lives never seemed to run on the usual tracks was because, so they felt, or might even say, they never met any men capable of seeing what they really were. As things were, they were regarded by women with a mixture of envy and hostility, and by men with emotions which—so they complained—were depressingly banal. Their friends saw them as women who positively disdained ordinary morality" (171). This sardonic claim of conventionality, then, alludes to the twin deficiencies of post-war domesticity as Anna and Ella understand them. On one hand, the lack of acceptable men thwarts their desire for an ostensibly normal home life. On the other hand, the pathologies evident in conventional domestic arrangements lead to questions about the value of such institutions. Anna does not renounce such pervasive narratives of domesticity outright—in fact, they continue to serve as markers of conventionality—but subverts them by satirizing them as the empty dreams of free women. The women who putatively abjure more normal lives seem pathetic, rather than heroic, in their renunciations. Such critiques are offered in the negative: Anna's freedom is less a choice than a lack, her domestic life a poor imitation of the one she craves.

To underscore the paucity of alternatives, "Free Women" chronicles, in tragicomic relief, the family history of Molly, Anna's best friend. Like Anna, Molly divorced young and was left to care for her son, Tommy, now aged nineteen. Her ex-husband, Richard, the top executive of one of Britain's largest multinational corporations, is now remarried, unhappily, to Marion. Marion, rejected by Richard and paralyzed by a drinking problem, eventually moves in with Molly and Tommy. Tommy suffers from acute depression and blinds himself while trying to commit suicide with a firearm. Together, son and stepmother begin to dominate Molly's home. After his accident, Tommy moves down to the ground floor and rarely leaves the house, "dominating it" in his obdurate solitude, "conscious of everything that went on in it, a blind but all-conscious presence" (377). Eventually, an exasperated Molly appeals to Anna for help with Marion and Tommy. Though she lives "like a guest" in her own home, "sneak[ing] upstairs" after work "so as not to disturb" them, she finds it difficult to speak to Marion because, emotionally speaking, "she isn't there" (510). With the assistance of such socially dysfunctional characters, the novel quickly dons the garb of a dark, domestic comedy.

Ironically, Molly's home becomes a refuge for those shut out of more conventional family situations. In the process, she herself becomes more uncomfortable in her own home as the traumas of failed relationships spill into her own life. Despite the narrative's critique of conventional domesticity, the nuclear family continues to serve as a normative material and imaginative reference point for both Molly and Anna, the two principal agents whose lives seem to belie such tropes.

In Anna's case, her home provides less and less psychological security as the novel progresses. Early in the novel, she takes comfort in the routines of her domestic roles, particularly in the care of her child, Janet. It is Ivor, her gay lodger, who first disrupts the relative tranquillity of her home life. The trouble begins when Ivor's lover, Ronnie, makes Anna's flat his de facto residence. Much more effeminate than Ivor, Ronnie's open cultivation and display of his homosexuality make Anna uncomfortable. Feeling ashamed of her homophobia and knowing that they will have a hard time finding another place to live, she cannot summon up the courage to ask Ronnie to leave. What right does she have, she asks herself, to "ask a couple of young men who were disturbing her peace of mind to leave?" Anna's maternal instincts eventually convince her that Ronnie's presence demands immediate action. "I'm going to protect Janet," she reasons angrily, thinking that her daughter ought to learn how to recognize a "real" man. Growing up in England, "a country full of men who are little boys and homosexuals and half-homosexuals," Janet will find it hard enough to find a suitable mate without the undue influence of Ronnie confusing her sexual orientation (404).

In the end, Anna forces them out, but her behavior is more complicated than simple homophobia. The display of open homosexuality in her home offends her domestic sensibilities. Threatened, she rushes to justify her emotional response by invoking matriarchal privilege. Because Ronnie's presence has such symbolic importance for Anna, her analysis inflates the significance and degree of his abnormalities as she sees them. Ronnie is not simply a man she does not like but a man who represents what is wrong with England; his localized pathologies resemble those of a generation of Englishmen. His sexuality makes Anna uncomfortable, but it is the fact that he is a kept man, entirely dependent on Ivor for his material existence, that pushes her over the edge. His effeminate clothes and use of makeup disgust Anna less because they imply a gay aesthetic than because they subvert her sense of appropriate domestic roles. Ironically, Anna's feelings of repulsion gesture toward the exaggerated models of heterosexual, masculine Englishness from which the novel as a whole instinctively recoils.

After her lodgers depart, and her daughter, around whom Anna arranges her life, elects to try boarding school, Anna's life devolves into utter chaos. "For twelve years," she thinks to herself after her daughter has left, "every minute of every day has been organised around Janet" and her needs (577). Anna knows that Janet's absence is "very bad" for her, realizing that Janet's presence and the responsibility it entails have provided "an outer shape to [her] life" (554). She selfishly asks Janet to come home because she gives her a sense of "normality" (543). In the months following Janet's departure, Anna begins to experience the full intensity of the mental illness with which she identifies Englishness. In scenes reminiscent of "The Yellow Wallpaper," Anna's home resembles a prison cell, a sinister inversion of the comforting domestic scenes she had planned when she first moved there. Anna describes the walls of the flat closing in on her while the darkness, once exterior to her room, becomes a fellow tenant (611). During the worst stretches, the bed and the floor seem to heave, while "the walls were losing their density," at which point she recognizes that she "was moving into a new dimension, further away from sanity than [she] had ever been" (613). Her room, once a "comfortable shell," becomes an antagonist, attacking her "from a hundred different points" as each stain, speck of dust, or unpolished door knob "assaulted" her "with hot waves of rocking nausea" (633). In a cruel reversal, Anna's domestic life—now devoid of the people with whom she once shared it—becomes the occasion and site for severe physical and psychological traumas. The altered circumstances of her family situation, which has never been satisfactory, help propel the collapse of her emotional architecture. Although the novel makes plain the deficiencies of her domestic arrangements, as her ironic use of the term "free women" indicates, she is no more ready to cope with a total abandonment of her family or a stable home. To be sure, Lessing's novel satirizes and makes problematic the domestic melodrama of her earlier work, but it does not find satisfaction in the explicit rejection of such social narratives. The novel refuses an either-or proposition: it neither accepts nor refutes the modern myth of domesticity outright.

Anna's madness assumes an unusual form in "Free Women: 5," the novel's final section. Her daughter leaves for school, and Anna turns down several offers from prospective tenants, so she is left alone in her large home. She habitually reads newspapers and journals of all kinds, her native intellectual curiosity growing into a compulsion. She rarely leaves her room, preferring the company of "half a dozen daily newspapers" and "a dozen weekly journals" to human contact of any kind. After perusing any articles with significant political information, Anna "carefully cut out the patches of print from newspapers and journals and stuck them on the walls with drawing-pins." Her passion soon turns into a pitched battle: the world of information against her capacity to organize it, to make sense of it. She leaves the house only to obtain food and more thumbtacks; before long, she covers the walls of her large room with clippings and begins on a second room. Feeling a strong urge to assimilate cognitively the events of the world, she "*had* to know what was going on everywhere" (649–50). Like the red and yellow notebooks, the novel's "Free Women" frame, the domestic narrative, concludes with Anna's informational obsession. Rather than write, the difficulty of which she reluctantly admits, she invests intellectually in reading. Far from providing a solution to her crippling writer's block, however, it only compounds her creative blockage.

It would be relatively easy to perform a Jamesonian reading of Anna's madness as a crisis of cognitive mapping. We could understand her condition as a metaphor for political and social consciousness in the confusing, debilitating, post-1956 world. Having lived through the familiar "modernist" traumas of the Holocaust, Stalinism, or even colonialism — when friends and enemies were clear, or in Jameson's terms, when class politics still offered a stable point of reference—Anna registers a loss of political bearings. The old coordinates have been dislodged, former languages compromised. Using space both literally and metaphorically, Jameson argues that "we ourselves, the human subjects who happen into this new space, have not kept pace with that evolution; there has been a mutation in the object unaccompanied as yet by any equivalent mutation in the subject. We do not yet possess the perceptual equipment to match this new hyperspace, as I will call it, in part because our perceptual habits were formed in that older kind of space I have called the space of high modernism" (*Postmodernism* 38–39). According to Jameson, there is no easy way out of this quandary. Cleverly, he moves to reestablish the credentials of academia by suggesting that it, by applying Leavisite "close reading" techniques to contemporary culture (informed, of course, by astute and progressive political motives), could educate and warn students about the insidious workings of late capitalism:

An aesthetic of cognitive mapping—a pedagogical political culture which seeks to endow the individual subject with some new heightened sense of its place in the global system—will necessarily have to respect this now enormously complex representational dialectic and invent radically new forms in order to do it justice. This is not then, a call for a return to some older kind of machinery. . . . The political form of postmodernism, if there ever is any, will have as its vocation the invention and projection of a global cognitive mapping, on a social as well as spatial scale. (54)

Surreptitiously, without any commotion and relatively little theoretical elaboration, Jameson reignites a long-standing debate on the competing and complementary functions of art and criticism. Cognitive mapping will be a "pedagogical political culture" in which skilled critics equip their students with a new, updated perceptual apparatus capable of deciphering the "enormously complex representational dialectic" which is contemporary art. No one should expect art to resolve the representational dialectic that it has helped create and depict—that will be the "vocation" of cognitive mapping practitioners and cultural theorists. It is enough that literature, art, and architecture document the political crises we now face: we should not expect cultural objects to solve them as well. Novels like *The Golden Notebook,* then, tend to exhibit, rather than resolve, the dialectic of postmodernity.

This reading is very seductive because it promises to explain the significance and idiosyncrasies of individual works by situating them in a nuanced historical logic. Jameson's work offers more than a technique for historicizing cultural artifacts. His theory both contextualizes and analyzes social conditions that create and become embedded in processes of cultural production. His argument is compelling because it does justice to the "enormous complexity" that readers encounter in novels like *The Golden Notebook.* The novel's confusing representational strategies seem to submit easily to Jameson's supple arguments. He makes his case, however, by suggesting that such texts participate in the "representational dialectic" of postmodernity. That task of apprehending and critiquing the postmodern condition, he insists, is the province of theory—in this particular circumstance, a theory that explains the conscious and unconscious drives of near-omnipotent multinational capital. *The Golden Notebook,* however, fits less comfortably into this analytic formula. Lessing's reverse ethnographic narratives are primarily concerned with those who are *excluded,* politically and socially, from the workings of mainstream culture. Far from representing postmodernity as the condition caused by submitting to, or being overwhelmed by, the allure of late capitalism—the apotheosis of postmodern hyperspace, of course, being late-capitalist architecture such as the Bonaventure Hotel—Lessing's work presents narratives of subjects left out of the cultural mix, such as lapsed Marxists, feminists, and anti-imperial agitators. Lessing even turns metropolitan subjects, now an endangered species in the age of postimperial England, into one of the minorities bewildered by changes in global culture. In a world in which multinational capital is supposedly breaking down cultural barriers, Lessing represents English culture as a peculiar and resilient back-formation, an anachronistic imperial remainder. As I discuss in the next chapter, however, the coincidence of globalization and the cultural trappings of the nation alert us to the tenaciousness of national identity in our supposedly postnational moment.

Lessing's reliance on postmodern devices is less a reflection of spatial confusion or cognitive dissonance than a self-conscious effort to defamiliarize metropolitan geography. Each of the novel's inner narratives is a frustrated search for cultural authenticity—a "real" man, the "true" working class, the "normal" English family. *The Golden Notebook*'s postmodern turn reflects an explicit attempt to particularize and satirize the foundations of English domestic space. Furthermore, the novel's commitment to experimental techniques should be set in the context of postwar immigration and the reformation of the metropolitan literary imagination during the period of imperial contraction. Although we can read Lessing's work as symptomatic of a historical moment, as is the wont of postmodern theory, her specific engagement with colonial romance and Conrad's modernist techniques requires an approach more attentive to matters of literary history as well. While many of her English colleagues were recycling domestic fiction as a way to reject the effete pretensions of interwar high modernism, Lessing's novel affirms a stylistic affinity with more formally innovative writers of that earlier period (something that would have surprised readers who knew her as a strong advocate of narrative realism). But neither is the novel's investment in aesthetic experimentation an unreconstructed resurrection of modernist techniques or its supposedly elitist politics: it can be read productively as the workings of a leftist, postcolonial migrant sifting through the detritus of the metropolitan literary scene. Without conflating postmodernity and postcoloniality, *The Golden Notebook* demonstrates how deeply the imagination of the postwar avant-garde is indebted to the reconfiguration of metropolitan culture by postcolonial writing.

As I turn, in the following chapter, to Salman Rushdie's *The Satanic Verses,* this pattern of postcolonial migrants sorting through the scrap heap of metropolitan culture will take the form of a particularly explosive confrontation. Like Lessing, Rushdie unceremoniously empties out Englishness of any definitive, positive attributes. The streets and neighborhoods of London, in particular, play host to a series of figurative struggles over past and future definitions of national identity. After demolishing the imperial pretensions of the English, however, the novel, in striking echoes of Lessing, Selvon, and Orwell, hesitantly suggests that a more bounded and modest version of national culture exists in the metropolitan class system. More provocatively, perhaps, the novel implies that commonwealth immigrants and their children, rather than white Britons, now control the discourse of Englishness by participating in local rituals of class difference. Mastering and negotiating forms of domestic class affect, curiously enough, becomes a way for postcolonial migrants to both embrace and repudiate national culture.

6. MAD GOAT IN THE ATTIC
THE SATANIC VERSES AND
GLOBAL ENGLISHNESS

Most academics read *The Satanic Verses* (1988) as an extended meditation on cultural hybridity. As Gayatri Spivak argues, its mode of representation is "citation, reinscription, re-routing the historical," epitomizing postcoloniality because it systematically dislodges "every metropolitan definition" (104). The novel is predicated on this trope of postcolonial disruption, foregrounding the political and cultural fallout of imperial contraction and the immigration of former colonial subjects to the metropole. In *The Location of Culture,* Homi Bhabha famously reads Rushdie's novel as a testament to "culture's [inherent] *hybridity*" and the "indeterminacy of diasporic identity" (38, 225). Its main character, Saladin Chamcha, he says, "stands, quite literally, in-between two border conditions" (224). Rushdie sometimes frames his own defense of the novel on the grounds that it represents an earnest attempt to give "voice and fictional flesh" to London's immigrant communities, "of which I am myself a member," by writing about "migration, its stresses and transformations" (qtd. in Appignanesi and Maitland 62, 6). The novel's apparent celebration of cultural mixing, with its extended meditations on the tensions caused by new migratory patterns, make it a logical choice to help critics "denationalize" the study of English literature. Its narrative of global travel—Chamcha goes back and forth between Bombay and London in search of his true identity—suggests that the cultural boundaries of the nation have become untenable in our postcolonial, transnational moment. As Bhabha would have it, it is now the "*in-between* space . . . that carries the burden of the meaning of culture" (38). If we wanted a novel that demonstrates the limitations of our old literary-historical models, based in part on national sovereignty, cultural integrity, and geographical certainty, this text would be an ideal candidate.

At a moment when globalization, as both an economic reality and a body of scholarly knowledge, rivals, or has supplanted, nationalist paradigms, novels such as *The Satanic Verses* have special bearing on the way we theorize the relationship between space and culture. Most theorists of globalization now describe the world with a specialized set of highly flexible metaphors, using concepts like "networks," "flows," or "links" that tend to imply more horizontal, disaggregated geographic and political relationships. Anthony Giddens, one of the earliest theorists of this trend, emphasizes globalization's tendency toward the "development of disembedding mechanisms" that operate by "lifting social relations out of their 'situatedness' in specific locales" (53). For Saskia Sassen, this process has led to and been determined by a loss of autonomy for the nation-state; individual countries no longer have the ability to control the movement of capital, labor, and culture within and across their borders. In a more general sense, the idea of globalization gives rise to a whole range of cartographic anxieties about cognitive mapping, deterritorialization, and the erosion of place as a site of phenomenological stability or subjective anchoring.

With this in mind, it would be relatively easy to argue that *The Satanic Verses* demonstrates the urgent need for a properly literary theory of globalization.[1] The novel's plot suggests that international mobility increasingly serves as a model of contemporary existence. Like Sassen, who maintains that global systems of economic exchange and interdependence have undermined the autonomy of the nation-state, one would be tempted to read this novel as a literary representation of our postnational world. Along these lines, Michael Hardt and Antonio Negri argue that an anti-imperial agenda can no longer rely on the security of sovereign states but instead must address political inequality in an eminently global context. In *Empire,* they insist that a global political consciousness must learn from but ultimately supersede postcolonial struggles.[2] Many critics read *The Satanic Verses* as one of the first novels to introduce postcolonial literary studies to this critical terrain. The text appears to refute the autonomy of the nation-state and the metropole, at the same time exploring the possibility of global travel as an emerging site of political subjectivity.

Yet readers of the novel are forced to confront the fact that struggles over London and Englishness are the basis of the confrontation between Saladin Chamcha and Gibreel Farishta, Chamcha's deranged doppelgänger. Chamcha, toady, self-made man, more-English-than, attaches all forms of cultural value to his adopted nation: charm, learning, sophistication, restraint, common sense, justice, moral probity, and so on. As a boy in India, London was his fetish; as an adult, he dreams of absolute assimilation, conquering London by becoming one with it. In contrast, Gibreel, the unrepentant provincial, runs down London and its inhabitants at every opportunity. He yearns to "tropicalize" metropolitan space, converting London, mile by mile, into a teeming, postcolonial city. In a cruel twist of fate, Chamcha spends most of the novel being disowned and persecuted by the English, while Gibreel, an international film icon, is adored in the city he loves to hate. The novel's version of Englishness, in essence, is an argument about cultural geography: Gibreel longs to conquer and convert the city he loathes, principally because it epitomizes all that is wrong with England, whereas Chamcha loves London yet is abandoned by it. The narrative's unlikely pairing of these two migrants captures the Janus-faced quality of Englishness I have endeavored to describe in this book. The novel is at once repulsed by and fascinated with London and its urban class system, using Chamcha and Gibreel to evoke the complicated set of affirmations and denials that characterize modern Englishness, uncannily reminiscent of Orwell's ambivalent celebration of imperial decline and national rediscovery. The kind of cultural exceptionalism so typical of twentieth-century English literature is embedded in this running debate over London's particular combination of charms and limitations. Rushdie's London is a cruel companion but also a stubborn foe: Chamcha is punished for his pursuit of Englishness and love of London, yet the metropole defeats Gibreel, who goes mad in his attempt to transform the city. The novel's hesitant turning away from London, along with its equivocal rejection of Englishness in favor of a globalized political subjectivity, is also a powerfully essentializing gesture, reducing English culture to a perverse, inexplicable pertinacity. The novel's eventual disavowal of England and London strongly resembles the discourse of national exceptionalism with which it competes.

   The Satanic Verses also demonstrates how the modern idea of Englishness has become inseparable from the geography of metropolitan space. London comes to stand for Englishness precisely because it is a world city: the discourse of English exceptionalism flourishes in the tension between provincialism and transnationalism, an admixture of London's status as a center of global commerce and England's lingering sense of postimperial melancholy. The ambivalence I have described as the archetype of Englishness plays on the dialectical strings of national identity, which in this particular instance can be read in the context of imperial/global geographies. Like Doris Lessing, Rushdie systematically evacuates Englishness of any genuine, concrete reality. The text relentlessly debunks Chamcha's "picture postcard" image of national culture. In one of the novel's more clever jokes, his nostalgic yearning for a quaint Little England is no more than a global marketing ploy, a symbolic system trading in ersatz cultural objects, tour packages, and manufactured history. Chamcha gradually becomes disenchanted when he learns that the type of Englishness he craves is only available through forms of commodified affect. The global currency of London is guaranteed by the sale of provincial England. London becomes the location of globalized Englishness, suggested by improbable combinations of metropolitan self-importance and provincial humility. *The Satanic Verses* implies that economic and cultural globalization works, in part, on the basis of exaggerating and selling local color: London has managed the transition from imperial metropolis to global city by advertising Englishness to an international audience. Rushdie's novel suggests that London's special function as the avatar and arbiter of English culture is itself a product of global geographic change.

DAMN COLD FISH

We learn early in the novel that Chamcha aspires to Englishness, a condition that eludes him to the very end. His desire to become a "goodand-proper Englishman" has its roots in an Oedipal contest. He wants to run as far away from his father as he can, and he sees in metropolitan culture the negation of what he regards as his father's unfortunate provincialism (43). The London of his childhood imagination, whose name resounds phonetically in his head as "Ellowen Deeowen," exists in a series of Victorian literary scenes, a city of monumental dimensions and imperial self-assurance. By a stroke of luck, his father offers to send him to a metropolitan public school, where he begins the process of self-fabrication as an Englishman. His earliest school memory is kippers for breakfast. The young Chamcha, not knowing where to start with this exotic dish, struggles, at the insistence of his masters and to the delight of heckling schoolmates, for a full ninety minutes with the bony repast. The experience nearly drives him to tears, but rather than demystifying England, it only heightens Chamcha's resolve to master this alien terrain. England, he learns at that meal, "was a peculiar-tasting smoked fish full of spikes and bones, and nobody would ever tell him how to eat it" (44). As an adult, Chamcha becomes a laughable spokesperson for Little England-ism, a comical version of T. S. Eliot's notorious list of all things English in *Notes towards the Definition of Culture:* a bowler hat–wearing, warm beer–drinking, fish-and-chips-eating, queen-adoring cartoon of a man. His wife, Pamela, complains that England for him had never represented anything more complicated than a heritage site, belatedly realizing that Chamcha only married her on account of her fair skin and posh accent (like him, of course, she was running away from her upbringing, having married him precisely to alienate herself from the aristocratic society in which she was raised). It is difficult to tell precisely what Chamcha finds gratifying about his quest. Perhaps his obstinacy and lack of reflex-ivity perfectly match England's fading, elusive attractions. More often than not, Chamcha is the only character willing to defend contempo-rary England: nearly everyone else in the novel, immigrants and native Londoners alike, seems intent on pointing out the country's innumer-able shortcomings. Chamcha, of course, is persecuted for this ridiculous attempt to conquer London, leading eventually to a reunification with subcontinental culture and the city of his birth, Bombay.

In one of the novel's humorous ironies, Chamcha's lone ally in de-fending the English turns out to be a traitor to the cause. Hal Valance, an unabashedly philistine advertising executive and television producer, is a modernized, ruthlessly capitalistic incarnation of hyperbolic nation-alism. A rabid supporter of the Falklands War and "intimate" friend of Margaret Thatcher, Valance thrives on an absurdly jingoistic version of national pride, flying the Union Jack over office and home alike, even sporting a waistcoat patterned on the British flag. Sunday lunch at his Highgate mansion, a dwelling Chamcha's enviously and condescend-ingly thinks a "self-made man's paradise," consists of roast beef, York-shire pudding, and sprouts. Valance's virulent nationalism and insatiable greed are as much a parody of national culture in Thatcherite London as is Chamcha's defense of "traditional" English values. As Valance an-nounces to his guest, "I . . . love this fucking country. That's why I'm going to sell it to the whole goddamn world . . . I'm going to sell the arse off it. That's what I've been selling all my fucking life: the fucking nation. The *flag.*" Valance hollows out the essence of English culture by transforming it into a global commodity. As he points out to Chamcha, the idea to "sell the arse off" the nation is part and parcel of Thatcher's new England. The genius of Thatcher is that she and her followers have wrested the discourse of national identity from the "woolly incompetent buggers from Surrey and Hampshire," the old upper-middle class, the Oxbridge plutocracy of country gentlemen, businessmen, and retired colonial administrators after whom Chamcha models himself. In the ascendant are people like Valance, with the wrong education and wrong accent, whose only credentials are ambition and loyalty to Thatcher's "revolution," as he calls it. Later, when Valance unceremoniously fires Chamcha from the best acting gig of his career, the actor realizes that he should have understood the warning Valance offered that day: the England Chamcha "had idolized and come to conquer" was a fantasy, a collection of outdated myths in which no one but a sycophantic immigrant could put much faith (266–70).

Valance's barbaric capitalism and aggressive vulgarity denote the shifting ground of Englishness Rushdie attempts to parody throughout the novel. His version of national identity is a composite of unsustainable contradictions that tend to work against any coherent version of national culture. Valance demonstrates his love for the nation by prostituting it to the world, reducing it to a list of marketable components. The novel depicts national culture through just such a series of negations and evacuations: each version of Englishness offered by the narrative is more fraudulent and preposterous than its predecessor.

Despite their many differences, Valance and Chamcha employ a common language when they argue for their own inclusion in the national imaginary: their respective claims of national belonging rely on a discourse of class rights and obligations. In Valance's case, the most formidable obstacle to national greatness is not an external enemy—like immigrants—but an internal threat. Nor, as we might anticipate from a supporter of Thatcher, does he blame the working class for national decline. Valance lusts after the material comforts enjoyed by the bourgeoisie, and he is attracted to Thatcherism because it promises a lower-middle-class revolution:

> She's radical all right. What she wants—what she actually thinks she can fucking *achieve*—is literally to invent a whole goddamn new middle class in this country. . . . People without background, without history. Hungry people, people who really *want*, and who know that with her, they can bloody well *get*. Nobody's ever tried to replace a

whole fucking *class* before, and the amazing thing is she might just do
it. . . . It's going to be something to see. It already is. (270)

Thatcher's program, according to Valance, represents a form of domestic class warfare. Instead of calling for an uprising of the dispossessed,
however, the new Conservatives channel lower-middle-class resentment
and greed to smash the working-class/bourgeois welfare state consensus. Chamcha, of course, looks on with horror as Thatcher's minions run
roughshod over the last genuine vestiges of the old England he adores.
Valance vandalizes Chamcha's sacred upper-middle-class cultural venues, selling them as tourist trinkets and laughing as he pockets the considerable proceeds. Chamcha, who reveres the empty symbols of bygone
England, both envies and sniffs at Valance's straightforward, unsenti-
mental marauding of the national cultural archive. As a more comprehensive analysis of the narrative suggests, Chamcha's distaste for Valance
and his uncompromising Thatcherism is also based on class prerogatives. Chamcha's claims of belonging to the national body—like those of
Valance and many others in the novel—depend largely on a manipulating language of domestic class difference.

CLASS CONSCIOUSNESS

Chamcha, the assimilated immigrant, is continually scandalized that no
one, including fellow Englishmen, seems to hold the country's venerable
traditions in high esteem. The text depicts the "nightmare" of immigration, however, by challenging Chamcha's participation in the discourse
of national identity and stripping him of his class status. Chamcha's first
experiences the dilemma of the migrant condition during a confrontation with the British border police. Like many anti-Thatcherite narratives, *The Satanic Verses* begins with an examination of police brutality
and the state's outright hostility toward racial minorities and immigrants
throughout the 1980s.[3] Those familiar with the novel will remember its
ingenious narrative device: Chamcha, who survives a terrorist hijacking
and the subsequent explosion of his plane but gets mistaken for an illegal
immigrant, is subjected to a humiliating interrogation and a thorough
beating at the hands of overly aggressive police officers. As a result of
this physical and emotional trauma, Chamcha turns into a human goat,
nearly eight feet tall, replete with hooves and sharp horns on his forehead.
Aside from serving as a potent marker of his racial identity, Chamcha's

new satyrlike body sends the protagonist rapidly down the social ladder, transforming the once-wealthy voice actor into an impoverished immigrant. It is only then that Chamcha begins to comprehend the full magnitude of his postcolonial nightmare.

In the back of the police van where he is being interrogated and tortured, Chamcha begins to question the right of his accusers to stand in judgment of him. His racist antagonists, he gradually discovers, are comically deformed incarnations of provincial, working-class British culture, bellowing out their jibes in accents Chamcha imitates effortlessly in the recording studio. A voice actor with unparalleled range, Chamcha notices that each of the immigration officers and five constables looks and sounds like a regional stereotype. Officer Stein, who seems the most the most senior of the three immigration officials, "whom his colleagues called 'Mack' or 'Jockey,'" sprinkles his speech with copious vernacular that Chamcha finds "exaggeratedly Scottish." Officer "Kim" Novak— hardly the most British of names, as Chamcha unwisely mentions to his captors—whose drawn face reminds the actor of medieval icons, looks abnormally pale and chatters about his "favourite soap-opera stars and game-show hosts" during the whole procedure. Bruno, the youngest and most free-spirited of the three, professes a banal enthusiasm for "watchin' girls" instead (160). When the five regular policemen attempt to join the conversation, the ringmaster Stein patronizingly excludes them, so they initiate a competing conversation about televised darts, professional wrestling, and football (all coded working-class leisure activities). Comparing the relative merits of the Tottenham Hotspur "double"-winning side of 1961 with the 1980s Liverpool squad sparks a furious debate. Chamcha, prostrate and vulnerable in the back of the van, thinks they resemble nothing so much as the football hooligans they supposedly restrain on a weekly basis at matches up and down the country. The situation seems so implausible to him because these officers, official guardians of national sovereignty, offer no evidence of their legitimacy as representatives of English culture. In his words, they are not "goodandproper English," nor are they part of the country "he had idolized and come to conquer" as a young man. According to his estranged wife, Chamcha's version of England is "[h]im and [his] Royal Family, you wouldn't believe. Cricket, the House of Parliament, the Queen. The place never stopped being a picture postcard to him. . . . I was bloody Britannia. Warm beer, mince pies, common-sense and me" (175). From the perspective of Chamcha's retrograde version of national culture, it is easy to see why these officers, who demonstrate obvious traces of cultural/class otherness, seem insufficiently English for their appointed post.

Chamcha's version of Englishness does not depend on absolute racial or somatic uniformity, but social and cultural homogeneity. It is, after all, a narrative of cultural uniqueness that depends on its ability to exclude social inferiors as effectively as racial others: it is a class story. In Chamcha's mind, the narrative of Englishness is capacious enough to embrace racial diversity—at the very least, a form of multiethnic nationality premised on total assimilation—yet restrictive enough to judiciously police social boundaries. No longer able to tolerate the banality of their conversation or the humiliation to which these uncultured thugs are treating him, Chamcha snaps back and attacks their credentials as protectors of national sovereignty:

> Chamcha found a scrap of anger from somewhere. "And what about them?" he demanded, jerking his head at the immigration officers. "They don't sound so Anglo-Saxon to me."
>
> For a moment it seemed that they might all fall upon him and tear him limb from limb for such temerity, but at length the skull-faced Officer Novak merely slapped his face a few times while replying, "I'm from Weybridge, you cunt. Get it straight: *Wey*bridge, where the fucking *Beatles* used to live." (163)

Responding to their déclassé accents and the lowbrow content of their speech, Chamcha cannot stomach the rough treatment he receives at the hands of these coarse, working-class officers. The uncouth "lads" who assault him fail to adhere to his rigorous linguistic and cultural standards. Novak's claims of belonging ironically invoke more contemporary examples of globalized Englishness, such as pop music icons like the Beatles, who become worldwide exports (tellingly, he doesn't say he comes from Weybridge, where E. M. Forster lived while writing *Howards End,* as the educated Chamcha might). In effect, Chamcha protests against the kind of resurgent imperialist/racist nationalism so prevalent during the 1980s by invoking a form of class privilege as evidence of inclusion in the national community. Thatcher and her allies regularly appealed to Britain's imperial legacy—especially in disputes with leftists about the Falklands, immigration policy, and labor issues—in an attempt to polarize the electorate and demonize internal enemies. Chamcha's guarded protest against this style of racism—he does, after all, support the broad outlines, if not the fine details, of the new Conservatism—paradoxically mobilizes a form of particularized Englishness against a discourse of exclusionary Britishness. Chamcha appeals to a largely bourgeois version of English exceptionalism to demand, however provisionally or problematically, his rights as a citizen. Chamcha's Englishness includes London's intelligentsia and the Home Counties' bourgeoisie, not provincial working-class England or the Celtic periphery. In a curious inversion, his arguments proceed by rejecting a more culturally heterogeneous—but generally racist—discourse of Britishness in favor of a culturally bounded, status-conscious form of Englishness grounded in class prerogatives.

As his futile retort implies, being systematically beaten by the police is not, however, what really galls Chamcha: it is being ritualistically shamed and taunted by his social inferiors. More disconcerting, however, is losing command of his polished voice, on which he has worked so diligently over the years to remove any trace of provincial, "non-University" undertones. His diffident protests mutate embarrassingly into rough animal squeals. His unlikely fall from the aircraft and physical transformation into a massive goat translate into a precipitous decline in class status. As he puts it to himself, he cannot fathom how a man of his accomplishments could be subjected to such forms of abuse: "The humiliation of it! He was—had gone to some lengths to become—a sophisticated man! Such degradations might be all very well for some riff-raff from villages in Sylhet or the bicycle-repair shops of Gujranwalla, but he was cut from a different cloth!" (159). The injustice and shame of being beaten cannot fully explain the depth of Chamcha's indignation; ultimately, it is his loss of status that completely unmoors him. By his reasoning, poor Bengali immigrants might expect, even deserve, this kind of treatment from justifiably suspicious police, but his efforts to cultivate more delicate sensibilities ought to spare him such embarrassments. In yet another ironic switchback, Chamcha spends the middle sections of the novel learning what it means to be a working-class Bengali immigrant in London. His ideological sentencing reaches its zenith when his goatish form gets adopted as a symbol of class and racial oppression by his new neighbors there. Much to his surprise, most of the working-class minorities he meets in inner-city London also think of themselves as English. Chamcha learns to question his adoration of the English, interestingly enough, through this provocative class fantasy.

"ELLOWEN DEEOWEN" SPELLS GENTRIFICATION

After a few days of illegal confinement and some aimless wandering, Chamcha eventually makes his way to the tough streets of Brickhall, a mythical borough in the heart of London's East End, finding refuge in its working-class Bengali community.[4] Nonwhite local residents, we soon learn, have been subject to increasing racial harassment, which effectively galvanizes the community in protest. "Best place for you is here," Sufyan, his benefactor, tells him: "Where else would you go to heal your disfigurements and recover your normal health? Where else but here, with us, among your own people, your own kind?" (253). Lacking the courage to tell folks at the Shaandaar rooming house what he really thinks of them, Chamcha only mumbles the declaration, "I'm not your kind," after his generous hosts have left the attic room. "I've spent half my life trying to get away from you" (253). Even the family's London-born daughters, Anahita and Mishal, who mockingly call their parents' homeland "Bungleditch," do not seem to qualify as true English in Chamcha's mind. They, like their unusual guest, have nothing but bad things to say about the subcontinent, though they have never been there. When Chamcha objects to the "foreign" food cooked by their mother, whose South Asian restaurant is a London landmark, the girls concur, sympathetically expressing a strong preference for bangers and mash. They enact Englishness by performing class membership: they see themselves as part of the national community because they adopt the rituals of urban, working-class life. It is their specific style of class affect—not their identity as second-generation Bengalis—by which Chamcha excludes them from his version of national culture. Chamcha does not accept their English identity because they, like the officers who abuse him, do not emulate bourgeois styles of speech and decorum. These troubling scenes illustrate most clearly the anxious articulation—the unsettled expression of two social forces—of race and social class in Thatcherite London. Chamcha's tenuous claims of belonging operate, after all, by invoking class prestige. These girls, who, unlike their guest, were born in England, could never fully inhabit Chamcha's national community because they do not share his social world. It is a class position—rather than a racial or cultural heritage—that sets these people apart in his mind.

The miserable boarding house turns a tidy profit by offering makeshift housing to the steady supply of local homeless families, most of

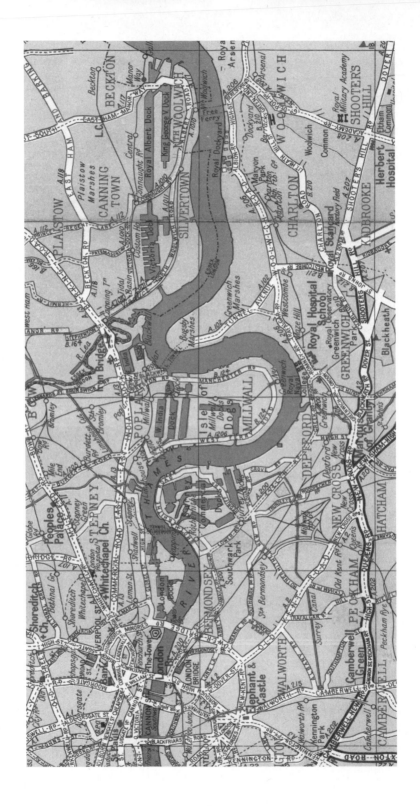

whom are recent immigrants. One of the teenage girls later explains to Chamcha, still quite goatish, how the "family business" works. Though the Shaandaar rooming house, upstairs from the eponymous café, is technically a bed-and-breakfast establishment, it essentially functions as a state-subsidized flop house. Owing to the severe crisis in public housing, its proprietors can cram indigent families of five into single rooms, ignoring health, fire, and public safety regulations, all the while claiming sizable "temporary" lodging allowances from the central government. Generating £10 revenue per person per night from the state in compensation, the Shaandaar represents the ideal investment in the tight housing market of the late 1980s. Chamcha immediately realizes the absurdity of the whole thing: for that kind of money, he reckons, the local council could afford to place an entire family in a reasonably sized home in the private sector. "But that wouldn't be classified as temporary accommodation," he notes, meaning "no central funding for such solutions. [Such measures] would also be opposed by local politicians committed to fighting the 'cuts'" in public expenditures, especially those in social services (264).

The East End housing squeeze depicted in the novel, however, was not the simple affair Chamcha imagines. The text uses "the Street" as a metaphor for London's ethnic conflicts of the 1980s, a place of struggle between white, xenophobic Britons, their working-class, predominantly South Asian neighbors, and the police—who do little to protect such embattled minorities from racist attacks and often, as Chamcha's case illustrates, actively work against them. The motif becomes particularly salient when we read the Street as a historical-geographic site of struggle between competing claims on metropolitan, and national, space. Through the use of "Enterprise Zones" or urban regeneration projects, Thatcher and her allies attacked the problem of urban poverty by evicting the poor from their homes. The Isle of Dogs, part of the borough of Tower Hamlets in the heart of the East End (but only a mile from the City of London), was the largest and most ambitious redevelopment scheme of its kind and one of Thatcher's pet projects (see fig. 7).[5] The

Figure 7. *(opposite)* Map of East London and Docklands. The far west edge of the map shows the City of London, the traditional home of the financial industry. The Isle of Dogs, in the borough of Tower Hamlets, is the peninsula created by the southward bend of the Thames. (Courtesy of the Map Collection, Yale University Library)

London Docklands Development Corporation (LDDC), a joint venture between the government and private investors, used its powers of compulsory land purchase to turn one of London's poorest areas into thousands of homes for the affluent and the most capacious, expensive, and ostentatious office building in Europe. The LDDC, under the government's auspices, helped destabilize immigrant communities by transforming the places in which they lived and worked into luxury housing and high-rise office buildings (Tower Hamlets still has one of the most concentrated minority populations in the country). Any discussion of the city's class politics during this decade must be accompanied by an understanding of the city's geography of urban renewal, because it was one of the most important ways in which all Londoners, whether living in opulence or in poverty, experienced class dynamics. As *The Satanic Verses* suggests, the ideological import and material experience of race in 1980s London were directly affected by massive geographic change embedded in class conflict.

This does not imply, however, that race and class are somehow identical, that there exists some homology or relatively simplistic correspondence between these two social categories in the novel. In order to expose the thinly veiled racism of Thatcher's ideological agenda, the text uses running feuds over the urban landscape to dramatize larger arguments about national belonging. As Rushdie's novel adroitly demonstrates, Thatcher's urban agenda exacerbated racial tensions because it forced working-class whites and minorities to compete for scarce resources. By exploring the problematic terms of national identity in this setting, the text offers a biting critique of Thatcherite racism, but it fails to fully examine the class dynamics through which racism becomes materially operational. The narrative relies on a complicated articulation of race *and* class politics; as the novel implies, Thatcherite racism is most effective when it pits working-class constituencies against one another. But after destabilizing claims of national belonging and diagnosing the racism those claims enable, the novel fails to critique the class machinery on which those exclusionary arguments depend. After visiting inner-city Brickhall and experiencing the frustrations of its inhabitants firsthand, Chamcha miraculously recovers his human form and returns to the comforts of his bourgeois life. His experience of class warfare in Brickhall eventually becomes an occasion for self-knowledge—tellingly, not an incident that encourages the protagonist to think of race in relation to forms of economic exploitation. In short, Chamcha himself makes claims of belonging by emulating a class position; the text scrupulously exposes the contradictions inherent in those claims by transporting him to working-class London, forcing him to realize that England may not be the safe haven he thinks. Ultimately, however, the novel transports Chamcha back to India, where he rediscovers an affinity for the culture of his birth, thousands of miles (literally and figuratively) from the place where his "nightmare" began.

As a result of the Docklands development scheme, initiated in 1981 when Thatcher and Secretary of Environment Michael Heseltine incorporated the LDDC, thousands of East Enders either lost their homes or found it impossible to place their growing children in homes of their own. Still one of the most uniformly working-class areas in the country in the early 1980s, 95 percent of Isle of Dogs residents were tenants in state-owned social housing. Within eight years, 44 percent of the housing stock was occupied by owners, almost all of them new, more affluent residents.[6] In Tower Hamlets, home of the Isle of Dogs and a borough with a significant Bangladeshi population, homelessness more than tripled during the Thatcher years, compared with a rise of 66 percent in all of Greater London.[7] The Docklands Forum recorded similar figures in the Docklands, and the LDDC responded by openly acknowledging the need for more social housing.[8] The abolition of the Greater London Council (GLC) in 1986 did not help matters, resulting in a 92 percent reduction of the public housing budget in the area (Brownill 78). Such cuts hit the impoverished local population particularly hard, and many Bengali families, anchored to the bottom of council housing lists for a variety of reasons, were left homeless for indefinite periods of time. Even when established residents were not forced out of their homes by construction of new buildings or infrastructure, attrition of the public housing stock made the market increasingly difficult during the 1980s.[9] Michael Hebbert calls the land speculation frenzy of the mid-1980s "an orgy of property development" (128). Perhaps most alarming was the precipitous increase in the market value of land: while one acre sold for about £35,000 in 1981, plots of the same size were being traded for £450,000 only eight years later. Speculation was so rampant that ownership on some residential properties changed hands five times before construction was completed, raising property values in some estates by 500 percent (J. Foster 122).[10] And because the area's predominantly working-class residents were almost all council tenants, few could ever profit materially from the development going on around them. Considering the average annual income figures for the area, fewer than 5 percent of homes on LDDC land were deemed affordable by local standards.[11]

Residents of the Docklands boroughs (parts of Greenwich, Southwark, Lewisham, Newham, and Tower Hamlets) were no strangers to redevelopment projects and wildly speculative building schemes. As Anne Kershen points out, the area known today as the Docklands was built in response to the growth of British industry and the expansion of empire during the eighteenth and nineteenth centuries. In more recent times, irreversible decline at the docks provided the opportunity for its spatial reincarnation. Located on the edge of the crowded City, London's historic center of the financial industry, the eight and a half square miles of land near the center of the metropolis offered unique development opportunities. At least ten years before the docks closed permanently in 1980, the GLC had been seriously investigating and publishing plans for regeneration. Most plans called for better infrastructure and more affordable housing for the area's working-class residents. With the election of Thatcher and the Conservatives in 1979, however, the logic of urban renewal in service of private enterprise acquired political urgency. Hoping to attract private investment to inner-city London, the Tories created urban development corporations (UDCs) and enterprise zones (EZs) in Docklands and elsewhere by using planning legislation developed for New Towns during the postwar period.[12] In a fascinating political reversal, Thatcher utilized the legislation created for New Towns— for her regime, one of the great anachronistic relics of the welfare state era—in order to create UDCs (during her leadership, the Conservatives sold all the New Town corporations, decades ahead of schedule). Parliament appoints UDCs directly, and UDCs are responsible only to that body, eliminating the need to obtain local planning permission in areas of parliamentary domain. UDCs have unilateral authority to purchase property, resell it to private bodies, and develop the land themselves. EZs create property-tax havens for a period of ten years; the Isle of Dogs' Canary Wharf, the gleaming office tower and centerpiece of Docklands redevelopment (fig. 8), was erected in the most well known EZ in the country and did not generate any tax revenue during its first decade of existence.

Although Thatcher's planning strategies utilized legislation that had been on the books for thirty years or more, there was a definite air of excitement and sense of novelty about the new development scheme.

Figure 8. Canary Wharf, Isle of Dogs, London. (Courtesy of Canary Wharf Group plc)

John R. Short, a highly skeptical urban planner, derisively calls it "the New Urban Order," while geographer Neil Smith uses the metaphor of the "final frontier" to describe the changes wrought by gentrification and redevelopment in places like the Docklands. Coming from the opposite end of the political spectrum, Caspar Weinberger views the Docklands as the outstanding legacy of Thatcher's rule (33), and James Bredin describes UDCs as "one of her first major innovations" (16). Shortly after the LDDC received its charter, Heseltine brimmed with confidence when asked about the future at Docklands:

> The area displays more acutely and extensively than any area in England the physical decline of the urban city and the need for urban regeneration. It represents a major opportunity for the development that London needs over the last twenty years of the 20th century— new housing, new environments, new industrial development, new facilities for recreation, new commercial development, new architecture— all calculated to bring these barren areas back into more valuable use. (qtd. in LDDC)

In almost no time at all, the Conservative Party reclaimed the Docklands area, especially Canary Wharf, offering it as a high-profile symbol of Tory inner-city strategy. Combining a "tough" urban policy with the rhetoric of laissez-faire capitalism, the Docklands became the centerpiece of Thatcher's plans for London. By the time she opened the 1987 Conservative electoral campaign at Canary Wharf's building site, the project had become a prominent symbol of Tory ideology: smashing the welfare state consensus, encouraging entrepreneurs rather than increasing public subsidies or "handouts" to the needy, and creating new physical, intellectual, and political environments designed to attract global capital.[13]

The ideological complexity and rich historical ironies of the Docklands serve as a dense metaphor for the politics of space in Thatcherite England. The redevelopment of the East End enacts, paradoxically, a repudiation, celebration, and reconceptualization of Britain's imperial culture. Ostensibly, the Docklands area, which was built to serve as a vast metropolitan entrepôt of colonial commerce, fell victim to declining imperial fortunes. No longer technologically viable or commercially necessary, the docks closed one by one from the 1960s onward, not long after the functional end of empire. The large working-class communities that had settled there, employed primarily in processing factories, warehouses, or on the ships and docks themselves, became redundant as well, the human consequences of a rapidly changing economic and political world system. London's ability to transform itself into a global city— rather than an imperial capital— depended on its willingness to make inexpensive land available for redevelopment. With the city's financial district already filled to capacity, London's success in expanding its financial services economy and attracting global capital necessitated significant infrastructural investment. Just as the geographic expansion of empire—and the resulting concentration of imperial wealth in the metropole—required a radical restructuring of London, so too did the remaking of London as a global finance center demand a spatial reordering of the city itself. Tory economic policy during the 1980s roughly followed this agenda: during the currency crises, the government consistently favored a strong British pound, effectively preserving the integrity of London's financial markets while functionally strangling British industry, which was already in dire straits. In general, it was a period in which the English turned away from an economic model based on industrial-colonial production (which was followed by the move for national self-sufficiency during welfare capitalism) and toward a system based on London's ability to compete on the global finance stage.

Culturally speaking, however, the 1980s were also a moment of ostentatious imperial celebration. The Docklands, for instance, are littered with architectural tributes to empire and industry, aesthetic reminders of the area's historic participation in an earlier incarnation of the world economy. Even as the Tories were turning away from old-style imperialism and industrialism as an economic model, they were eagerly reviving jingoistic imperialism as a system of political symbolism. Rather than weaken the country's reliance on a nationalist and imperialist imaginary, the Tories coupled Britain's material integration in global circuits of economic exchange with a cultural resurgence of patriotism and exclusionary nationalism. The Falklands War is probably the most obvious example of this trend, but Rushdie himself, in *Imaginary Homelands,* attributed similarly troubling motives to the "Raj revivalism" in the arts during Thatcher's reign. In retrospect, this seeming contradiction between the government's economic policies (increasing the trend toward globalization) and ideological discourse (exaggerating British nationalism) probably makes a good deal of sense. The coincident rise of economic globalization and resurgent nationalist nostalgia allowed the Tories to maintain the illusion of national self-sufficiency even as domestic industrial concerns—and the country's working class—came under increasing pressure from overseas competition.

WORD ON THE STREET

Although this Valance-style new bourgeoisie may have tried to sever links to the area's working-class past—perhaps preserving a superannuated crane or a decommissioned ship as a tribute to the Docklands' industrial legacy—it could not do so without inciting acrimony from locals. *The Satanic Verses,* in its own fashion, offers a counternarrative, fictionally recording the frustrations of a group of people caught between an invasive bourgeoisie and racist, working-class neighbors. Mishal, the elder Sufyan daughter, begins to observe the chaos around her almost comically, having "developed the habit of talking about the Street as if it were a mythological background and she, on high at Chamcha's attic window, the recording angel and the exterminator, too." Unaware of the increasingly violent nature of the area in which he has taken refuge, Chamcha listens inattentively to Mishal's stories about "the white racists and black 'self-help' or vigilante posses starring in this modern *Mahabharata.*" At the end of the block, she recounts, he could see for himself where "the Brickhall Three were done over by the police" and then framed, blamed for their own injuries. Around the corner he could tour "the scene of the murder of the Jamaican, Ulysses E. Lee," and in the local pub, "the stain on the carpet marking where Jatinder Singh Mehta breathed his last" (283–84).

For the most part, Chamcha remains an unsympathetic observer, failing to make the connection between this new, aggressive middle class and the inflammatory racism encountered by Brickhall's minority residents. Most racist attacks were committed against poor minorities who were new to the area, perpetrated by working-class whites and the police—what did urban redevelopment schemes have to do with racist violence? Rushdie's novel fictionalizes the forms of racial conflict that became commonplace in the Docklands area during the housing crises of the 1980s. As Janet Foster points out, rapid gentrification on the Isle of Dogs created a tripartite division among residents: an older, established, white working class living in council estates; newer working-class residents moving into the area's diminishing stock of social housing; and the new affluent professionals snapping up luxury quayside housing (251). And while the more established residents protested, at times quite strongly, against the redevelopment plans implemented by the LDDC, it was newer residents who competed successfully for council flats, many of them poor Bengali families, who became the primary targets of racist aggression.[14]

It was when some Bengali families from other parts of Tower Hamlets were placed in Isle of Dogs council housing that racial tensions really escalated. According to Foster, longtime white residents began to agitate against Asians, who had traditionally received the poorest accommodation, when they were allotted places in some of the more desirable estates after a court ruling banned such forms of housing discrimination (265). Ironically, most Bangladeshis, well aware of the Isle of Dogs' reputation for acute racism, had no desire to come to the area but were forced to do so by the local council's inflexible housing policy.[15] By 1993 things had deteriorated to the point where the British National Party, a neofascist outfit, won the local council seat for the Isle of Dogs. Though many called the victory a "protest vote" over housing issues and correctly predicted that Labour would regain the seat in the next election, no one could dispute the palpable level of tension. One journalist, offering his opinion about the area's reputation for racism, voiced popular sentiment when he said, "You get the feeling it's a bit of a powder keg" (qtd. in Foster 253). Despite a long history as a heterogeneous community, many established residents expressed open resentment of "new" Asians while vehemently denying the charge of racism. In the words of one resident, the impotence of local politicians, who were stripped of any power to change the situation (the LDDC held unilateral development authority), only exacerbated matters: "Quite a lot of anger's building up. . . . People feel embittered or endangered . . . [and] they're likely to sort of fling out. People react . . . when they feel they can't win" (qtd. in Foster 261). In short, the local Bengali population, rather than the LDDC or new affluent residents, became targets of racist abuse. Many considered this unfortunate situation predictable. In the face of a severe housing shortage and other reductions in social services, the local white population and poor South Asians were in direct competition for limited resources. Immigrants and minorities were cornered by an unsympathetic state and the violent reprisals of their white neighbors.

It was not long before members of the Bengali community started to fight back, in the process becoming more politically sensitive to the mobilization of race as a discourse of national belonging. Feeling abandoned by the police and otherwise helpless against increasingly violent racist attacks, Asian "gangs" became a formidable urban presence by the early 1990s. In the words of one Bengali youth whose father had been assaulted: "Ten, fifteen years ago, nobody used to bother, they just used to take it. . . . It's not that way any more. We are prepared to defend ourselves."[16] In this area of London, it was class relationships embedded in the Docklands' urban redevelopment that conditioned the historical experience of race during the 1980s. Thus, to paraphrase Stuart Hall's oft-quoted formulation about the relationship between racism and class in metropolitan societies, race is the experiential modality through which class is lived in the novel's Brickhall, as well as 1980s London.[17] As Hall puts it, racism is not simply a conspiracy from above: it becomes an important, sometimes the dominant, ideological means by which black, white, and other fractions of the working class represent themselves, confronting both global capital and one another. The South Asian community became racially marked in the context of global patterns of labor migration, the composition of transnational capital, and metropolitan geography.

This material conjunction of racial conflict, class relationships, and battles over urban space shapes the themes of cultural mobility and hybridity in *The Satanic Verses*. While the epistemological significance of Chamcha's journey cannot be reduced to his experience of racism in London's East End—he has the means to leave Brickhall and return to India—his time there structures the narrative development of race as both a local and an international condition. Chamcha's knowledge of race depends on his experiences in the metropole, but, narratively speaking, that part of his development stands in contradiction to his intercontinental journey and his quest for intellectual and spiritual regeneration. While the novel's material economy of race is immersed in London's working-class Bengali community, its narrative and symbolic economies of race lead Chamcha to seek renewal by returning "home," as he says, to India.

The text's Brickhall community bears a striking material and emotional likeness to the South Asian constituencies in Spitalfields, centered at Brick Lane, made famous in recent years by Monica Ali (fig. 9). When Anahita, the youngest member of the Sufyan clan, quips, "Thatcherism has its effect," she refers not only to the employment of racist rhetoric by political elites and their working-class allies but also to the urban policies being pursued in London. Chamcha, a new and unwilling member of Brickhall's poor minority community, remains unconvinced by Anahita's explanation of their plight. "No pitched battles these days," her sister reminds their intractable guest, sensing the indifference with which Chamcha reacts to their analysis: "The emphasis is on small-scale enterprises. . . . In other words, five or six white bastards murdering us, one individual at a time." The narrator renders it thus: "These days the posses roamed the nocturnal Street, ready for aggravation. 'It's our turf,' said Mishal Sufyan of that Street without a blade of grass in sight. 'Let

Figure 9. Corner of Princelet Street and Brick Lane, also known as "Little Bangladesh." Spitalfields, Tower Hamlets, London. (Author's collection)

'em come and get it if they can'" (284). By the time Chamcha arrives on the scene, tempers in Brickhall are already frayed. The temperature on the Street has been rising for weeks; "beatings-up, attacks on property," and other typical crimes against the city's minorities inflame passions (289). At Club Hot Wax, local residents incinerate effigies of notorious racists from Britain's past and present—predictably, wax figurines of Margaret Thatcher, Enoch Powell, and Oswald Mosley are crowd favorites—in the disco's on-stage microwave oven.[18]

Chamcha, himself a victim of racist policing, becomes an unlikely rallying cry for frustrated neighborhood residents. People mobilize around his demonic appearance, sporting T-shirts with his likeness and fake horns, adopting an image of themselves "that white society had rejected for so long, inhabit[ing] it, reclaim[ing] it," making it their own. Middle-class whites, protective of the beachhead they have established in a less affluent area of the city, begin to fear the image of the goat, "a sulphurous enemy crushing their perfectly restored residences." The police look even less favorably on such expressions of youthful exuberance, circulating the official explanation that a growing and dangerous devil cult is afoot. Chamcha becomes a potent symbol for indigent and embattled Asians, "twisted up by fate class race history, all that, but getting off his behind, bad and mad, to kick a little ass" (286). As if confirm-ing the story, the neighborhood's elderly women are being preyed upon and ritually slaughtered by an unknown serial killer; packs of vigi-lante Sikhs patrol the area, hoping to find the culprit. The police arrest Uhuru Simba, a local activist, on suspicion of the murders. He dies in custody, and the police offer a transparently false explanation of his death. Days later, when vigilantes apparently catch the real killer in the act, ru-mors spread immediately that the authorities are refusing to charge the suspect with the killings; the streets of Brickhall, predictably, erupt in violence.

Following the lead of Ian Baucom, it would be tempting to read the disturbance as a "riot of Englishness" in which the empire's scattered subjects, already inhabiting metropolitan space, rise up and demand their rights as citizens. Baucom situates these scenes in a long history of urban protest in which English rioters seek to correct contemporary injustices and remind the national community of its idealized self. He reads the novel's rioters as postcolonial redeemers, those who both de-mand their rights as citizens and insist that the nation make good on its own promises—justice, equality, and equal protection under the law. Such rioters are not desecrators but saviors and reformers, forcibly en-suring that the nation protect individual and collective rights. Rushdie's migrants represent a particularly fascinating condition because they are postcolonial operatives, a diverse people who seek not, as we might ex-pect, to disband the nation but to recuperate it for collective enjoyment and belonging (190–218).

Though compelling in a general sense, this reading downplays the extent to which England's urban class system, in conjunction with the novel's understanding of ethnicity and metropolitan racism, informs the novel's discussions of national inclusion and exclusion. If we read the riot only as a protest against more restrictive immigration policies and unofficial, tacitly condoned harassment—forms of on-the-ground rac-ism that effectively police the borders of the national community—we understate the degree to which racial exclusion depends on and mobi-lizes class affect. When Hanif Johnson, a Brickhall councilor, complains that "the level of aggression bubbling just under the skin of this town gets me really scared" (287), we cannot feel the full weight of his fears without also understanding the connections between race, gentrifica-tion, and the crisis in public housing. The text conveys the magnitude of the threat posed by Thatcher's political ideology by describing the fears, not of all Asians, but of poor Asians in particular. While the Tory program may represent a unilaterally and unambiguously racist platform, we must acknowledge that it realizes its maximum intensity through the medium of social class. Similarly, it is clear that Brickhall's residents make a counterclaim of belonging by embracing a working-class English tradition: popular revolt. The fact that Chamcha confronts "his own kind," his own people, as a goat is not accidental—it could not happen any other way—because his metamorphosis is the class vehicle through which he experiences and acknowledges racism for the first time. Only as a goat, an outcast hurled down the social ladder by his magical transformation, can Chamcha see the efficacy of Thatcherite racism.

Another obstacle to reading the uprising as an act of productive occupation and redemption of metropolitan space is the text's overwhelmingly satirical portrayal of the Brickhall community and its attempt to organize political protests. Although the portly Dr. Uhuru Simba, the activist who becomes a victim of police brutality, styles himself as a community spokesperson, it is not always clear to what extent he has the support of the people on whose behalf he purportedly agitates. He tends to assault "uppity" neighborhood women, including Mishal, whom he has punched in the mouth at a public meeting (Mishal had the audacity to point out that he wasn't actually from Africa, merely Sylvester Roberts from the less exotic New Cross Way). His adopted name is a joke—taken from the lion in Tarzan, not an "African" language—and so is his academic title, yet no one, aside from Chamcha, the reactionary interloper, seems much troubled by these inconsistencies. Hanif Johnson, the slick lawyer who affects a Trinidadian accent when adducing instances of oppression, is, like Simba, a purely local product. He channels immigrant discourse to mobilize the experience of disenfranchisement, often for personal, rather than collective, gain. Likewise, the two Sufyan girls are not, strictly speaking, working class themselves, but embrace the argot of the Street in an effort to reject their parents' excessive and unfashionable Bengaliness. Chamcha's wife, Pamela, who works as a community relations officer in Brickhall, offers a parody of white guilt–inspired lefty activism. As John McLeod observes, the novel seems deeply troubled by the use of American and African civil rights discourse by Brickhall activists, ultimately questioning the virtue of rioting as a means of voicing dissent or demanding inclusion in the national imaginary (152–57). Even more politically detached residents of Brickhall, such as Hind Sufyan, Mishal and Anahita's bitter, stereotypically conservative Asian mother, are lampoons: she has little to say about (or interest in) anything outside the four walls of the Shaandaar and S. S. Sisodia's Bombay films.

As many commentators have pointed out, nearly every character and shade of political position represented in the novel is the object of satiric joking. The sentiments of Valance, arch Thatcherite, are no more or less laughable than those of Simba, who organizes protests against Valance's hit television program, *Maxim Aliens*. The police and the immigrants they beat up, likewise, are reduced to equally hyperbolic ethnic and cultural stereotypes. This tendency to exaggerate class and cultural differences has the paradoxical effect of collapsing political differences. The novel represents the relationship between class and race—textual markers of both difference and belonging—as the dynamic interplay of highly stylized discursive positions and cultural attributes. The novel's sustained use of parody effectively delegitimizes forms of political speech by turning them into elaborate jokes. Although the narrative calls attention to the material effects of class and racial oppression— Chamcha learns how foolish he has been in his pursuit of Englishness by becoming a living symbol of working-class minority politics—its political spokespersons are frauds who simply appropriate the discourse of disenfranchisement. The Brickhall sections of the novel show us that the real victims of poverty and racism are the nameless, monstrous creatures lurking in the dark halls of the Shaandaar. Those who purportedly claim to speak on their behalf—such as Simba and Johnson—are merely scam artists who appropriate the language of oppression to advance their own interests.

Worse yet, Brickhall's political leaders are more or less indistinguishable from their opponents—the police, politicians, and their racist supporters.[19] The fraudulence of Brickhall's activists and the class otherness of the police reduce them to comic inversions of one another. In other words, the novel satirizes both xenophobic nationalists and minority activists by making irreconcilable the material and affective poles of class politics vis-à-vis the problem of racial difference: the police are too ethnic to be English, the ethnics too English to legitimately protest against racist oppression. The novel undercuts the claims of belonging advanced by Valance and the police, the ideological representatives of neoimperialist nationalism, by making them bearers of excessive class and regional difference, despite their eagerness to erase, ignore, or overcome their exaggerated provincialism. Similarly, the radical politics of most Brickhall residents—including Simba, Johnson, and the Sufyan girls—seems out of step with their "real" class position: unlike the rest of Brickhall, they mimic and appropriate, rather than live, working-class experience. In the logic of the narrative, neither the police nor Brickhall's community leaders have the ethical right to their political positions because they are hypocritical satires of the cultural values they supposedly defend.

The Brickhall riot also brings some closure to the running debate between Chamcha and Gibreel about London and contemporary forms of Englishness, an argument that offers the novel's most sustained discussion of space and metropolitan culture. Gibreel, who wears the sneer of an "inverted Podsnap, for whom all things English are worthy of derision instead of praise," zealously sets about the task of tropicalizing London (425–26). With the help of the popular city atlas *London A to Z,* he attempts to systematically transform the city, square by square on the map, into the antithesis of itself: an equatorial, postcolonial metropolis. He suffers, of course, from wild delusions that drive him to suicide—his hallucinatory wish to transform London is another manifestation of the madness that precipitates the novel's infamous dream sequences—a fact that complicates any attempt to read his actions in a purely recuperative light. Gibreel's reclamation project culminates with the Brickhall riot, during which he imagines himself engaged in an apocalyptic mission of retribution and salvation. But London roundly defeats Gibreel in his efforts to master its terrain and convert its inhabitants. The anthropomorphic city shifts its form at will, bending its streets and changing their names to confuse the archangelic actor, making it impossible to "approach his quest in the systematic manner he would have preferred" (327). Reminiscent of the young Lessing, for whom London and the English prove annoyingly evasive, both Gibreel and Chamcha find the task of mapping and dominating metropolitan space far more challenging than they had anticipated. For these postcolonial conquerors, the desire to particularize and "de-imperialize" London's cultural geography evacuates metropolitan space of any concrete material reality. The city not only survives Gibreel's attempt to save and transform it but also effectively resists his efforts by destabilizing his cartographic impulses and cognitive maps.

The foggy, ambiguous London evoked here by Rushdie, and the literary city I have described in this book, have become highly ritualized representations of metropolitan culture. The kinds of obstacles encountered by Gibreel allude not to a flattened, postmodern hyperspace but to a superdense, highly convoluted, self-aware geographic system that can protect itself from unwanted appropriation. The city's function as a representational space is both embedded in and highly resistant to its material reality. London stands in for both the empty center of late imperial culture (whose mouthpiece is the pretransformation Chamcha) and the plenitude of meaning associated with migration and a working form of postcoloniality. London's dual function as the capital of provincial Englishness and host of transnational culture suggests that every attempt to particularize the local through the mapping of space proceeds on the basis of evacuation and reclamation, the simultaneity of urban decay and regeneration. The politics of space in 1980s London is a miniature version of modern Englishness, here figured as an insular yet paradoxically cosmopolitan culture, embodied in its urban class system, precariously oscillating between imperial implosion and postimperial rejuvenation. Rushdie's version of Englishness rehearses the dialectical tension of postimperial London in which the city is figured as both the epitome and the negation of an emerging global culture. London's particularity is itself a manifestly international condition, a global cultural formation in which the paradoxes of the local are made available to a worldwide audience. As many of the texts in this study suggest, modern Englishness resides in exasperating combinations of local culture couched in global experience, of endless displacements and insistent specificities, of gleeful disavowals and reluctant affirmations.

OF RACISM AND REINCARNATION

The novel's protagonist, Salahuddin Chamchawalla, does not begin the story, nor does he end it, as a satyr whose magical disfigurements were precipitated by the extremities of violence and hatred.[20] As I suggested in the introduction to this chapter, the novel subjugates and depoliticizes its deployment of London's class culture, using it as an important, but circumscribed, facet of a grand narrative of national identity and postcolonial migration. Although the novel relies on London's working class—both white and black—to narrate Chamcha's metropolitan nightmare, the text refuses to generate a narrative language capable of reconciling Chamcha's recovery of Indianness with England's class geography. The narrative hinges on social and political mobility: without Chamcha's atavistic deterioration and ultimate rebirth, the text could not fully explore the vicissitudes of cultural translation and disjuncture. In the logic of the narrative, Chamcha cannot find out what it means to be Indian by returning to Bombay because he first learns that he is Indian in England. His Indianness is a condition not only of his national origin, his race, or his cultural affiliations, but also of the class dynamics of London. The plot attempts to mediate the contradiction between narrative representations of space—London as a stage in Chamcha's journey—and the historical-geographic conditions constitutive of the novel's existence.

In the days before the Brickhall riot, Chamcha regains his fully human form, transformed, as it were, "by the fearsome concentration of his hate" (294). Just as Thatcher and the LDDC brought new vitality to the "barren areas" of which Heseltine complained, Chamcha, revisiting the novel's theme of reincarnation, determines that he will "come back to life," making himself anew (401). Moving back to the restored Notting Hill home he and his wife had shared before his "accident," Chamcha calls the bank to inquire about his accounts and then his agent, who assures him that, with time, he could continue his successful career. Although the "red tape surrounding his return to life proved more obstructive than he expected," Chamcha remains confident and effervescent, making every effort "to resume his old life of delicate sensibilities, taking himself off to concerts and art galleries and plays, and if his responses were rather dull;—if these pursuits singularly failed to send him home in the state of exultation which was the return he expected from high art;—then he insisted to himself that the thrill would soon return; he had had 'a bad experience,' and needed a little time" (407). Surrounding himself with the familiar (and tasteful) objects in his den, Chamcha settles confidently into his old armchair, congratulating himself that he finds it difficult to sustain hatred over long periods of time. Looking forward rather than back, "everything which had befallen [him] of late that was irreconcilable" with his renewed ambitions appears "somehow irrelevant, as even the most stubborn of nightmares will once you've splashed your face, brushed your teeth, and had a strong, hot drink" (406). Now that his horns have receded, he goes about the business of being a "goodandproper" Englishman once again.

But it would not be accurate to suggest that Chamcha emerges wholly unchanged from his unsettling encounter with working-class life. The concerts, plays, galleries, and acquaintances he enjoyed so much before his nightmare—the cultural trappings of bourgeois, metropolitan

Englishness—no longer captivate him. He also vows revenge on Gibreel Farishta, his fellow crash survivor who elected to remain quiet when a timely word could have saved him. More importantly, his thoughts drift toward "home," the India he left as a young man, when he learns that his father has fallen terminally ill with cancer. For the first time in several decades, his feelings begin to soften toward the place, and even the people, with whom he grew up: "Chamcha's head whirled. What strange meanings words were taking on. Only a few days ago that *back home* would have rung false. But now his father was dying and old emotions were sending tentacles out to grasp him. Maybe his tongue was twisting again, sending his accent East along with the rest of him" (514). The moment of truth arrives when Chamcha stands in front of the stately home in which he was reared. Ironically, his old digs will afford even greater opportunities for the social exclusivity he craves in London: during his absence, his father has installed an imported video monitoring system to keep out unwanted visitors (520). As the mature actor returns to comfort his ailing parent, he begins to respect and even admire the man whom he hated only months before, the one with whom he had not communicated in years:

> To fall in love with one's father after the long angry decades was a serene and beautiful feeling; a renewing, life-giving thing, Saladin wanted to say, but did not, because it sounded vampirish. . . . Although he kept it quiet, however, Saladin felt hourly closer to many old, rejected selves, many alternate Saladins—or rather Salahuddins—which had split off from himself as he made his various life choices, but which had apparently continued to exist, perhaps in the parallel universes of quantum theory. (523)

Chamcha, like the novel itself, beats a hasty retreat from England and its postcolonial nightmares. The mean streets of Brickhall represent at best a fading memory; Chamcha's present involves forgiveness, reconciliation, and a return to "roots." Unlike the relatively poor immigrants on whom he relies during his "breakdown," he has the luxury to flee Brickhall, its smoldering buildings and overcrowded boarding rooms.

Only a few days after returning to Scandal Point, the family compound, Chamcha sadly watches his father die. The novel's end, after all, is fairly conventional: never removed from the dying man's will, he inherits the whole of his father's considerable fortune. Such a resolution, however, raises some disturbing questions about the novel's use of class politics and social mobility. Our protagonist, we know, will be just fine. Although we can only guess that it will take him some time to recover from his "illness" and the shock of his father's death—in short, to recapture the Indianness he had shorn himself of so many years ago—we know that he is headed down the right path. Where does that leave the "riffraff from villages in Sylhet or the bicycle repair shops in Gujranwalla," or the homeless Bengali families back in London? The narrative never entertains that question. Chamcha leaves town just after the riot reaches its conclusion—after all the fun has ended—and when the hard work of rebuilding begins. The narrative transforms the uncomfortably real experiences of the South Asian community in East London into a kind of dream with Chamcha at its center.[21] The time he spends there is an epiphany, but it is somehow foreign to him. His metamorphosis, the "granny ripper" murders, the groups of young vigilantes, the incidents of police brutality, and the apocalyptic riot all contribute to the hallucinatory texture of these sections of the novel.

Although most critics barely mention the novel's conclusion, preferring instead the explosive deconstruction of Englishness offered by the middle sections of the narrative, the palpable unreality of London implies that we ought to take the novel's resolution a little more seriously. If we consider these sections as part of a more elaborate narrative economy, we must recognize Chamcha's time in Brickhall as one stop on a much longer journey. His metamorphosis and his experiences in Brickhall are narratologically significant because they force the protagonist into an existential crisis, not because the narrative has the means or desire to create a language capable of reconciling Chamcha's experience of immigration with those of the Brickhall community. Brickhall is not real in the logic of the novel because it is a stage through which the transmogrified Chamcha must pass in order to regain his Indianness. The narrative tendency to depoliticize class in service of discussions about national identity fits perfectly well with the novel's concluding scenes. For Chamcha, working-class Brickhall is a place of comedic interludes and self-discovery. It is Chamcha whom the novel redeems, not Brickhall, London, or English culture. By examining the complicated spatial history and class dynamics behind the metaphor of the Street, I have tried to demonstrate how London's political geography has real material consequences for the participants in this ideological struggle. For London's poorer immigrant communities, the Street is not a glib metaphor for the neighborhoods in which they live and work, nor is "the nightmare" of immigration a clever construction from which they can awake and flee as they choose.

This narrative movement reveals both the appeal of globalization as an explanatory model for contemporary social, economic, and cultural conditions as well as its complexity when it is deployed as a metaphor for new forms of political awareness. Although we can no longer assume the sovereignty of the nation-state or treat it as a privileged mechanism of political rule, we should be careful not to assume that globalization either eradicates local difference or assimilates easily into postcolonial politics. A model of globalization adequate for literary studies should help explain how international political and economic conditions produce radically different local conditions, accounting for the ways in which texts explore and exploit those circumstances. On one hand, the narrative movement of *The Satanic Verses* provides, especially in its Brickhall sections, an engaging account of the way immigrants *are subjected to* global political, economic, and cultural systems of exclusion and exploitation. Similar to many academic accounts of globalization, the novel provides a sophisticated critique of the immigrant condition under the regime of international capital. It links metropolitan racism and the struggle for enfranchisement with much broader historical and political trajectories. It is very good at diagnosing, in other words, the most deleterious effects of globalization. On the other hand, the narrative imagines a very limited form of political subjectivity within our globalized world. The novel's path toward political consciousness relies on its ability to traverse and manipulate an increasingly complex international landscape. Unlike the types of political subjection we encounter in the earlier parts of the novel, Chamcha's political awakening is predicated on forms of social, intellectual, and physical mobility. While the narrative depends on a language of oppression and class subjection to fuel Chamcha's nascent self-awareness, he achieves a measure of political awareness and agency by leaving behind London's inner city.

I find this narrative trajectory so problematic because social mobility circumscribes the formal resolution of the story—which in this case coincides with the political resolution of the story. While the novel needs a working class in order to access questions about racial identity and postcolonial anxieties, it must similarly disentangle itself from the painful class dynamic—the nightmare, for short—it deploys to this effect. The novel "contains," in both senses of the word, the class narrative around which it coheres. The story requires a discussion of social class and would not make sense without it, yet it does not fully explore the ramifications of this problem, containing the situation by leaving it altogether. The narrative orchestrates Chamcha's reincarnation by failing to examine the consequences of such an act, perpetrating a willful disengagement from the realities of social life in England's immigrant communities. Just as the novel achieves an intensity and momentum it will never regain, the narrative abruptly pulls back, following Chamcha's rather solipsistic return to Bombay. Meanwhile, his encounter with class, as magically as his horns, disappears from view. Like many of Thatcher's strongest critics, the novel leaves the most trying questions unanswered.

This narrative ambivalence, I have been suggesting, reflects a split between the text's understanding of race (and its articulation with class) as a reflection of material circumstances and the novel's imaginative projection of race as a problem that can be resolved by Chamcha's cultural reintegration in Bombay. For Chamcha, and the novel as a whole, the question of race produces a subjective crisis when it is manifested as an embodied and material racism, or as racial segregation and exploitation as a function of the metropolitan environment. The novel's travel story, however, reflects a deep narrative tension between the text's treatment of racism as historically contingent and race as a transnational, even existential, condition. The novel implies that Chamcha achieves a form of self-awareness and political agency not by considering the complex interaction of race and class in metropolitan space but by contemplating his personal relationship with his father and the city of his birth—a sort of transnational resolution of localized systems of inequality, and certainly not an option available to most of Brickhall's residents. A term such as globalization, if it is to become a productive addition to our critical vocabulary, must be able not only to decipher the material conditions in which fiction is conceived but also to critique the way texts such as *The Satanic Verses* mobilize the idea of globality to imagine political consciousness. As this novel demonstrates, the tension between the real and imaginary manifestations of race (and class) politics often becomes encoded in a structure of narrative ambivalence, a symbolic enunciation of the contradiction between racism as a narrative of lived experience and race as an ideological construction designed to establish a basis for collective (or individual) political action.

So what is really at stake in novels such as *The Satanic Verses* is the way fiction uses narrative to imagine political subjectivity. The novel articulates its postcoloniality by problematizing the political sovereignty and cultural legitimacy of England and seemingly embracing hybridity and international mobility. It critiques England's nationalistic xenophobia and racism as naive, reactionary responses to the country's loss of imperial hegemony and its resulting decline of status in the world political order. Like Hardt and Negri, the authors of *Empire,* who find postcolonialism an insufficient model for contemporary political theory, *The Satanic Verses* turns to an emerging global environment to resolve the legacy of colonial domination and exploitation. Unlike *Empire,* however, the novel imagines political subjectivity as a way to escape from, rather than attend to, both local and transnational systems of inequality. For transnational theory to become truly useful for postcolonial literary studies, scholars must be able to use globalization as a historical and theoretical model for describing contemporary systems of political and cultural exchange, but also to evaluate the ways that literary texts mobilize and manipulate such conditions. Globalization is not simply a form of political theory; it can help literary studies understand the ways in which narratives imagine political subjectivity today. This chapter, and indeed the book as a whole, does not represent an attempt to assert the primacy of the local over and against the international, for there is no necessary contradiction between immediate social conditions and global political structures. Rather, I have tried to demonstrate how fiction can be used to conceive political consciousness by moving within and beyond the cultural coordinates of the nation. It is a challenge to postcolonial literary studies to both map and interpret the arc of this narrative imagination.

CONCLUSION

In the past ten or fifteen years, there has been an upsurge of scholarly and popular interest in Englishness, London, and the special relationship between the two. Witness, for instance, Peter Ackroyd's recent work in *London: The Biography* (2000) and *Albion: The Origins of the English Imagination* (2002). Pointing out the various peoples and cultures that have settled and influenced England, he observes that this ineffable sense of national belonging "has more to do with location and with territory, therefore, than with any atavistic native impulses." The country's painting, literature, music, and architecture, like the people themselves, may be the "apotheosis" of "mixed style," but England's coherence and perdurability can be attributed to the fact that its physical borders have remained more stable than any of its Continental neighbors—a debatable point, given the importance of imperialism and the fraught relationship between Britain and England (*Albion* xxix). Nevertheless, this particular and contested construction of Englishness—what Ackroyd calls a "territorial imperative"—exists in a composite of cultural fluidity and spatial fixity, as if national identity were produced through a practice of cultural-geographic necromancy in which the host feeds on and thereby magically digests the habits and traditions of new arrivals (464). In a broader historical context, we know that landscape has a special place in the production of England's national imaginary, but a fascination with urbanity, particularly London, has become more salient in recent times. In late Victorian and Edwardian literature, in contrast, London and its teeming masses were often figured as a swollen, cancerous growth on the national body. During the modernist period, I have argued, representations of the city began to acquire more legitimacy as invocations of national space, and this characterization has become more pervasive in postwar literature.

As Ackroyd's writing suggests, it is now commonplace—though by no means universally accepted—to describe Englishness as a flowering garden of cultural diversity planted in the familiar soil of an extant social geography. Postwar immigration and the rise of postcolonial literature about metropolitan culture have accelerated this trend toward writing Englishness through London's cultural mélange. This confluence allows us, broadly speaking, to observe more continuity between, and rethink the ideological compatibility of, modernist and postcolonial narrative strategies of utilizing metropolitan geography.

Contemporary English fiction suggests that the dialectical tension between metropolitan decay and regeneration has become a standard trope in depictions of London and urban England. In novels such as *Bleeding London* (1997), by Geoff Nicholson, *London Fields* (1989), by Martin Amis, and *Hawksmoor* (1985), by Ackroyd, the geography of London is closely identified with violence, criminality, and narratives of detection. This type of imaginative work draws on the long tradition of British crime fiction—which, starting with Sherlock Holmes, has deep roots in the late Victorian obsession with metropolitan degeneracy—and in this respect revisits many of the tropes I discussed in chapter 2. But these novels also combine narrative, spatial, and sexual desires in such a way that the pleasure of solving a mystery is coupled with intellectual mastery of a city that is regularly represented as a corporeal, anthropomorphic, and erotic space. Like Ackroyd, who offers a "biography" rather than a more straightforward history of London, these texts turn metropolitan space into a vast but knowable, resilient yet frequently vulnerable body. Fetishizing London's geography becomes a metaphor for the perverse combinations of death and rebirth that are the defining features of contemporary urbanity. As Lewis Mumford argues in *The Culture of Cities*, modern cities "must not be monuments, but self-renewing organisms"; the dead should not be immortalized with lasting structures, but ought to fertilize the ground for new forms of life (439–40). London can be mastered because it is a decomposing corpse, but its expiring body also gives life and sustenance to a variety of parasites and scavengers feasting on the remains of an imperial metropolis. The discourse of English exceptionalism, so closely linked to the physical and cultural geography of London, works through the paradox of disavowal and identification symbolized by death and reincarnation.

As the editors of *The Empire Writes Back* observe, the theme of demolition and renovation is also "a recurring and evocative figure for the problematic of post-colonial identity" (Ashcroft, Griffiths, and Tiffin 28). An array of postcolonial writers have grafted the themes of urban destruction and creativity into their work, a trope with strong roots in early twentieth-century representations of London. Along these lines, Rosemary Marangoly George argues that examining "the concepts and structures we recognize as 'home' in the context of global English generates a reassessment of our understanding of belonging" (1). The idea of home building and destroying, in other words, has taken on global significations: real homes may localize global conditions, but fictions of domesticity have globalized the local by taking up transnational problems of belonging, exclusion, and identity. For instance, in Kate Pullinger's first novel, *When the Monster Dies* (1989), a group of commonwealth immigrants spend much of the narrative fixing up their illegal squats, making something useful—and homey—out of London's vacant, unwanted, surplus spaces. The narrative climaxes, however, with an ambivalent act of destruction: some of the main characters, striking out against capitalist developers, attempt to blow up Battersea Power Station, which has been rebuilt as an American-style amusement park. The novel's dying monster, of course, is the British Empire, and its scattered subjects occupy London with the aim of both destroying and remaking metropolitan space. Lessing's *The Good Terrorist* (1985) works with similar materials. Anarchist squatters ruthlessly pillage the homes of wealthier friends and relatives in order to support their revolutionary objectives, which include relatively unsuccessful bomb-throwing exploits.

Beyond Pullinger, Lessing, and Rushdie, whose novel culminates with similarly apocalyptic scenes of metropolitan violence, this obsession with a crumbling and renascent London appears in various guises: in *Rotting Hill* (1951), Wyndham Lewis takes his own neighborhood of Notting Hill—tellingly, also a center of immigration from the West Indies during the 1950s—as symptomatic of postwar London, "a monstrous derelict of a city" (96); Colin MacInnes's London trilogy, *City of Spades* (1957), *Absolute Beginners* (1959), and *Mr Love and Justice* (1960), traverses the city's poorer ethnic enclaves in search of a new, postimperial beginning; Buchi Emecheta's first two novels, *In the Ditch* (1972) and *Second-Class Citizen* (1974), wade through the slums of north London while their protagonists search for better housing, jobs, and relationships; Penelope Fitzgerald's *Offshore* (1979) moves back and forth between Swinging London of the King's Road, circa 1960s, and a community of social misfits making homes out of dilapidated boats on Chelsea Reach; Iain Sinclair's *Downriver* (1991) maps, with loving care and pangs of nostalgia, the decrepit corners of the Docklands area on the cusp of its Thatcherite makeover; Zadie Smith's *White Teeth* (2000) begins with an aborted suicide on London's outskirts and ends with the birth of a mixed-race child; Monica Ali's *Brick Lane* (2003) visits the impoverished Bengali community living in the housing estates of east London to connect metropolitan space with global forms of exchange and exploitation. Narratives of World War II and the Blitz have a special place in this genealogy: Graham Greene's *The End of the Affair* (1951) puts sexual desire and religious devotion in conflict against the backdrop of wartime blackouts; Thomas Pynchon's *Gravity's Rainbow* (1973) makes the link between eroticism, paranoia, random violence, and London's geography even more explicit; Francis Wyndham's *Out of the War* (1974) and *The Other Garden* (1987) linger over the fine details of class difference and mobility during the years of fighting; William Golding's *Darkness Visible* (1979) stages a contest between good and evil while the capital burns; Michael Moorcock's *Mother London* (1989) offers a palimpsest of World War II–era London through a small collection of eccentric mind readers, focusing on the city's experience of and recovery from the attacks. Some of this fascination with destruction and rebuilding can be explained by extensive wartime damage and efforts to rebuild London, which lasted well into the 1960s, but the persistence of this theme invites a more complicated reading.[1] As Marshall Berman argues so persuasively in *All That Is Solid Melts into Air,* the restless interplay of creativity and destruction of urban space represents nothing other than the dialectic of modernity itself. Yet in twentieth-century England, these jarringly intense conjunctions have become part of conversations about the plight of the nation.

As this eclectic list suggests, the desire to represent metropolitan space by rehearsing the metaphorical death and rebirth of the metropolis is not an exclusively postcolonial phenomenon. Broadly speaking, this manner of imagining London coincides with representations of England and national culture in its postimperial phase. The literal and figurative forms of London's reconstruction evoke the dilemma of imperial collapse and national rediscovery. Given London's sheer size and importance, the city has figured prominently in understandings of regional and national culture for several centuries. Yet only a hundred years ago it was relatively common to represent the growth of metropolitan space, at least in literary terms, as inimical to the country's well-being. Use of London as a synecdoche for national space has become even more widespread in recent years, but contemporary literary representations of the urban environment tend to be remarkable for their distinctive forms of ambivalence. Both imperial collapse and postimperial rebuilding are frequently depicted through inextricable mixtures of wild hope and abject despair, startling newness and oppressive familiarity. Often it is hard to say for sure what is being celebrated and what is being mourned, making it difficult to neatly segregate politically conservative writers, who might welcome the retrieval of an exclusive, bounded Englishness, from their more radical, postcolonial colleagues, many of whom attempt to demythologize imperial England by turning it into a provincial outpost of regional quirkiness. This type of collusion points to one of the more subtle ironies of this transformation: just as the functional end of imperialism forced the English to narrow the parameters of national culture, English fiction became even more reliant on representations of London, the material and ideological center of a rapidly contracting empire, when alluding to the idea of national culture. The space most directly implicated in imperial expansion, administration, and commerce has become the place most closely associated with the postimperial nation, helping to rewrite England, stripped of its imperial ambitions, as the global city of London and its humble provinces.

The trend of describing Englishness as a distinctively urban condition has been facilitated by the contradictory deployment of class as a marker of both unassimilated difference and cultural cohesion. *The Buddha of Suburbia* (1990), by Hanif Kureishi, illustrates this point as emphatically as any of the texts I have examined so far. In the novel's frequently quoted opening sentences, the narrator ambivalently claims an English identity: "My name is Karim Amir, and I am an Englishman born and bred, almost. I am often considered a funny kind of Englishman, a new breed as it were, having emerged from two old histories. But I don't care—Englishman I am (though not proud of it), from the South London suburbs and going somewhere" (3). Most critics read this passage, and the novel as a whole, from a postcolonial perspective, emphasizing Karim's hybrid cultural background (born of an English mother and an Indian father) and his encounters with various forms of racism. It is tempting, in fact, to place too much emphasis on Karim's disclaimer, his "almost," when arguing the position that the category of Englishness remains fundamentally exclusionary, the property of xenophobic, politically conservative whites. But most critics cut this passage short, turning away before Karim reiterates his claim to be an Englishman, unambiguously, "though not proud of it." It is his embarrassment—the shame associated with being English, we can see, but also the shame of being an awkward semiprovincial, from the nearby suburbs—that fully explains the source of his reluctance. The tortured oscillation embedded in these few lines epitomizes the modern form of Englishness in which the need to condemn is as strong as the desire to confess, resulting in a heady mixture of contrition and resignation. Karim's "almost" refers as much to himself as to the category of Englishness, which emerges as a state of perpetual negation and affirmation. It is a category almost, but not quite, alien to itself and its constituents.

The "somewhere" Karim dreams of going at the beginning of the novel is London, the place where he can escape the narrow-mindedness of the suburbs and enjoy the full privileges of Englishness. Karim first moves to London while working on home restoration projects with his father and stepmother, Eva. Like Karim, Eva goes through a process of self-transformation, shedding her identity as a forty-something suburban divorcée and methodically "constructing an artistic persona for herself" (150). Her creative medium is domestic: she is a property speculator and house renovator, buying dilapidated buildings in edgy neighborhoods ripe for gentrification, fixing them up, then selling them for a profit. By the end of the novel, being on intimate terms with London's geography and tenaciously clinging to the remains of English culture are the only things about which Karim seems confident: "And so I sat in the centre of this old city that I loved, which itself sat at the bottom of a tiny island. I was surrounded by people I loved, and I felt happy and miserable at the same time. I thought of what a mess everything had been, but that it wouldn't always be that way" (284). Like so many late- and postimperial invocations of England, the nation's maddening and endearing smallness becomes a noteworthy cultural and geographical attribute, as does the allure of its capital city. Karim's final words succinctly recapitulate many of the themes I have touched on, reinforcing the importance of London, the quaintness of the nation, and this acute sense of pathos. The novel's provincial-to-metropolitan narrative trajectory is not, of course, a new development in English fiction—postcolonial fiction has readily incorporated the plotline of provincial aspirants. Worth noting, however, is the fact that so many postcolonial texts seem eager to invest in metropolitan space. Such novels offer subtle, contemporary replies to late

Victorian slum narratives, as if to say that enclaves of urban immigrants offer pockets of hope and vitality, not physical and moral deterioration. The close literary relationship between London and Englishness can be attributed, in part, to the lasting impact of postcolonial writing on metropolitan space. Rather than dispense with the idea of Englishness altogether, many postcolonial writers work within—better yet, now dominate—the discourse of national distinctiveness by claiming urban space, particularly London.

Karim's embarrassment and hesitancy, figured in the novel's opening salvo as the indelible but unwanted stamp of Englishness, allude less to the question of race, however one might define it, than to class and geography. This is not to say that the novel offers no depictions of racism, which are peppered throughout the narrative, but to insist that Karim's desire—or his ineluctable need—to identify as English comes from an inside knowledge of England's urban class system. Karim operates, in his own words, as "a class detective" (198). As Rita Felski observes, he becomes "hypersensitive to the complex and often confusing codes of class distinction," all of which become painfully apparent as he adjusts to life in the city (38). We follow the narrator, the son of a badly paid civil servant and a shoe saleswoman, as he moves from the lower-middle-class suburb of Orpington to New York and London in pursuit of an acting career. Karim displays all the anxieties of a young man full of dreams but perpetually short of financial and cultural capital. More than anything, he envies and is disgusted by the ease with which his more affluent colleagues negotiate the shabby chic world of high culture. His first wealthy love interest, Eleanor, and her lefty bohemian set, for example, befriend a street-sweeper called Heater, who regales them with stories of working-class life before moving on to his real interests, classical music and Continental philosophy. Karim, naturally, despises this man who deliberately exaggerates his political authenticity as a member of the revolutionary proletariat. What infuriates Karim most, we learn, is that Eleanor likes them both for the same reasons, more or less: her cross-class liaison with Karim gratifies her social conscience and fans the flames of her desire, and the fact that he is not white, we surmise, is an added bonus. Karim's "cute" accent, she tells him, is "street voice . . . like cockney, only not so raw. . . . It's different from my voice, of course" (178). From that moment, Karim resolves to lose the class character of his accent, just as he attempts to conceal or erase every trace of his provincial background. Ironically, London is not the place where Karim can escape the prison of class difference, but the space where subtler and more pernicious forms of social distinction are endlessly reinforced.

Despite his eagerness to climb the social ladder, Karim incessantly calls attention to the phoniness of the metropolitan art scene, pointing out that its meticulously ragged clothes, progressive politics, and intellectual banter simply provide cover for vanity, social exclusivity, and an inner vacuity. This satiric portrayal of the metropolitan world of high culture puts *The Buddha of Suburbia* in the distinctly English tradition of comedic, social-climbing novels such as Orwell's *Keep the Aspidistra Flying* (1936) and Kingsley Amis's *Lucky Jim* (1954). Orwell's lower-middle-class protagonist, Gordon Comstock, is a struggling poet whose lack of cultural and material resources consigns him to failure. The novel's lone representative of a flourishing bohemian artist type, Ravelston, is not a genuine artist himself but a wealthy patron of the arts who has the luxury to embrace a fashionable, toothless communism. Amis's title character, Dixon, labeled a "shabby little provincial bore" by a bitter colleague, finds himself immersed in the absurd world of higher education at a new, less prestigious "redbrick" university (158). An assortment of embarrassingly public gaffes mark him as an outsider, yet one whose genuineness underscores the farcically pedantic behavior of his fellow university teachers. Karim's class background and social hopes, likewise, represent a form of decidedly English honesty that debunks the pretentiousness of the metropolitan cultural elite: he is ashamed of embarrassing, undesirable things (such as his lack of taste and cultural capital), and he desires, unashamedly, social graces, leisure, and money. His philistinism—ironically, the suburban stigma he hopes to efface— offers a commonsense rejoinder to the laughable trappings of the high-brow metropolitan milieu.

The novel relies on the experience of class difference and the notoriously elusive prospect of social mobility, in other words, to explain the vicissitudes of Englishness, a form of collective identity to which Karim thinks himself inescapably yoked. Class in *The Buddha of Suburbia* functions less as a marker of political antagonisms (or material position) and more as a system of organizing desire and anxiety. The novel's depictions of sexual relationships, like its explorations of the metropolitan art scene, are dominated by instances of class-crossing fears and fantasies. Karim desperately longs to escape the dreary, anonymous suburbs, but he is utterly dismayed to learn that his best chance of access to (if not acceptance in) the upside-down world of bohemian London involves playing up, rather than playing down, his racial and class difference. But Karim scrupulously avoids or rejects opportunities for political action that involve protesting against the instances of petty discrimination at which he bristles throughout the narrative; he repeatedly announces his indifference toward progressive political organizations. This is not to say that the novel totally depoliticizes class, but that the narrative deployment of class is more complicated than a simple mapping of available political positions and conflicts. Class in the text is not merely an index of political resistance and conformity, disenfranchisement and influence, or deprivation and affluence: understanding the novel's use of class means carefully attending to the forms of desire inscribed in the narrative. Reducing Karim's shame to a form of false consciousness doesn't take us very far if we hope to make sense of class in its literary condition. The novel's representation of class is embedded in this tension between class as a reflection of material conditions and class as a system of affect. Karim's lower-middle classness both defines what he is—it is a stain he wants to erase but finds he cannot—and the thing against which he defines himself. This disjuncture is typical of class as a literary object. As I have argued, these distinctive combinations of desire and anxiety frame the modern discourse of English exceptionalism. The narrative's particularizing gesture—its ambivalent but unambiguous proclamation of Englishness—is embedded in Karim's participation in the rituals of domestic class difference, portrayed through this specific blend of shame and aspiration. Class acts simultaneously as a means of representing privilege, status, wealth, and difference, and also as a way to project shared forms of longing and abjection characteristic of national consciousness in the postimperial moment.

Karim's memorable "almost" calls to mind Orwell's image of haunted domesticity with which I began this book. The English class system is a strange house in which everyone, even the departed, seems destined to live but no one wants to own. The term "English exceptionalism," I hope, captures the sense of trepidation with which most of these texts approach the question of national belonging. Karim's story resides in this mysterious collection of almosts and negations, taking both class and national identity as principal sites of wavering. His clever personal exemption, or his reluctance, comes with the knowledge that there is always something leftover, extraneous in this construction. Even as he invokes the discourse of English exceptionalism by enacting rituals of class membership and difference, he returns us to the figure of the intransigent clerk from *Howards End* and *Mrs. Dalloway* by way of a clerk's son. It is frequently the ambiguous position of the lower-middle-class character, perpetually looking in both directions, that illustrates the vexed workings of class along its material, ideological, and symbolic axes. Each of the primary texts I examine in this book, in fact, works with the raw narrative material of class mobility. Perhaps this fundamental observation will inspire more studies of class in motion—too often, class in the British context leads to fairly rigid treatments of "the" working class. Connecting class in its literary forms with modern expressions of national identity points to many of the successes and failures of postwar scholarship on class politics. Arguments "for" and "against" the relative importance of class have become tendentious, but there is still plenty of room to think about class as a polyvalent relation, one that is constantly managed through acts of disavowal and affiliation. If studying class can tell us something about the shifting terms and conditions of national culture in twentieth-century England, perhaps considering forms of cross-class identification—including national identity—can enrich our understanding of class in and as context. Recognizing the broad historical outlines, cultural tropes, and geographical specificities implied by this transition does not, I think, present a clear political solution, but instead a compelling intellectual opportunity, one that may allow us to see with more clarity the class content embedded in our literary traditions.

NOTES

I. ENGLISH, ALL TOO ENGLISH

1. For an extended analysis of the "class is dead" paradox of modern British culture, see Cannadine, *Rise and Fall of Class*. Cannadine makes the point that "class" has become a dated concept, blaming overenthusiastic academics as much as anyone. He cites Thompson, easily the most important scholar of class in Britain, as evidence of this oversaturation problem: "Even some of the old-guard Marxist historians seem to have retracted and recanted. . . . [In] one of his last essays, E. P. Thompson declared that '"class" was perhaps overworked in the 1960s and 1970s, and it had become merely boring. It is a concept long past its sell-by date'" (16).

2. Hitchcock, "They Must Be Represented?" Hitchcock has published several essays and books that argue this point from a number of different positions; see also "'Work Has the Smell of Vinegar'" and *Working-Class Fiction*.

3. See in particular Dimock and Gilmore's introduction to *Rethinking Class*. See also Kaplan's "Millennial Class," the introduction to *PMLA*'s special issue on class; and Ross's introduction to a similar volume from *Modern Fiction Studies*.

4. Although my approach emphasizes the work of class as a system of literary representation, I rely on a loosely Marxist understanding of class relationships in capitalist societies. Aside from Althusser, Lefebvre, and Thompson, to whom I refer directly on several occasions, Marx, Lukács, and Gramsci have had the greatest influence on my thinking about class. Marx, of course, elaborates on class as an economic condition in *Capital*, volume 1 (455–91, 914–30), and elsewhere, and his most insightful writing on class in its political form is *The 18th Brumaire*. In *Capital*, he writes, "The foundation of every division of labour which has attained a certain degree of development, and has been brought about by the exchange of commodities, is the separation of town from country" (472). This particular emphasis on the spatial dimensions of class relationships informs this book as a whole.

5. King, *Bungalow*.

6. Gilroy, *Black Atlantic.* See especially his critique (to which this introductory chapter responds) of the British New Left and its culpability in this discourse of national and ethnic exclusivity (3–14).

7. For fuller discussions of ethnography and metropolitan societies, see Esty, *Shrinking Island;* Buzard, "Ethnography as Interruption"; Manganaro, *Modernist Anthropology;* and Pratt, *Imperial Eyes.* For a history of the Mass Observation movement in Britain, whose findings were the compilation of work done by amateur ethnographers, see Sheridan, Street, and Bloome, *Writing Ourselves.*

8. In addition to the scholars mentioned in the following notes, see Nairn, *Break-Up of Britain;* Gilroy, *"There Ain't No Black";* Tabili, *"We Ask for British Justice";* Mercer, *Welcome to the Jungle;* Paul, *Whitewashing Britain;* and Morley and Robbins, *British Cultural Studies,* particularly Catherine Hall's essay, "British Cultural Identities."

9. The question of England's specific relationship with its Celtic neighbors, Scotland, Wales, and Ireland, though obviously important, falls beyond the scope of this book. Practically speaking, I could not do this thorny problem justice in a book of this length, though I hope my project may stimulate dialogue with others working on this issue. Furthermore, what I describe as the discourse of English exceptionalism became particularly evident in the mid-century period, say between 1947 and 1970, when Britain was losing its overseas colonies rapidly. Because Eire broke away in the 1920s, while the rest of the United Kingdom remained functionally intact until the end of the twentieth century, the acute sense of pathos I associate with Englishness is not necessarily evident in Anglo-Celtic relations.

10. Baucom's introduction to *Out of Place* provides one of the most succinct analyses of this process. See also Gilroy, *"There Ain't No Black."*

11. See Baucom, *Out of Place;* and George, *Politics of Home.*

12. Esty's study of late modernist writers such as Woolf and Eliot, however, demonstrates that there was a strong interest in rural revivalism during the period of national retrenchment in the 1930s. As I argue in chap. 2, pastoral themes, part of an elaborate endgame played out by the late modernists, were largely abandoned by their postwar successors.

13. Esty's account of British cultural studies offers a detailed examination of the early New Left's "blind spots . . . with regard to race and empire" (198). As he argues, "demetropolitanizing" impulses were present in the early, middle, and late strands of cultural studies. The Hoggart-Williams-Thompson group used anthropological holism to restore English particularity, which paradoxically made England a "first among equals" in the pecking order of the nations. Nairn and Anderson launched a more systematic attack on English parochialism. Said, Gilroy, and others continue to pick at the frayed edges of the English national fabric.

14. Although this book focuses on England's relationship with a crumbling empire, the "threat" of Americanization was also a prominent refrain in the discourse of cultural exceptionalism during the 1950s in particular. Working-class "affluence" and the influx of cultural products, such as film and popular music, from the

United States prompted fears about American hegemony in England. See Abravanel, "Atlantic Modernism."

15. In "When Was 'the Postcolonial'?" Stuart Hall makes a similar argument when he says that postwar English intellectuals have been continually engaged in an attempt to "recover an alternative set of cultural origins not contaminated by colonising experience" (246).

16. See S. Hall, "Supply of Demand," and Laing, *Representations of Working-Class Life*, respectively.

17. For more on the narrative of the affluent working class of the 1950s and '60s, see Goldthorpe, *Affluent Worker*; Goldthorpe et al., *Affluent Worker*; and chap. 4 of this book.

18. For an examination of "status dilution" in the modern period, see Bourdieu, *Distinction*.

19. Nairn, "English Working Class" 48. For more on the exchanges between Anderson, Nairn, and Thompson, see Thompson, "Peculiarities of the English"; Nairn, "Nature of the Labour Party," parts 1 and 2; and Anderson, "Left in the Fifties," and "Socialism and Pseudo-Empiricism."

20. In *Retreat from Class*, Ellen Wood offers a detailed critique of the "new" intellectual socialism. She essentially blames high theory for the intellectual left's hollow center, tracing the erosion of class-based analysis to the influx of Continental Marxism in Britain.

21. Qtd. in Easthope, *Englishness and National Culture* 113.

22. See Macherey, *Theory of Literary Production* 61–68, 85–89.

23. For a brief summary of this concept, which Williams developed over the course of his career, see *Marxism and Literature* 128–35.

24. Hitchcock, "They Must Be Represented?" 29. See also Althusser and Balibar, *Reading Capital* 83–198.

25. Eagleton, *Criticism and Ideology* 89. See also Macherey, *Theory of Literary Production* 122; and Eagleton, *Ideology of the Aesthetic*, and *Ideology: An Introduction*.

26. Althusser and Balibar complain of exactly this confusion between the idea of the object and the object itself, or between theory and actual material practices, in *Reading Capital* 11–69.

27. Some of the most important academic considerations of globalization include Hardt and Negri, *Empire*; Sassen, *Losing Control?*; Appadurai, *Modernity at Large*; Harvey, *Spaces of Hope*; Bauman, *Globalization*; King, *Global Cities*; and Giddens, *Consequences of Modernity*.

28. "Cognitive mapping," of course, is Jameson's term. See "Postmodernism."

29. For one of the most influential books on space in the modernist period, see Kern, *Culture of Time and Space*; for recent books covering the "space vs. place" debate, see Casey, *Fate of Place*; Thacker, *Moving through Modernity*; Carter, Donald, and Squires, *Space and Place*; Kort, *Place and Space in Modern Fiction*; in addition to Tuan's classic *Space and Place*. For more on "public vs. private," consult

Massey, *Space, Place, and Gender;* and Landes, *Feminism.* For a recent consideration of the "local vs. global" discussion, see M. Smith, *Transnational Urbanism.*

30. Esty, "National Objects" 12.

31. See McLaughlin, *Writing the Urban Jungle.*

32. For a thorough examination of "postcolonial" London, see Ball, *Imagining London.*

33. See Williams, *Politics of Modernism;* and Simmel, "Metropolis and Mental Life." "Metropolitan perception" as a term captures the urban, imperial, and cultural implications of metropolitan life. When Esty discusses postcolonial writers of the 1950s who challenge the terms and conditions of metropolitan perception, he uses the term "demetropolitanization."

34. This observation complicates the "neoimperial" model of postcolonial literature offered by Huggan, for example, in *Postcolonial Exotic.*

35. My desire to read geography as a means of cultural production builds on the extremely suggestive work of Lefebvre, especially *Production of Space* and *Critique of Everyday Life.*

36. See Foucault, *Discipline and Punish.*

37. For example, see Rose, *Feminism and Geography;* Armstrong, *Desire and Domestic Fiction;* Parsons, *Streetwalking the Metropolis;* and Massey, *Space, Place and Gender.*

38. Most Marxist geographers read space as the reflection of capitalist accumulation. For example, see Harvey, *Social Justice and the City;* and Certeau, *Practice of Everyday Life.*

39. See Said, *Orientalism,* and *Culture and Imperialism* 3–14.

40. For more on the connection between narrative plotting and space, see Brooks, *Reading for Plot* 11–12.

2. BROKEN FENCES

1. The dividing line between more and less sympathetic accounts of urban poverty is sometimes difficult to establish in retrospect. Turn-of-the-century accounts of the urban poor, whether penned by moral crusaders with a progressive agenda or by reactionary thinkers advocating eugenic solutions, usually offered sensationalistic material. Particularly interesting is the direct connection many texts make between colonial subjects and the distinct "culture" of urban, working-class England.

2. Greenslade, "Fitness and Fin de Siècle" 47–48.

3. In addition to Greenslade, see Soloway, "Counting the Degenerates" 137; Searle, *Eugenics and Politics;* and Jones, *Outcast London.*

4. Masterman, *Heart of the Empire* 8. Also see Gilbert's thorough introduction for a more extended discussion of the relationship between the urban class system and imperialism.

5. English, *Comic Transactions* 31–66.

6. During periods of internal crisis, advocates of "empire migration" argued that colonies should be utilized to disperse surplus capital and people (as well as mitigate social tension). See Cohen, "'Get Out!'" Cohen, of course, cites the famous Cecil Rhodes sound bite: "My cherished idea is a solution for the social problem, i.e., in order to save the 40,000,000 inhabitants of the United Kingdom from a bloody civil war, we colonial statesmen must acquire new lands to settle the surplus population, to provide new markets for the goods produced by them in the factories and mines. The Empire, as I have always said, is a bread and butter question. If you want to avoid civil war, you must become imperialists" (qtd. in Lenin, *Imperialism* 79). Also see Magubane, *Bringing the Empire Home* 79–87.

7. For more on the idea of the pastoral aesthetic as an expression of English distinctiveness, see Williams, *Country and the City* 279–88; and Mercer, *Welcome to the Jungle* 287–307. For a fuller discussion of the deep connection between pastoral literature and imperialism in the nineteenth century, see Said, *Culture and Imperialism* 62–110. Esty, *Shrinking Island* 41, and Ranger, "Invention of Tradition," discuss the value of the pastoral form as an educational export to the colonies.

8. The work of Anthony King is the one possible exception to this categorization, but he does not consider Garden Cities directly. Meacham, in *Regaining Paradise,* pursues an argument similar to my own: he suggests that the panic over the physical and moral deterioration of the working class led to a rearticulation of Englishness through spatial reform. He even points to Masterman's *Heart of Empire* as a text that spurred the English to take action (2). Despite Masterman's title, however, nowhere does Meacham connect the potential collapse of empire as relevant to the study of land reform discourse in turn-of-the-century England.

9. Additionally, the empire had long been an aesthetic and cultural resource out of which the metropole could draw inspiration. As early as 1858 — coincidentally, at the tail end of the Indian Mutiny — Ruskin was asking "what lessons India could supply for the reform of art and architecture in Britain" (Metcalf, *Imperial Vision* 141).

10. For instance, see Morgan, *Danger of Deterioration.*

11. In recent years, the South African War and its effect on domestic politics have received a great deal of scholarly attention. See Krebs, *Gender, Race, and Writing Empire;* Schneer, *London 1900;* Magubane, *Bringing the Empire Home;* and Breward, "Sartorial Spectacle."

12. See T. Smith, "'Grand Work of Noble Conception.'"

13. There were analogous efforts in the colonies: the British attempted to consolidate and "naturalize" their position in South Africa and India by constructing new types of colonial architecture, mimicking indigenous forms. See Metcalf, *Imperial Vision.*

14. For fuller discussions of Lutyens's work, both imperial and domestic, see Arts Council of Great Britain, *Lutyens;* Stamp and Goulancourt, *English House, 1860–1914;* O'Neill, *Lutyens Country Houses;* Jane Brown, *Lutyens and the Edwardians;* Morris and Winchester, *Stones of Empire;* and Metcalf, *Imperial Vision.*

15. King, *Bungalow;* see also Briggs (known as "Bungalow Briggs"), *Bungalows and Country Residences.*

16. For a complementary discussion of landscape art during England's period of imperial expansion, see Mitchell, "Imperial Landscape."

17. Blatchford, *Merrie England.*

18. For one of the better modern readings of the novel's liberal imagination, see Born, "Private Gardens, Public Swamps."

19. Also see Outka's excellent discussion of Lutyens's ersatz country-house aesthetic devices in connection with "commodified nostalgia" in *Howards End.* As Outka argues, Forster's novel does not simply embrace the easy charms of Lutyens's style but instead explores the social costs attendant on an uncritical acceptance of the pastoral solution. Hegglund also argues that Edwardian country houses like *Howards End* were made to appear older and more established than they actually were ("Defending the Realm" 404–5).

20. The novel's complex misgivings about London's swollen suburbs have been picked over by a variety of commentators. For two of the best discussions, see Thacker, *Moving through Modernity* 55–59; and Hegglund, "Defending the Realm." Likewise, in "Suburbia, *Ressentiment,* and End of Empire," Kutcha discusses Forster's antipathy toward suburban development in *Passage to India.* For an excellent historical overview of suburban development in England, see F. M. L. Thompson, *Rise of Suburbia.*

21. The abstract idea of fairness has long been a staple of middle-class political ethics in England. See McKibbin, *Classes and Cultures,* especially chap. 9, "The Sporting Life" 332–85. Middle-class forms of sociability usually discouraged competitive situations and emphasized instead the importance of "fair play" and "putting on a good show." Among other things, McKibbin links this attitude and the middle class's prominent role in sports management to Britain precipitous decline in international athletic prowess.

22. Much of my discussion of the relationship between imperialism and automobiles in the novel follows Thacker's excellent consideration of this link (*Moving through Modernity* 62–74); see also Weissman, "*Howards End:* Gasoline and Goddesses."

23. See also Tabili, "*We Ask for British Justice,*" especially chap. 4, "Blot on Our Hospitality" 58–80.

24. As many commentators have suggested, the novel's interest in resolving Anglo-German tension in the years before the Great War is relevant to this discussion. The Schlegels, whose father was German, regularly think of themselves as cosmopolitan and Continental in their outlook. The Wilcoxes, in contrast, are English to the core; as Charles explains, the family remains deeply skeptical of "cosmopolitans": "I can't stand them, and German cosmopolitanism is the limit" (100). And as Henry makes embarrassingly clear to the Schlegel sisters, the Anglo-German rivalry is a direct consequence of imperial aspirations: "Unless we get firm in West Africa, Ger—untold complications may follow" (124).

25. See Williams, *Country and the City* 9–45.

26. See, for instance, Su, "Refiguring National Character"; and Littlejohn, *Fate of the English Country House.*

27. In fact, many country estates were effectively taken over by the state in the postwar period, becoming an important part of the heritage industry. Such manors were usually donated by aristocratic families for tax reasons. Sally Potter's film adaptation of Virginia Woolf's *Orlando* shows an interesting perspective on this transition, in which the aristocratic title character, who lives through several centuries, visits the country manor her family had once owned as it is being converted into a public conservation site.

28. Featherstone, "Nation as Pastoral" 167. Featherstone suggests that this use of the pastoral goes back to World War I, citing Fussell, *Great War and Modern Memory.*

29. Sinfield, *Literature, Politics,* especially chap. 2, "War Stories" 6–22.

30. For the most comprehensive historical overview of the welfare state in Britain, see Timmins, *Five Giants.*

31. In *Brideshead* 200–208, Waugh provides an interesting account of the General Strike of 1926 from the perspective of the aristocracy. A young Ryder, who had been abroad, returns from France to lend a hand. He is disappointed to find that it "had not been worth leaving Paris" (207).

32. Jameson uses those words to describe the second part of Joseph Conrad's *Lord Jim* (*Political Unconscious* 206). He suggests that *Lord Jim* represents a point of departure for twentieth-century literature. On the one hand, Conrad's novel makes important contributions to the emergent field of high modernism, which had a formative influence on the academy and the canon. On the other hand, the novel, particularly its second half, uses a more mass-culture formula. Jameson credits the Frankfurt School (thinkers like Adorno and Marcuse) with first discussing this trend. See particularly Horkheimer and Adorno, *Dialectic of Enlightenment.*

33. Granada Television, of course, turned this novel into a successful miniseries. My edition of the text provides the most dramatic representation of this process: the front cover calls it the "companion to the PBS television series."

3. STRANGERS IN THE PARK

1. For fuller treatments of the novel's oppositional pairs, see the following sources: J. H. Miller, "Woolf's All Souls' Day" (past and present); Froula, "*Mrs. Dalloway*'s Postwar Elegy," and Clewell, "Consolation Refused" (life and death); Levenback, *Woolf and the Great War* (war and peace); Zwerdling, *Woolf and the Real World* (wealth and poverty); Squier, *Woolf and London* (sexuality and gender).

2. See Boehmer's introduction to *Scouting for Boys,* Baden-Powell's enormously popular guide to the scouting movement. The scouting movement was motivated by fears of urban degeneracy in its early days at the turn of the century. Boehmer calls the guide "an imperial self-improvement text par excellence" (xviii).

Baden-Powell was himself a military hero of the South African War, the conflict that led to so much soul-searching over empire and the urban class system.

3. Baudelaire's figure of the *flâneur,* and Benjamin's illuminating work on it, rely too much on the notion of bodily and psychological self-possession of the urban subject to function as a useful *general* model of the urban experience in modernist literature. Adaptations of Benjamin's work on the *flâneur* to decipher *Mrs. Dalloway* are widespread. See Bowlby, "Walking, Women and Writing"; McCue, "Confronting Modernity"; Lord, "Frames of Septimus Smith"; Brownstein, "Silver Spoons and Knives"; J. Marcus, "Thinking Back through Our Mothers"; and Parsons, *Streetwalking the Metropolis.*

4. See Schneer, *London 1900* 97–106; and Ritvo, *Animal Estate.*

5. See Preston, "'Scenery of the Torrid Zone'"; and Conway, *People's Parks* 169–70.

6. See Meynell, "Royal Botanic Society's Garden." The Royal Botanic Society was often criticized for being merely a fashionable salon for wealthy dilettantes (rather than a "serious" botanical society). Most avid horticulturalists thought Kew Gardens and the Horticultural Society of London in Chiswick far superior.

7. See, for instance, Metcalf, *Imperial Vision* 176–80.

8. For more on London's turn-of-the-century plans for an "imperial quarter," see Driver and Gilbert, "Heart of Empire?"; Gilbert, "'London in All its Glory'"; Driver and Gilbert, *Imperial Cities;* and Beaufoy, "'Order out of Chaos.'"

9. Also see Davin, "Imperialism and Motherhood"; and Thane, "Late Victorian Englishwomen" 183.

10. See Conway, *People's Parks* 21; and Jordan, "Public Parks" 86.

11. C. L. R. James wrote about cricket and politics in *Beyond a Boundary.* Recently, many historians have followed his lead by considering the relationship between sporting culture, class, and imperialism. See Mangan, *Games Ethic and Imperialism;* Bailey, *Leisure and Class;* McKibbin, *Classes and Cultures* 332–85; Appadurai, *Modernity at Large* 89–113; Baucom, *Out of Place* 135–63; and Lazarus, *Nationalism and Cultural Practice.*

12. In fact, A. Wood, in "Walking the Web," demonstrates that while the novel's representation of London itself may be more or less realistic, Woolf manipulates the city by not allowing nearly enough time for characters to walk in the way she describes.

13. Clarissa and Septimus do have similar physical features, but I read this as a symbolic rather than a "social" or direct personal connection—the distinction with which I am most concerned here. The narrative works on the principle that they remain anonymous to one another but have a spiritual/symbolic connection.

14. For an excellent cultural studies reading of this moment in the novel, see North, *Reading 1922* 81–86.

15. The novel began as a short story called "Mrs Dalloway in Bond Street," which first appeared in the *Dial* in 1923. The character of Septimus Smith was

added as a kind of unconscious twin of Clarissa. See McNichol's introduction to *Mrs Dalloway's Party* 9–17.

16. D. K. Reed, "Merging Voices" 118–19. Like Reed, Zwerdling and Squier offer fairly sympathetic readings of the novel and Clarissa Dalloway as a character; all point to Woolf's diary, in which she describes her goals for the work: "I want to give life & death, sanity & insanity; I want to criticise the social system, & to show it at work, at its most intense" (June 19, 1923, *Diary* 248).

17. *Between the Acts* in particular reflects on this ambivalent attitude toward the avant-garde and its appropriateness to English customs, but *Jacob's Room, Orlando, The Waves,* and *To the Lighthouse* are all invested in adapting experimental forms to the English literary tradition.

18. Wirth-Nesher, *City Codes* 18–21, elaborates on this point; see also Snaith, *Virginia Woolf;* and C. Reed, *Bloomsbury Rooms,* especially chap. 13.

19. See Lamming's *Pleasures of Exile,* in which he argues that "[w]riters like Selvon . . . they never really left the land" and therefore write with a "peasant sensibility" (45, 225). See also Ramchand, "Songs of Innocence"; and Procter, *Dwelling Places* 46–49.

20. I am skeptical of attempts to use the *flâneur* or its theoretical offspring to explain the urban aesthetics of postcolonial texts. As my discussion of *Mrs. Dalloway* suggests, the figure is marked by the illusion of bodily and psychological integrity—a perception not available to most female, working-class, or nonwhite characters. See Ball's otherwise strong book, *Imagining London* 135–43; and Procter, *Dwelling Places* 96–100.

4. CITIES OF AFFLUENCE

1. John Barber, review of *Look Back* in the *Daily Express,* qtd. in J. R. Taylor, *John Osborne* 46.

2. Most accounts of postwar British theater describe the atmosphere of the early 1950s as moribund. Rebellato, in part to suggest that this widely accepted categorization is a form of revisionist history, parodies it: "By 1956, British theatre was in a terrible state. The West End was dominated by a few philistine theatre managers, cranking out emotionally repressed, middle-class plays, all set in drawing-rooms with French windows, as vehicles for stars whose only talent was to wield a cigarette holder and a cocktail glass while wearing a dinner jacket" (*1956* 1).

3. John Mander, from *The Writer and Commitment* (London: Secker and Warburg, 1961), qtd. in J. R. Taylor, *John Osborne* 143. For more on Osborne's personal commitment to socialism, which was short-lived and largely a matter of personal freedom, see Maschler, *Declaration.*

4. In "Small Personal Voice," for instance, Lessing expresses sympathy with the Angry Young Men when she calls social realism "the highest form of prose writing" (4). Implicitly, it is also an attack on high modernism. See also Sinfield's reading

of the relationship between Angry writers, modernism, and the literary-critical establishment in n. 7 below.

5. I use the term "domestic melodrama" to describe the basic generic conventions at work in this otherwise heterogeneous group of texts, which includes both plays and novels. The idea of domesticity has a dual meaning: the setting in these texts is quite often domestic, but more importantly, the main dramatic problem usually involves a heterosexual love affair. Most Angry works end with a young male protagonist settling down into marriage, hence the concept of domesticity. "Melodrama," of course, connects these texts with one of the most persistent and adaptable genres in popular culture. I use melodrama to signify the way protagonists are usually situated: they typically struggle against long odds in a hostile, unsympathetic society. Rather than deploy an antagonist of some kind to create dramatic tension, most Angry texts have a protagonist battling against the fates, which tend to conspire against him.

6. J. Osborne, "That Awful Museum" 216. Quigley, "The Personal, the Political," comments on the apparent contradiction between the play's conventional form and the vitality it conveyed to the audience as well as the impact it had on a whole generation of postwar playwrights.

7. See Sinfield, *Literature, Politics* 60–85; and English, *Comic Transactions* 128–59. Sinfield argues that the repudiation of high culture can be traced, through a specific cultural history, to the misogyny and homophobia of Angry writers. In trumpeting the new "hard" style of literary realism, they frequently used such figures as Virginia Woolf, Lytton Strachey, and Evelyn Waugh as targets. In order to represent this axis schematically, he creates a small chart in which he aligns the terms "dominant, the state, the working class, and masculinity" across a horizontal axis, opposing them to the terms "literary, the personal, the leisure class, and femininity." Each term represents the antithesis of its corresponding partner; thus "the state" and "the personal" are oppositional categories, as are "working class" and "leisure class" (66). Although Sinfield's diagram presents a useful starting point for the investigation of gender in Angry writers, I argue that a category such as "the state" does not fit so easily into any strictly oppositional paradigm. The state plays an active, complicated role in the production of gender identities through the field of domesticity. Given Sinfield's position of "the personal," we might also guess that he would place "the domestic" in opposition to terms like masculinity and the state. Considering the importance of the state within the domestic sphere and its centrality in the creation of "masculinity," it might make more sense to discuss how terms achieve meaning by working through other categories rather than opposing them.

8. See also Sinfield's reading of jazz politics, chap. 8, "Making a Scene" 152–81.

9. For an insightful examination of the Arts Council and postwar drama, see Rebellato, *1956* 37–69, 101–26.

10. *The Charter of Incorporation Granted by His Majesty The King to the Arts Council of Great Britain Ninth Day of August 1946* 3; qtd. in Harris, *Government Patronage* 41–42.

11. The English Stage Company played a central role in the emergence of the new postwar drama. John Osborne, Arnold Wesker, N. F. Simpson, Harold Pinter, Ann Jellicoe, John Arden, Shelagh Delaney, and later Caryl Churchill all wrote for the company, with most of them premiering several plays there. Though *Look Back* had a great deal of success, most of the company's original plays lost money. In the years 1956–61, the Arts Council supported the company with grants of £30,000. But the commercial acumen of the group should not be underestimated: in the same period of time, they earned £50,000 by selling rights to screenplays from *Look Back* and other original productions. See J. R. Taylor, *Anger and After* 37.

12. See McKibbin, *Classes and Cultures* 98–105. This anxious attitude was typical of the lower-middle class, especially in the postwar settlement. While the lower-middle class had done comparatively well between 1926 and 1940 (the labor crises of the 1920s, notably the General Strike, helped consolidate their position), it fared considerably worse, in comparison with other groups, during the 1950s.

13. I use several related terms almost interchangeably throughout this chapter. In most instances, I use "the welfare state" to refer to government as well as the institutions, many in the service industries, established by the state during the postwar settlement. "Keynesian" refers to the philosophical and economic strategies developed by John Maynard Keynes, the British Nobel Prize–winning economist who advocated and helped legislate the social "safety net" of the welfare state. I use "welfare capitalism" to describe the cooperation between the state and industry with respect to medium-term capital growth strategies. These included social security measures but also state subsidizing of less profitable but essential industries such as energy, public transportation, and housing construction. Fairly recent detailed histories of the welfare state include John Brown, *British Welfare State;* Timmins, *Five Giants;* and Lowe, *Welfare State.*

14. The Beveridge Report reached an unprecedented audience for a document of its kind, selling over 600,000 copies in its initial release. For a more detailed account of it, see John Brown, *British Welfare State.* See also Beveridge, *Full Employment.*

15. See Routh, *Occupation and Pay* 5. See also HMSO, *Census 1951* and *Census 1961.*

16. After the Tory election victory of 1951, many Labour leaders expressed alarm that widespread material prosperity would erode working-class support for the party—even though Labour had won more votes (though a lower percentage of the vote) than at any time in its history. See my chap. 1.

17. Before World War I, only 10 percent of homes were owned by their occupants, and this figure did not rise appreciably until after World War II, when subsidized housing programs made home ownership possible for many working-class families. See Short, *Housing in Britain* 118–20.

18. Fyvel, "Stones of Harlow" 15. For historical reviews of New Towns and welfare state urban planning systems, see Cullingworth, *Town and Country Planning;* Schaffer, *New Town Story;* Ravetz, *Remaking Cities;* and Burns, *New Towns for Old.*

19. See Philipson, *Aycliffe and Peterlee* 123–24.

20. For a complete discussion of collective consumption and its role in post-war economies, see Castells, *City, Class, and Power,* especially chap. 2, "Collective Consumption" 15–36.

21. For example, in *Lucky Jim,* set in the late 1940s, the main character, Jim Dixon, carefully rations his cigarettes. Only a few years later, Arthur Seaton consumes them, and other "luxury" items, with gleeful abandon. Tobacco became a common way to think about material deprivation because it was expensive for years after the war. In Lessing's *In Pursuit of the English,* set in 1949, cigarettes become a contentious part of the domestic economy.

22. In contrast, in *Working-Class Fiction* Hitchcock reads *Saturday Night* as an instance of "counter-literary" tradition. He argues that it embodies its relationship to both class politics and the literary tradition in its deployment of radical, highly politicized literary techniques. I suggest, on the other hand, that the novel encodes its political coordinates through its adaptation of fairly conventional literary forms.

23. For a succinct but thorough discussion of nineteenth-century housing, see S. Marcus, *Apartment Stories* 83–132. Her discussion pulls evidence from a variety of sources—including hygienists, architects, philanthropists, and urban cartographers—to demonstrate the English bourgeois obsession with single-family homes and the potential for discretion that they promise. In an ingenious turn, Marcus reads popular ghost stories to show the impracticability and instability of this largely unrealized domestic ideal. As I discuss below, this English fascination with the single-family dwelling persists well into the twenty-first century.

24. For a fairly complete history of working-class housing in Britain, see Burnett, *Social History of Housing.*

25. In *Uses of Literacy,* Hoggart argues that marriage constitutes the one inviolable social code of working-class life. "Working-class men and women still accept marriage as normal and 'right,' and that in their early twenties," he claims. This feeling remains so strong that it even pervades codes of humor: although "working-class people have a host of jokes about marriage," never does one encounter a joke "against marriage" (37). "Sin," on the other hand, "is any act against the idea of home and family," such as conducting extramarital affairs or conceiving a child without the intention to marry (18). In this sense, Hoggart might be tempted to argue that Arthur's behavior breaks all acceptable codes of conduct; as the novel demonstrates, however, even he achieves "full" masculinity within the bonds of marriage.

26. Castells, *City, Class, and Power,* points out that distribution of resources in welfare-capitalist economies often leads to higher than "necessary" levels of consumption. In the case of housing, for instance, many families were forced, by slum clearances, to move into new homes. Although the quality of such housing represented a dramatic improvement, poor families were also compelled to pay higher portions of their income in rent, even with state housing subsidies. This also

happens with transportation, with roads and public transportation facilities often being built and operated in places where residents might have opted to spend the money elsewhere. Moving families into homes on the periphery of urban areas, where most new homes at this time were constructed, only exacerbated the problem: not only were families paying higher rent, albeit for improved accommodation, but they also had to spend more money on travel. See also Ravetz, *Remaking Cities* 63–97.

27. Like many of his New Left colleagues, Hoggart complains that the "new" acquisitiveness of the working class was eroding older popular forms of art and entertainment. More traditional pastimes, such as club singing and storytelling, were being replaced by vacuous jukebox songs and an insipid, "candy-floss" press (*Uses of Literacy* 157–87).

28. See the Parker Morris Report: Department of Environment, *Homes for Today and Tomorrow* 1–2. The statistics for domestic appliance ownership come from Burnett, *Social History of Housing* 283.

29. See Hoggart, *Uses of Literacy* 48–63. Hoggart explains that the "Us/Them" attitude "arises partly from a feeling that the world outside is strange and often unhelpful, that it has most of the counters stacked on its side, that to meet it on its own terms is difficult" (48). Unlike Sillitoe, Hoggart characterizes working-class people's relationship with the police as often "good," though most regard the force as an "authority which has its eye on them, rather than as a member of the public services whose job it is to help and protect them." He extends this attitude to cover most civil servants and social workers, with whom, "though they may be kindly and well disposed," most working-class people tend to avoid all contact (49).

5. THE ELUSIVE ENGLISHMAN

1. Marlow says as much about Kurtz, whose access to certain types of obscure and restricted knowledge inspires Marlow's respect and admiration: "And said he [the colonial administrator to whom Marlow reports], 'Mr. Kurtz's knowledge of unexplored regions must have been necessarily extensive and peculiar—owing to his great abilities and to the deplorable circumstances in which he had been placed: therefore—' I assured him Mr. Kurtz's knowledge, however extensive, did not bear upon the problems of commerce or administration" (286).

2. Said, of course, has argued in many places that the colonies were an essential space for "playing out" Western fantasies. Beebee suggests that this was a common feature of modernist treatments of remote geographical and cultural spaces. See chap. 4, "Birth of the Prose Poem," in *Ideology of Genre* 113–47.

3. In the four Notebook sections of the novel, we always see the black notebook first, followed by the red, yellow, and blue in turn.

4. According to the text, *Frontiers of War,* a novel about an illicit love affair between an African woman and a British Royal Air Force pilot stationed in Rhodesia during World War II, was published in 1951 and achieved some success, allowing

Anna to live comfortably for several years from the proceeds. The black notebook also includes a hypothetical review that Anna would have written had she been asked to react to that novel: "A first novel which shows a genuine minor talent . . . the novelty of its story, a love affair between a young Englishman thrown into the Colony because of the war and a half-primitive black woman, obscures the fact that this is an unoriginal theme, scantily developed" (59–60).

5. Although Anna introduces him as "the young American writer James Schafter" (436), a few pages later she quotes a letter from a publisher that addresses him as "Mr Schaffer" (440). I take it that the first spelling is a typographical error.

6. In the inner Golden Notebook, Saul Green gives Anna the first line of the frame, "Free Women": "The two women were alone in the London flat" (3, 639). One way to read this is to assume that Anna writes the "Free Women" sections after overcoming her writer's block, using it as a frame for her notebooks.

7. For examples of postmodern theory that use space as a key theoretical concept, see Jameson, *Postmodernism;* Harvey, *Condition of Postmodernity;* and Soja, *Postmodern Geographies.* Perhaps none of these texts consider decolonization because their work tends to focus on America, which was acquiring colonies just as Britain was losing them.

8. There are several more detailed analyses of Lessing's uneven relationship with leftist politics at this time. See Jenny Taylor, "Introduction." Much of my brief discussion follows English, *Comic Transactions* 60–70.

9. E. P. Thompson, preface to McEwen's *Greening of a Red* x.

10. As nearly every history of cultural studies and the British New Left mentions, 1956 was a watershed political year in Britain. The Suez crisis, the Soviet invasion of Hungary, and the revelation of Stalinist atrocities (at the 20th International) combined to produce a crisis of confidence on the left, resulting in a mass exodus from the Communist Party. The New Left formed amid the fallout.

6. MAD GOAT IN THE ATTIC

1. One of the best and earliest efforts to write about literary forms of globalization is Moses, *Novel and Globalization.* See also recent issues of *PMLA* 116.1 (2001), ed. Gunn; *South Atlantic Quarterly* 100.3 (2001), ed. O'Brien and Szeman; and *Modern Fiction Studies* 48.1 (2002), ed. Bérubé.

2. Here is how Hardt and Negri describe the relationship between postcolonial studies and globalization theory:

We suspect that postmodernist and postcolonialist theories may end up in a dead end because they fail to recognize adequately the contemporary object of critique, that is, they mistake today's real enemy. What if the modern form of power these critics (and we ourselves) have taken such pains to describe and contest no longer holds sway in our society? What if these theorists are so intent on combating the remnants of a past form of domination that they fail to recognize the new form that is looming over them in the present? . . . In short, what if a new paradigm of power, a postmodern sovereignty, has come to replace the modern paradigm and rule through differential hierarchies of the hybrid and fragmentary subjectivities that these theorists celebrate? (*Empire*, 137–38)

See in general their part 2, sec. 4, "Symptoms of Passage" 137–59.

3. There is an extensive body of literature on the "tradition" of police brutality and mistreatment of minorities in general, either through overly aggressive surveillance tactics or a failure to respond to minority complaints. For a classic treatment of this topic, see Stuart Hall, et al., *Policing the Crisis;* and Gilroy and Sim, "Law, Order." For the official report on the Brixton "riots," see Scarman, *Scarman Report*. For more recent accounts of police neglect of minority complaints, see Cathcart, *Case of Stephen Lawrence.*

4. Rushdie's Brickhall is a mythical place, and it would be inaccurate to suggest that it can be equated with the Isle of Dogs. The "etymology" of the name might come from combining Brixton and Southall. Brixton, in south London and home to a large Afro-Caribbean population, was the site of several disturbances during the late 1970s and 1980s. Southall, in west London, has one of the largest and oldest South Asian settlements in Britain. The nonexistent postal code for the mythical place is cited as NE1 in the novel, which could put it in the vicinity of Tower Hamlets. The name's first syllable might also refer to Brick Lane, also known as "Little Bangladesh." Brick Lane is in Spitalfields, adjacent to the Isle of Dogs and part of the borough of Tower Hamlets but just beyond the purview of the London Docklands Development Corporation (LDDC) (see figs. 7 and 9). Most importantly, the experiences of many of the South Asian residents resemble those of the minority communities in the Docklands area.

5. The City of London is the geographical center of London and the financial capital of the nation. Until the deregulation of the financial industry in the 1980s (a key component of Docklands redevelopment), all securities trading in Britain was confined by law to the City.

6. Between 1981 and 1989 at least 80 percent of homes built by the LDDC were designed for private ownership. It was only after the crash in the housing market in 1987–88 that the corporation made any attempt to provide social housing at all. Many of the homes started only a year previously had become unsalable on the public market, forcing the LDDC to sell the homes to local councils instead. See Brownill, *Developing London's Docklands* 67–68.

7. To be exact, homelessness rose by 304 percent in Tower Hamlets between 1981 and 1989, a few years less than the whole of Thatcher's reign as prime minister (Brownill, *Developing London's Docklands* 80).

8. The Docklands Forum, a local activist group, claimed that the rate of homelessness in Docklands had risen by 335 percent between 1981 and 1987, compared with a rise of 74 percent in inner London. See Docklands Consultative Committee, *Priced Out* 15.

9. For a brief summary of the infrastructure developments at Docklands, see Williamson, *London Docklands* 54–55. Before incorporation of the LDDC, the area was poorly served by public transportation of any kind (e.g., only one draw-bridge—with one bus route—connected the Isle of Dogs with the rest of London for most of the twentieth century). A light railway, finished in the mid-1980s, was the first major transportation improvement, followed by the Jubilee Line extension. The Limeshouse Link, the most expensive stretch of road in the country, connects the inner Docklands with London's arterial highway system. Its construction necessitated the demolition of many homes in the area.

10. See also Jacobs, *Edge of Empire* 70–102.

11. Hall and Ogden set £40,000 as the price for an "affordable home" during this period. In 1982–83, 99 percent of homes in Docklands fell in this category; in 1987, the figure had dropped to 5 percent. See "Social Structure of New Migrants" 157–58.

12. In *Cities of Tomorrow,* Sir Peter Hall says that there is "a rich historical irony here" (354). The legislation for New Town development corporations was written during the immediate postwar years by a Labour government interested in managing long-term economic growth strategies. They hoped to accomplish this by centralizing economic planning and land development powers. For many years, the Tories resisted such measures, especially in the Home Counties, by appealing to principles of local democracy and accountability. By 1980 those traditional roles had been reversed as the new Conservatives centralized many land-use programs, while local Labour councils, such the GLC, and later the individual boroughs formed a vigorous opposition. Perhaps even more ironic was the rhetoric of "privatisation." The central government poured at least £2 billion into the area by supporting the LDDC directly as well as by offering huge tax exemptions, and this figure does not take into account almost £5 billion spent on infrastructure (LDDC, *Starting from Scratch*). The Conservatives encouraged the private sector by giving land away, the biggest subsidy of them all. For a concise discussion of EZs and the Conservative agenda behind them, see Shutt, "Tory Enterprise Zones."

13. Ironically, Docklands developers were subsidized more heavily than almost any project in the country's history. Most subsidies came in the form of free land and infrastructure improvements. Although Bredin estimates that "more than 78% of the financing has come from private sources" ("Rising from Rubble" 18), the public has funded the project to the tune of £2 billion to date in the form of tax concessions and other gifts (Weinberger, "Good Economic News"); when we include the figures for infrastructure, the ratio of public/private spending is much closer to 50/50. For more on the most expensive highway in the country, see Kershen, "Docklands"; on the Jubilee Line extension, O'Connor, "Transit Facelift." Even *The Economist,* one of the Tories' most loyal media supporters, complained that the government was throwing good money after bad as it expanded plans and budgets in the area ("London Docklands" 1990).

14. Early protests against the LDDC were lodged through the courts, most notably the House of Lords, which hesitantly gave their approbation to the corporation. At stake was the total absence of local accountability. For more, see Ledgerwood, *Urban Innovation*. Later, protesters concentrated on rallying the affected communities, with varied degrees of success (Foster, *Docklands* 249–86).

15. Scholars have long identified the East End as a center of xenophobic and racist activity. In the early part of the twentieth century, Jewish immigrants were targeted. Later, Oswald Mosley's fascist groups used the area as a political base. As black immigrants came to the East End, they became the focal point of racist activity. See Husbands, "East End Racism." Making matters worse, Tower Hamlets instituted a one-offer-only housing policy during the 1980s. Families who refused accommodation would not be offered anything else, effectively forcing them to take what was on offer.

16. Qtd. in Thompson, *Gangland Britain* 108. Thompson's rather sensationalistic account of London's gangs should be taken with a grain of salt. He suggests that the "third generation of disaffected Bengali youth . . . rapidly formed themselves into a second wave of vigilantes in order to fight their oppressors [racists]. Tall, stronger and sassier than those who had gone before, this generation had seen their parents suffer at the hands of thugs and were determined not to follow suit" (107).

17. See S. Hall, "Race, Articulation": "Race is thus, also, the modality in which class is 'lived,' the medium through which class relations are experienced, the form in which it is appropriated and 'fought through.' This has consequences for the whole class, not specifically for its 'racially defined' segment" (55). See also his *Policing the Crisis:* "It is in the modality of race that those whom the structures systematically exploit, exclude and subordinate discover themselves as an exploited, excluded and subordinated class. Thus it is primarily in and through the modality of race that resistance, opposition and rebellion *first* expresses itself" (347).

18. Pinkwalla, the DJ, sums up the frustrations of the club's clientele thus: "Now-mi-feel-indignation-when-dem-talk-immigration-when-dem-make-insinuation-we-no-part-a-de-nation-an-mi-make-proclamation-a-de-true-situation-how-we-make-contribution-since-de-Rome-Occupation" (292–93).

19. It is interesting that the one Brickhall activist whom the novel seems to take seriously is Jumpy Joshi, a local karate instructor and poet who alludes to Enoch Powell's famous anti-immigrant metaphor "rivers of blood" in his own political verse. As Joshi says, he wants to "[r]eclaim the metaphor . . . make it a thing we can use" (186). Even in this reversal, however, we can see how closely the language of political protest resembles its opposite, the discourse of political oppression.

20. Chamcha reverts to his full Indian name when he returns to Bombay in the latter stages of the novel.

21. As many of the other quoted passages suggest, this dream motif recurs throughout the novel. In *Rushdie File,* ed. Appignanesi and Maitland, Rushdie himself suggests that the novel's dreamlike qualities correspond to the contemporary experience of Britain (8–9).

CONCLUSION

1. A quick survey of postwar British film, especially from the Thatcher era, suggests that similar themes of metropolitan destruction and rebuilding are at work there, too. See John Mackenzie's *The Long Good Friday* (1979); Hanif Kureishi and Stephen Frears's *Sammy and Rosie Get Laid* (1987); Ken Loach's *Riff-Raff* (1990), or any number of Mike Leigh's films.

BIBLIOGRAPHY

Abravanel, Genevieve. "Atlantic Modernism: Americanization and English Literature in the Early Twentieth Century." Diss. Duke U, 2004.

Ackroyd, Peter. *Albion: The Origins of the English Imagination.* 2002. New York: Anchor, 2004.

———. *Hawksmoor.* London: Penguin, 1985, 2002.

———. *London: The Biography.* 2000. New York: Anchor, 2003.

Ali, Monica. *Brick Lane.* New York: Scribner, 2003.

Allsop, Kenneth. *The Angry Decade: A Survey of Cultural Revolt of the Nineteen-Fifties.* London: Peter Owen, 1969.

Althusser, Louis. *For Marx.* Trans. Ben Brewster. New York: Pantheon, 1969.

———. "Ideology and Ideological State Apparatuses (Notes Towards an Investigation)." *Lenin and Philosophy and Other Essays.* Trans. Ben Brewster. New York: New Left Books, 1971. 127–86.

Althusser, Louis, and Etienne Balibar. *Reading Capital.* 1970. Trans. Ben Brewster. London: Verso, 1997.

Amis, Kingsley. *Lucky Jim.* 1954. London: Penguin, 1992.

Amis, Martin. *London Fields.* London: Jonathan Cape, 1989.

Anderson, Perry. "The Left in the Fifties." *New Left Review* 29 (1965): 3–18.

———. "Origins of the Present Crisis." *New Left Review* 23 (1964): 26–53.

———. "Socialism and Pseudo-Empiricism." *New Left Review* 35 (1966): 2–42.

Appadurai, Arjun. *Modernity at Large: Cultural Dimensions of Globalization.* Minneapolis: U of Minnesota P, 1996.

Appignanesi, Lisa, and Sara Maitland, eds. *The Rushdie File.* Syracuse: Syracuse UP, 1990.

Armstrong, Nancy. *Desire and Domestic Fiction: A Political History of the Novel.* New York: Oxford UP, 1987.

Arts Council of Great Britain. *Lutyens: The Work of the English Architect Sir Edwin Lutyens (1869–1944).* London: Arts Council, 1982.

Ashcroft, Bill, Gareth Griffiths, and Helen Tiffin, eds. *The Empire Writes Back: Theory and Practice in Post-Colonial Literatures.* London: Routledge, 1989.

Bachelard, Gaston. *The Poetics of Space.* Trans. Maria Jolas. Boston: Beacon, 1969.

Baden-Powell, Robert Stephenson Smyth. *Scouting for Boys: A Handbook for Instruction in Good Citizenship.* 1908. Ed. Elleke Boehmer. Oxford: Oxford UP, 2004.

Bailey, Peter. *Leisure and Class in Victorian England: Rational Recreation and the Contest for Control, 1830–1885.* London: Routledge & Kegan Paul, 1978.

Ball, John Clement. *Imagining London: Postcolonial Fiction and the Transnational Metropolis.* Toronto: U of Toronto P, 2004.

Barrell, John. *The Dark Side of the Landscape: The Rural Poor in English Painting, 1730–1840.* Cambridge: Cambridge UP, 1980.

Baucom, Ian. *Out of Place: Englishness, Empire, and the Locations of Identity.* Princeton: Princeton UP, 1999.

Bauman, Zygmunt. *Globalization: The Human Consequences.* New York: Columbia UP, 1998.

———. *Memories of Class: The Pre-History and After-Life of Class.* London: Routledge & Kegan Paul, 1982.

Beaufoy, Helena. "'Order out of Chaos': The London Society and the Planning of London, 1912–1920." *Planning Perspectives* 12 (1997): 135–64.

Beebee, Thomas. *The Ideology of Genre: A Study of Generic Instability.* University Park: Pennsylvania State UP, 1994.

Beevers, Robert. *The Garden City Utopia: A Critical Biography of Ebenezer Howard.* Basingstoke: Macmillan, 1988.

Berman, Marshall. *All That Is Solid Melts into Air: The Experience of Modernity.* New York: Penguin, 1982, 1988.

Bérubé, Michael, ed. *Postmodernism and the Globalization of English.* Spec. issue of *Modern Fiction Studies* 48.1 (2002): 1–228.

Beveridge, William H. *Full Employment in a Free Society.* London: HMSO, 1944.

———. *Social Insurance and Allied Services, Report by Sir William Beveridge* [Beveridge Report]. London: HMSO, 1942.

Bhabha, Homi. *The Location of Culture.* New York: Routledge, 1994.

Blatchford, Robert. *Merrie England.* 1894. New York: Monthly Review Press, 1966.

Booth, William. *In Darkest England and the Way Out.* London: International Headquarters for the Salvation Army, 1890.

Born, Daniel. "Private Gardens, Public Swamps: *Howards End* and the Revaluation of Liberal Guilt." *Novel: A Forum on Fiction* 25 (1992): 141–59.

Bourdieu, Pierre. *Distinction: A Social Critique of the Judgement of Taste.* Trans. Richard Nice. Cambridge, MA: Harvard UP, 1984.

Bowlby, Rachel. "Walking, Women and Writing: Virginia Woolf as Flaneuse." *New Feminist Discourses: Critical Essays on Theories and Texts.* Ed. Isobel Armstrong. London: Routledge, 1992. 26–47.

Braine, John. *Room at the Top.* 1957. Harmondsworth: Penguin, 1959.

Bredin, James. "Rising from Rubble." *Industry Week* 18 Mar. 1996: 16–18.

Brennan, Timothy. *Salman Rushdie and the Third World: Myths of the Nation.* New York: St. Martin's, 1989.

Breward, Christopher. "Sartorial Spectacle: Clothing and Masculine Identities in the Imperial City, 1860–1914." Driver and Gilbert, *Imperial Cities* 238–53.

Brideshead Revisited. Dir. Michael Lindsay-Hogg and Charles Sturridge. 1981. Videocassette. Acorn Media, 2002.

Briggs, Robert. *Bungalows and Country Residences.* London: Batsford, 1891.

Brooks, Peter. *Reading for the Plot: Design and Intention in Narrative.* Cambridge, MA: Harvard UP, 1984.

Brown, Jane. *Lutyens and the Edwardians: An English Architect and His Clients.* London: Viking, 1996.

Brown, John. *The British Welfare State: A Critical History.* London: Blackwell, 1995.

Brownill, Sue. *Developing London's Docklands: Another Great Planning Disaster?* London: Chapman, 1990.

Brownstein, Marilyn L. "Silver Spoons and Knives: Virginia Woolf and Walter Benjamin (Some Notes on a Practical Approach to Cultural Studies)." *Virginia Woolf: Emerging Perspectives.* Ed. Mark Hussey and Vara Neverow. New York: Pace UP, 1994. 204–9.

Buder, Stanley. *Visionaries and Planners: The Garden City Movement and the Modern Community.* New York: Oxford UP, 1990.

Bunce, Michael. *The Countryside Ideal: Anglo-American Images of Landscape.* London: Routledge, 1989.

Burnett, John. *A Social History of Housing, 1815–1985.* London: Methuen, 1986.

Burns, Wilfred. *New Towns for Old: The Techniques for Urban Renewal.* London: Leonard Hill, 1963.

Buzard, James. "Ethnography as Interruption: *News from Nowhere,* Narrative, and the Modern Romance of Authority." *Victorian Studies* 40 (1997): 445–74.

Callinicos, Alex. *Against Postmodernism: A Marxist Critique.* New York: St. Martin's, 1990.

Cannadine, David. *The Rise and Fall of Class in Britain.* New York: Columbia UP, 1999.

Carter, Erica, James Donald, and Judith Squires, eds. *Space and Place: Theories of Identity and Location.* London: Lawrence & Wishart, 1993.

Casey, Edward. *The Fate of Place: A Philosophical History.* Berkeley and Los Angeles: U of California P, 1997.

Castells, Manuel. *City, Class, and Power.* Trans. Elizabeth Lebas. London: Macmillan, 1978.

———. *The Rise of Network Society.* Cambridge: Blackwell, 1996.

Cathcart, Brian. *The Case of Stephen Lawrence.* London: Penguin, 2000.

Certeau, Michel de. *The Practice of Everyday Life.* Trans. Stephen Rendall. Berkeley and Los Angeles: U of California P, 1984.

Chun, Lin. *The British New Left.* Edinburgh: Edinburgh UP, 1993.

Clewell, Tammy. "Consolation Refused: Virginia Woolf, The Great War, and Modernist Mourning." *Modern Fiction Studies* 50 (2004): 197–223.

Cohen, Scott. "'Get Out!': Empire Migration and Human Traffic in *Lord Jim*." *Novel: A Forum on Fiction* 36 (2003): 374–97.

Colley, Linda. "Britishness and Otherness: An Argument." *Journal of British Studies* 31 (1992): 309–29.

———. *Britons: Forging the Nation, 1707–1837*. New Haven: Yale UP, 1992.

Conrad, Joseph. *Heart of Darkness*. 1899. *Great Short Works of Joseph Conrad*. New York: Harper & Row, 1966. 208–92.

———. *The Secret Agent*. 1907. Harmondsworth: Penguin, 1983.

Conway, Hazel. *People's Parks: The Design and Development of Victorian Parks in Britain*. Cambridge: Cambridge UP, 1991.

Cooper, William. *Scenes from Provincial Life*. 1950. Harmondsworth: Penguin, 1961.

Cullingworth, J. B. *Town and Country Planning in Britain*. Hemel Hempstead: George Allen & Unwin, 1964.

Davin, Anna. "Imperialism and Motherhood." *History Workshop Journal* 5 (1978): 9–65.

Deleuze, Gilles, and Félix Guattari. *A Thousand Plateaus: Capitalism and Schizophrenia*. Trans. Brian Massumi. Minneapolis: U of Minnesota P, 1987.

Department of Environment. *Homes for Today and Tomorrow* [Parker Morris Report]. London: HMSO, 1961.

Dimock, Wai Chee, and Michael T. Gilmore, eds. *Rethinking Class: Literary Studies and Social Formations*. New York: Columbia UP, 1994.

Disraeli, Benjamin. *Sybil; or, The Two Nations*. 1845. London: Oxford UP, 1926.

Docklands Consultative Committee. *Priced Out of Town: A Conference on the Future of Housing in East London*. London: DCC, 1989.

Driver, Felix, and David Gilbert. "Heart of Empire? Landscape, Space, and Performance in Imperial London." *Environment and Planning D: Society and Space* 16 (1998): 11–28.

———, eds. *Imperial Cities: Landscape, Display and Identity*. Manchester: Manchester UP, 1999.

Eagleton, Terry. *Criticism and Ideology: A Study in Marxist Literary Theory*. London: Verso, 1975.

———. *Ideology: An Introduction*. London: Verso, 1991.

———. *The Ideology of the Aesthetic*. Oxford: Basil Blackwell, 1990.

Eagleton, Terry, Fredric Jameson, and Edward W. Said. *Nationalism, Colonialism, and Literature*. Intro. Seamus Deane. Minneapolis: U of Minnesota P, 1990.

Easthope, Anthony. *Englishness and National Culture*. London: Routledge, 1999.

Eliot, T. S. *Notes towards the Definition of Culture*. London: Faber & Faber, 1962.

———. *The Waste Land: A Facsimile and Transcript of the Original Drafts Including the Annotations of Ezra Pound*. Ed. Valerie Eliot. London: Faber & Faber, 1971.

Emecheta, Buchi. *In the Ditch*. London: Barrie & Jenkins, 1972.

———. *Second-Class Citizen*. London: Allison & Busby, 1974.

Empson, William. *Some Versions of Pastoral*. London: Chatto & Windus, 1935.

Engels, Friedrich. *The Condition of the Working Class in England.* 1845. London: Penguin, 1987.

English, James F. *Comic Transactions: Literature, Humor, and the Politics of Community in Twentieth-Century Britain.* Ithaca: Cornell UP, 1994.

Esty, Jed [Joshua D.]. "National Objects: Keynesian Economics and Modernist Culture in England." *Modernism/Modernity* 7 (1999): 1–24.

———. *A Shrinking Island: Modernism and National Culture in England.* Princeton: Princeton UP, 2004.

Featherstone, Simon. "The Nation as Pastoral in British Literature of the Second World War." *Journal of European Studies* 16 (1986): 155–68.

Felski, Rita. "Nothing to Declare: Identity, Shame, and the Lower Middle Class." *PMLA* 115 (2000): 33–45.

Finnegan, Ruth. *Tales of the City: A Study of Narrative and Urban Life.* Cambridge: Cambridge UP, 1998.

Fitzgerald, Penelope. *Offshore.* London: Collins, 1979.

Forster, E. M. *Howards End.* 1910. Ed. Alistair M. Duckworth. Boston: Bedford, 1997.

Foster, Janet. *Docklands: Cultures in Conflict, Worlds in Collision.* London: U College London P, 1999.

Foucault, Michel. *Discipline and Punish: The Birth of the Prison.* Trans. Alan Sheridan. New York: Vintage, 1979.

Fox, Pamela. *Class Fictions: Shame and Resistance in the British Working-Class Novel, 1890–1945.* Durham: Duke UP, 1994.

Frank, Joseph. *The Idea of Spatial Form.* New Brunswick: Rutgers UP, 1991.

Froula, Christine. "*Mrs. Dalloway*'s Postwar Elegy: Women, War, and the Art of Mourning." *Modernism/Modernity* 9 (2002): 125–63.

Fussell, Paul. *The Great War and Modern Memory.* New York: Oxford UP, 1975.

Fyvel, T. R. "The Stones of Harlow." *Encounter,* June 1956: 11–17.

George, Rosemary Marangoly. *The Politics of Home: Postcolonial Relocations and Twentieth-Century Fiction.* Berkeley and Los Angeles: U of California P, 1996.

Giddens, Anthony. *The Consequences of Modernity.* Stanford: Stanford UP, 1990.

Giedion, Sigfried. *Space, Time, and Architecture: The Growth of a New Tradition.* Cambridge, MA: Harvard UP, 1967.

Gikandi, Simon. *Maps of Englishness: Writing Identity in the Culture of Colonialism.* New York: Columbia UP, 1996.

Gilbert, David. "'London in All its Glory—or How to Enjoy London': Guidebook Representations of Imperial London." *Journal of Historical Geography* 25 (1999): 279–97.

Gilroy, Paul. *The Black Atlantic: Modernity and Double Consciousness.* Cambridge, MA: Harvard UP, 1993.

———. *"There Ain't No Black in the Union Jack": The Cultural Politics of Race and Nation.* Chicago: U of Chicago P, 1991.

Gilroy, Paul, and Joe Sim. "Law, Order, and the State of the Left." *Law, Order, and the Authoritarian State: Readings in Critical Criminology.* Ed. Phil Scraton. Milton Keynes: Open UP, 1987. 71–106.

Golding, William. *Darkness Visible.* New York: Farrar Straus Giroux, 1979.

Goldthorpe, John H. *The Affluent Worker in the Class Structure.* Cambridge: Cambridge UP, 1969.

Goldthorpe, John H., David Lockwood, Frank Bechhofer, and Jennifer Platt. *The Affluent Worker: Political Attitudes and Behavior.* Cambridge: Cambridge UP, 1968.

Gramsci, Antonio. *Selections from the Prison Notebooks.* Ed. and trans. Quintin Hoare and Geoffrey Nowell Smith. New York: International Publishers, 1971.

Greene, Graham. *The End of the Affair.* London: Heinemann, 1951.

Greenslade, William. "Fitness and Fin de Siècle." *Fin de Siècle/Fin du Globe: Fears and Fantasies of the Late Nineteenth Century.* Ed. John Stokes. New York: St. Martin's, 1992. 37–51.

Gunn, Giles, ed. *Globalizing Literary Studies.* Spec. issue of *PMLA* 116.1 (2001): 1–272.

Hall, Catherine. "British Cultural Identities and the Legacy of the Empire." Morley and Robbins 27–40.

Hall, Sir Peter. *Cities of Tomorrow: An Intellectual History of Urban Planning and Design in the Twentieth Century.* Oxford: Blackwell, 1988, 1996.

Hall, Ray, and Philip E. Ogden. "The Social Structure of New Migrants to London Docklands: Recent Evidence from Wapping." *London Journal* 17 (1992): 153–69.

Hall, Stuart. "Race, Articulation and Societies Structured in Dominance." *Black British Cultural Studies: A Reader.* Ed. Houston Baker, Manthia Diawara, and Ruth D. Lindeborg. Chicago: U of Chicago P, 1996. 16–60.

———. "The Supply of Demand." E. P. Thompson, *Out of Apathy* 56–97.

———. "When Was 'the Postcolonial'? Thinking at the Limit." *The Post-Colonial Question: Common Skies, Divided Horizons.* Ed. Iain Chambers and Lidia Curti. London: Routledge, 1996. 242–60.

Hall, Stuart, et al. *Policing the Crisis: Mugging, the State, and Law and Order.* London: Macmillan, 1978.

Hardt, Michael, and Antonio Negri. *Empire.* Cambridge, MA: Harvard UP, 2000.

Hardy, Denis. *From Garden Cities to New Towns: Campaigning for Town and Country Planning, 1899–1946.* London: E & FN Spon, 1991.

———. *From New Towns to Green Politics: Campaigning for Town and Country Planning, 1946–1990.* London: E & FN Spon, 1991.

Harris, John. *Government Patronage of the Arts in Great Britain.* Chicago: U of Chicago P, 1970.

Harvey, David. *The Condition of Postmodernity: An Enquiry into the Origins of Cultural Change.* Oxford: Blackwell, 1989.

———. *Social Justice and the City.* Baltimore: Johns Hopkins UP, 1973.

———. *Spaces of Hope.* Berkeley and Los Angeles: U of California P, 2000.

Hebbert, Michael. "One 'Planning Disaster' after Another: London Docklands 1970–1992." *London Journal* 17 (1992): 115–34.

Hegglund, John. "Defending the Realm: Domestic Space and Mass Cultural Contamination in *Howards End* and *An Englishman's Home*." *English Literature in Transition (1880–1920)* 40 (1997): 398–423.

Hitchcock, Peter. "They Must Be Represented? Problems in Theories of Working-Class Representation." *PMLA* 115 (2000): 20–32.

———. "'Work Has the Smell of Vinegar': Sensing Class in John Berger's Trilogy." *Modern Fiction Studies* 47 (2001): 12–42.

———. *Working-Class Fiction in Theory and Practice: A Reading of Alan Sillitoe.* Ann Arbor: UMI, 1989.

Hite, Molly. *The Other Side of the Story: Structures and Strategies of Contemporary Feminist Narrative.* Ithaca: Cornell UP, 1989.

HMSO. *Census 1951: Classification of Occupations.* London: HMSO, 1956.

———. *Census 1961, England and Wales: Occupation and Industry National Summary Tables.* London: HMSO, 1965.

Hoggart, Richard. *The Uses of Literacy.* 1957. New Brunswick, NJ: Transaction, 1992.

Horkheimer, Max, and Theodor Adorno. *The Dialectic of Enlightenment.* Trans. John Cumming. New York: Continuum, 1996.

Howard, Ebenezer. *Garden Cities of Tomorrow.* 1902. Cambridge: MIT P, 1965.

Huggan, Graham. *The Postcolonial Exotic: Marketing the Margins.* London: Routledge, 2001.

Husbands, Christopher T. "East End Racism 1900–1980: Geographical Continuities in Vigilantist and Extreme Right-Wing Political Behavior." *London Journal* 8 (1982): 3–26.

Ishiguro, Kazuo. *The Remains of the Day.* New York: Knopf, 1989.

Jacobs, Jane M. *Edge of Empire: Postcolonialism and the City.* London: Routledge, 1996.

James, C. L. R. *Beyond a Boundary.* 1963. Durham: Duke UP, 1993.

Jameson, Fredric. *The Cultural Turn: Selected Writings on the Postmodern, 1983–1998.* London: Verso, 1998.

———. "Modernism and Imperialism." Eagleton, Jameson, and Said, *Nationalism, Colonialism, and Literature* 43–66.

———. *The Political Unconscious: Narrative as a Socially Symbolic Act.* Ithaca: Cornell UP, 1981.

———. "Postmodernism, or The Cultural Logic of Late Capitalism." *New Left Review* 146 (1984): 53–92.

———. *Postmodernism, or, The Cultural Logic of Late Capitalism.* Durham: Duke UP, 1991.

Jones, Gareth Stedman. *Languages of Class: Studies in English Working Class History, 1832–1982.* Cambridge: Cambridge UP, 1983.

———. *Outcast London: A Study in the Relationship between Classes in Victorian Society.* Oxford: Clarendon, 1971.

Jordan, Harriet. "Public Parks, 1885–1914." *Garden History* 22 (1994): 85–113.

Kaplan, Cora. "Millennial Class." *PMLA* 115.1 (2000): 9–19.

———, ed. *Rereading Class.* Spec. issue of *PMLA* 115.1 (2000): 1–152.

Kern, Stephen. *The Culture of Time and Space, 1880–1918.* Cambridge, MA: Harvard UP, 1983.

Kershen, Anne. "Docklands: A Private City?" *History Today* 43 (1993): 7–12.

King, Anthony. *The Bungalow: The Production of a Global Culture.* London: Routledge & Kegan Paul, 1984.

———. *Global Cities: Post-Imperialism and the Internationalization of London.* London: Routledge, 1990.

Kort, Wesley A. *Place and Space in Modern Fiction.* Gainesville: UP of Florida, 2004.

Krebs, Paula. *Gender, Race, and the Writing of Empire: Public Discourse and the Boer War.* Cambridge: Cambridge UP, 1999.

Kureishi, Hanif. *The Buddha of Suburbia.* 1990. New York: Penguin, 1991.

Kutcha, Todd. "Suburbia, *Ressentiment,* and the End of Empire in *A Passage to India.*" *Novel: A Forum on Fiction* 36 (2003): 307–29.

Laclau, Ernesto, and Chantal Mouffe. *Hegemony and Socialist Strategy: Towards a Radical Democratic Politics.* London: Verso, 1985.

Laing, Stuart. *Representations of Working-Class Life, 1957–1964.* London: Macmillan, 1986.

Lamming, George. *The Emigrants.* 1954. Ann Arbor: U of Michigan P, 1994.

———. *The Pleasures of Exile.* London: Allison & Busby, 1960, 1984.

Landes, Joan, ed. *Feminism: The Public and the Private.* Oxford: Oxford UP, 1998.

Larkin, Philip. *Jill.* 1946. London: Faber & Faber, 1964.

Lawrence, D. H. *Lady Chatterley's Lover.* 1928. New York: Grove, 1959.

Lawrence, Roderick. "Domestic Space and Society: A Cross-Cultural Study." *Comparative Studies in Society and History* 24 (1982): 104–30.

Lazarus, Neil. *Nationalism and Cultural Practice in the Postcolonial World.* Cambridge: Cambridge UP, 1999.

Ledgerwood, Grant. *Urban Innovation: The Transformation of London's Docklands, 1968–84.* Brookfield, VT: Gower, 1985.

Lefebvre, Henri. *The Critique of Everyday Life.* Vol. 1. 1947. Trans. John Moore. London: Verso, 1991.

———. *The Production of Space.* 1974. Trans. Donald Nicholson-Smith. Oxford: Blackwell, 1991.

Lehan, Richard. *The City in Literature: An Intellectual and Cultural History.* Berkeley and Los Angeles: U of California P, 1998.

Lenin, V. I. *Imperialism: The Highest Stage of Capitalism.* New York: International Publishers, 1939.

Lessing, Doris. *Going Home.* London: Michael Joseph, 1957.

———. *The Golden Notebook.* 1962. New York: Bantam, 1973.

———. *The Good Terrorist.* New York: Knopf, 1985.

————. *The Grass Is Singing.* London: Michael Joseph, 1950.

————. *In Pursuit of the English.* New York: HarperCollins, 1960.

————. "Preface to the Golden Notebook." *A Small Personal Voice* 24–43.

————. "The Small Personal Voice." 1957. *A Small Personal Voice* 3–21.

————. *A Small Personal Voice: Essays, Reviews, Interviews.* Ed. and intro. Paul Schlueter. New York: Knopf, 1974.

Levenback, Karen. *Virginia Woolf and the Great War.* Syracuse: Syracuse UP, 1999.

Lewis, Wyndham. *Rotting Hill.* 1951. Ed. Paul Edwards. Santa Barbara: Black Sparrow P, 1986.

Littlejohn, David. *The Fate of the English Country House.* New York: Oxford UP, 1997.

Livingston, Robert Eric. "Glocal Knowledges: Agency and Place in Literary Studies." *PMLA* 116 (2001): 145–57.

London Docklands Development Corporation [LDDC]. *London Docklands Today.* London: LDDC, 1995.

————. *Starting from Scratch: The Development of Transport in London Docklands.* London: LDDC, 1997.

"London Docklands: High Time for a New Approach." Editorial. *The Economist* 20 Oct. 1990: 2.

The Long Good Friday. Dir. John Mackenzie. 1979. Videocassette. Anchor Bay Entertainment, 1996.

Lord, Catherine M. "The Frames of Septimus Smith: Through Twenty Four Hours in the City of Mrs. Dalloway, 1923, and of Millennial London: Art Is a Shocking Experience." *Parallax* 5 (1999): 36–46.

Lowe, Rodney. *The Welfare State in Britain since 1945.* London: Macmillan, 1993.

Lukács, Georg. *History and Class Consciousness: Studies in Marxist Dialectics.* Trans. Rodney Livingstone. Cambridge, MA: MIT P, 1971.

Lynch, Kevin. *The Image of the City.* Cambridge, MA: MIT P, 1960.

Lyotard, Jean-François. *The Postmodern Condition: A Report on Knowledge.* Trans. Geoff Bennington and Brian Massumi. Minneapolis: U of Minnesota P, 1984.

Macherey, Pierre. *A Theory of Literary Production.* Trans. Geoffrey Wall. London: Routledge, 1978.

MacInnes, Colin. *Absolute Beginners.* London: MacGibbon & Kee, 1959.

————. *City of Spades.* London: MacGibbon & Kee, 1957.

————. *Mr Love and Justice.* London: MacGibbon & Kee, 1960.

Magubane, Zine. *Bringing the Empire Home: Race, Class, and Gender in Britain and Colonial South Africa.* Chicago: U of Chicago P, 2004.

Mangan, J. A. *The Games Ethic and Imperialism: Aspects of the Diffusion of an Ideal.* 1986. London: Frank Cass, 1998.

Manganaro, Mark. *Modernist Anthropology: From Fieldwork to Text.* Princeton: Princeton UP, 1990.

Marcus, Jane. "Thinking Back through Our Mothers." *New Feminist Essays on Virginia Woolf.* Ed. Marcus. Lincoln: U of Nebraska P, 1981. 1–30.

Marcus, Sharon. *Apartment Stories: City and Home in Nineteenth-Century Paris and London.* Berkeley and Los Angeles: U of California P, 1999.

Marx, Karl. *Capital: A Critique of Political Economy.* Vol. 1. Trans. Ben Fowkes. Intro. Ernest Mandel. London: Penguin and New Left Review, 1976.

———. *The 18th Brumaire of Louis Bonaparte.* New York: International Publishers, 1963.

———. *Grundrisse.* Trans. Martin Nicolaus. London: Penguin and New Left Review, 1973.

Maschler, Tom, ed. *Declaration.* London: MacGibbon & Kee, 1957.

Massey, Doreen. *Space, Place, and Gender.* Minneapolis: U of Minnesota P, 1993.

Masterman, C. F. G. *From the Abyss: Of Its Inhabitants by One of Them.* 1902. New York: Garland, 1980.

———. *The Heart of the Empire: Discussions of Problems of Modern City Life in England. With an Essay on Imperialism.* 1901. Ed. Bentley B. Gilbert. New York: Harvester, 1973.

Mayhew, Henry. *London Labour and the London Poor.* 1861. 4 vols. New York: Dover, 1968.

McCue, Megan M. "Confronting Modernity: Virginia Woolf and Walter Benjamin." *Virginia Woolf and the Arts: Selected Papers from the Sixth Annual Conference on Virginia Woolf.* Ed. Diane Gillespie and Leslie K. Hankins. New York: Pace UP, 1997. 310–19.

McKeon, Michael. *The Origins of the English Novel, 1600–1740.* Baltimore: Johns Hopkins UP, 1987.

McKibbin, Ross. *Classes and Cultures: England 1918–1951.* Oxford: Oxford UP, 1998.

McLaughlin, Joseph. *Writing the Urban Jungle: Reading Empire in London from Doyle to Eliot.* Charlottesville: U of Virginia P, 2000.

McLeod, John. *Postcolonial London: Rewriting the Metropolis.* New York: Routledge, 2004.

McNichol, Stella. Introduction. *Mrs Dalloway's Party: A Short Story Sequence.* By Virginia Woolf. London: Hogarth P, 1973. 9–17.

Meacham, Standish. *Regaining Paradise: Englishness and the Early Garden City Movement.* New Haven: Yale UP, 1999.

Mercer, Kobena. *Welcome to the Jungle: New Positions in Black Cultural Studies.* New York: Routledge, 1994.

Metcalf, Thomas. *An Imperial Vision: Indian Architecture and Britain's Raj.* Berkeley and Los Angeles: U of California P, 1989.

Meynell, Guy. "The Royal Botanic Society's Garden, Regent's Park." *London Journal* 6 (1980): 135–46.

Miller, J. Hillis. "Virginia Woolf's All Souls' Day: The Omniscient Narrator in *Mrs. Dalloway.*" *The Shaken Realist.* Ed. Melvin Friedman and John Vickery. Baton Rouge: Louisiana State UP, 1970. 100–127.

Miller, Mervyn. *Letchworth: The First Garden City.* Chicester: Phillimore, 1989.

————. *Raymond Unwin: Garden Cities and Town Planning.* Leicester: Leicester UP, 1992.

Mitchell, W. J. T. "Imperial Landscape." *Landscape and Power.* 2nd ed. Chicago: U of Chicago P, 1994, 2002. 5–34.

Moorcock, Michael. *Mother London.* New York: Harmony, 1989.

Morgan, John Edward. *The Danger of Deterioration of Race from the Rapid Increase of Great Cities.* London: Longmans, Green, 1866.

Morley, David, and Kevin Robbins, eds. *British Cultural Studies: Geography, Nationality, and Identity.* Oxford: Oxford UP, 2001.

Morris, Jan, and Simon Winchester. *Stones of Empire: The Buildings of the Raj.* Oxford: Oxford UP, 1983.

Moses, Michael Valdez. *The Novel and the Globalization of Culture.* New York: Oxford UP, 1995.

Mumford, Lewis. *The Culture of Cities.* New York: Harcourt, Brace, 1938.

————. "The Garden City Idea and Modern Planning." Introduction. Howard 29–40.

Nairn, Tom. *The Break-Up of Britain: Crisis and Neo-Nationalism.* London: New Left Books, 1977.

————. "The English Working Class." *New Left Review* 24 (1964): 43–57.

————. "The Nature of the Labour Party—1." *New Left Review* 27 (1964): 38–65.

————. "The Nature of the Labour Party—2." *New Left Review* 28 (1964): 33–62.

Nicholson, Geoff. *Bleeding London.* London: Victor Gollancz, 1997.

North, Michael. *Reading 1922: A Return to the Scene of the Modern.* Oxford: Oxford UP, 1999.

O'Brien, Susie, and Imre Szeman, eds. *The Globalization of Fiction/The Fiction of Globalization.* Spec. issue of *South Atlantic Quarterly* 100.3 (2001): 603–854.

O'Connor, Robert. "A Transit Facelift: The Jubilee Extension." *Mass Transit* 20 (1994): 56–59.

O'Neill, Daniel. *Sir Edwin Lutyens: Country Houses.* New York: Whitney Library of Design, 1980.

Orlando. Dir. Sally Potter. Screenplay by Sally Potter. 1992. Videocassette. Columbia, 1994.

Orwell, George. *Keep the Aspidistra Flying.* 1936. San Diego: Harcourt Brace, 1956.

————. *The Road to Wigan Pier.* 1937. San Diego: Harcourt Brace, 1958.

Osborn, Frederic, and Arnold Whittick. *The New Towns: The Answer to Megalopolis.* Cambridge, MA: MIT Press, 1969.

Osborne, John. *Look Back in Anger.* New York: S. G. Philips, 1957.

————. "That Awful Museum." *Twentieth Century* 169 (1961): 212–16.

Outka, Elizabeth. "Buying Time: *Howards End* and Commodified Nostalgia." *Novel: A Forum on Fiction* 36 (2003): 330–50.

Parsons, Deborah L. *Streetwalking the Metropolis: Women, the City and Modernity.* Oxford: Oxford UP, 2000.

Paul, Kathleen. *Whitewashing Britain: Race and Citizenship in the Postwar Era.* Ithaca: Cornell UP, 1997.

Pennycook, Alistair. *English and the Discourses of Colonialism.* London: Routledge, 1998.

Philipson, Garry. *Aycliffe and Peterlee: New Towns, 1946–1988.* Cambridge: Publications for Companies, 1988.

Pike, Burton. *The Image of the City in Modern Literature.* Princeton: Princeton UP, 1981.

Pratt, Mary Louise. *Imperial Eyes: Travel Writing and Transculturation.* London: Routledge, 1992.

Preston, Rebecca. "'The Scenery of the Torrid Zone': Imagined Travels and the Culture of Exotics in Nineteenth-Century British Gardens." Driver and Gilbert, *Imperial Cities* 194–211.

Procter, James. *Dwelling Places: Postwar Black British Writing.* Manchester: Manchester UP, 2003.

Pullinger, Kate. *When the Monster Dies.* London: Jonathan Cape, 1989.

Pynchon, Thomas. *Gravity's Rainbow.* New York: Viking, 1973.

Quigley, Austin E. "The Personal, the Political, and the Postmodern in Osborne's *Look Back in Anger* and *Déjàvu.*" *John Osborne: A Casebook.* Ed. Patricia D. Denison. New York: Garland, 1997. 35–59.

Ramchand, Kenneth. "Songs of Innocence, Songs of Experience: Samuel Selvon's *The Lonely Londoners* as a Literary Work." *World Literature Written in English* 21 (1982): 644–54.

Ranger, Terence. "The Invention of Tradition in Colonial Africa." *The Invention of Tradition.* Ed. E. J. Hobsbawm and Ranger. Cambridge: Cambridge UP, 1983. 211–62.

Ravetz, Alison. *Remaking Cities: Contradictions of the Recent Urban Development.* London: Croom Helm, 1980.

Rebellato, Dan. *1956 and All That: The Making of Modern British Drama.* London: Routledge, 1999.

Reed, Christopher. *Bloomsbury Rooms: Modernism, Subculture, and Domesticity.* New Haven: Yale UP, 2004.

Reed, Donna K. "Merging Voices: *Mrs. Dalloway* and *No Place on Earth.*" *Comparative Literature* 47 (1995): 118–35.

Resnick, Stephen A., and Richard D. Wolff. *Knowledge and Class: A Marxian Critique of Political Economy.* Chicago: U of Chicago P, 1987.

Richards, J. M. "Failure of the New Towns." *Architectural Review* 114 (1953): 29–32.

Ricouer, Paul. *Time and Narrative.* Vol. 1. Trans. Kathleen McLaughlin and David Pellauer. Chicago: U of Chicago P, 1984.

———. *Time and Narrative.* Vol. 2. Trans. Kathleen McLaughlin and David Pellauer. Chicago: U of Chicago P, 1985.

Riff-Raff. Dir. Ken Loach. 1990. Videocassette. Turner Home Entertainment, 1993.

Ritvo, Harriet. *The Animal Estate: The English and Other Creatures in the Victorian Age*. Cambridge, MA: Harvard UP, 1987.

Rose, Gillian. *Feminism and Geography: The Limits of Geographical Knowledge*. Minneapolis: U of Minnesota P, 1993.

Rosenzweig, Roy, and Elizabeth Blackmar. *The Park and the People: A History of Central Park*. Ithaca: Cornell UP, 1992.

Ross, Stephen. "Introduction: Working-Class Fictions." *Modern Fiction Studies* 47.1 (2001): 1–11.

———, ed. *Working-Class Fiction*. Spec. issue of *Modern Fiction Studies* 47.1 (2001): 1–277.

Routh, Guy. *Occupation and Pay in Great Britain, 1906–79*. London: Macmillan, 1965, 1980.

Rubenstein, Roberta. *The Novelistic Vision of Doris Lessing: Breaking the Forms of Consciousness*. Urbana: U of Illinois P, 1979.

Rushdie, Salman. *Imaginary Homelands: Essays and Criticism, 1981–1991*. London: Granta, 1991.

———. *The Satanic Verses*. 1988. Dover, DE: The Consortium, 1992.

Said, Edward. *Culture and Imperialism*. New York: Vintage, 1993.

———. *Orientalism*. New York: Vintage, 1979.

Sammy and Rosie Get Laid. Dir. Stephen Frears. Screenplay by Hanif Kureishi. 1987. Videocassette. Hallmark Home Entertainment, 1997.

Sassen, Saskia. *Losing Control? Sovereignty in an Age of Globalization*. New York: Columbia UP, 1996.

Scarman, Sir Leslie George. *The Scarman Report: Report of an Inquiry*. New York: Penguin, 1982.

Schaffer, Frank. *The New Town Story*. London: MacGibbon & Kee, 1970.

Schneer, Jonathan. *London 1900: The Imperial Metropolis*. New Haven: Yale UP, 1999.

Searle, G. R. *Eugenics and Politics in Britain, 1900–1914*. Leyden: Noordhoff International, 1976.

Sheridan, Dorothy, Brian Street, and David Bloome. *Writing Ourselves: Mass-Observation and Literacy Practices*. Cresskill, NJ: Hampton, 2000.

Short, John R. *Housing in Britain: The Post-War Experience*. London: Methuen, 1982.

———. "Yuppies, Yuffies, and the New Urban Order." *Transactions, Institute of British Geographers* 14 (1989): 173–88.

Shutt, Jon. "Tory Enterprise Zones and the Labour Movement." *Capital and Class* 23 (1984): 19–44.

Sillitoe, Alan. *Key to the Door*. London: Macmillan, 1961.

———. *Saturday Night and Sunday Morning*. New York: Plume, 1958.

Simmel, Georg. "The Metropolis and Mental Life." *Classic Essays on the Culture of Cities*. Ed. Richard Sennett. Englewood Cliffs, NJ: Prentice Hall, 1969. 47–60.

Sinclair, Iain. *Downriver*. London: Paladin, 1991.

Sinfield, Alan. *Literature, Politics, and Culture in Postwar Britain.* Berkeley and Los Angeles: U of California P, 1989.

Smith, Michael Peter. *Transnational Urbanism: Locating Globalization.* Malden, MA: Blackwell, 2001.

Smith, Neil. "The Final Frontier." *Gentrification of the City.* Ed. Smith and Peter Williams. Boston: Allen & Unwin, 1986. 15–34.

Smith, Tori. "'A Grand Work of Noble Conception': The Victoria Memorial and Imperial London." Driver and Gilbert, *Imperial Cities* 21–39.

Smith, Zadie. *White Teeth.* London: Hamish Hamilton, 2000.

Snaith, Anna. *Virginia Woolf: Public and Private Negotiations.* New York: Palgrave, 2000.

Soja, Edward W. *Postmodern Geographies: The Reassertion of Space in Critical Theory.* London: Verso, 1989.

Soloway, Richard. "Counting the Degenerates: The Statistics of Race Deterioration in Edwardian England." *Journal of Contemporary History* 17 (1982): 137–64.

Spivak, Gayatri. "Reading *The Satanic Verses.*" *What Is an Author?* Ed. Maurice Biriotti and Nicola Miller. Manchester: Manchester UP, 1993. 104–34.

Sprague, Claire. "Doubles Talk." *Critical Essays on Doris Lessing.* Ed. Sprague and Virginia Tiger. Boston: G. K. Hall, 1986. 44–60.

Squier, Susan Merrill. *Virginia Woolf and London: The Sexual Politics of the City.* Chapel Hill: U of North Carolina P, 1985.

Stamp, Gavin, and André Goulancourt. *The English House, 1860–1914.* Chicago: U of Chicago P, 1986.

Stanley, Henry. *In Darkest Africa.* New York: Charles Scribner's Sons, 1890.

Steedman, Carolyn. *Landscape for a Good Woman.* New Brunswick: Rutgers UP, 1987.

Storey, David. *This Sporting Life.* 1960. Harmondsworth: Penguin, 1962.

Su, John J. "Refiguring National Character: The Remains of the British Estate Novel." *Modern Fiction Studies* 48 (2002): 552–80.

Suleri, Sara. *The Rhetoric of English India.* Chicago: U of Chicago P, 1992.

Tabili, Laura. *"We Ask for British Justice": Workers and Racial Difference in Late Imperial Britain.* Ithaca: Cornell UP, 1994.

Taylor, Jenny. "Introduction: Situating Reading." *Notebooks/Memoirs/Archives: Reading and Rereading Doris Lessing.* Boston: Routledge & Kegan Paul, 1982. 1–42.

Taylor, John Russell. *Anger and After: A Guide to the New British Drama.* London: Methuen, 1962.

———, ed. *John Osborne: "Look Back in Anger," a Casebook.* London: Macmillan, 1968.

Thacker, Andrew. *Moving through Modernity: Space and Geography in Modernism.* Manchester: Manchester UP, 2003.

Thane, Pat. "Late Victorian Englishwomen." *Later Victorian Britain, 1867–1900.* Ed. T. R. Gourvish and Alan O'Day. London: Macmillan, 1988. 175–208.

Thompson, E. P. *The Making of the English Working Class*. 1963. New York: Vintage, 1966.

———, ed. *Out of Apathy*. London: New Left Books, 1960.

———. "The Peculiarities of the English." *Poverty of Theory and Other Essays*. New York: Monthly Review P, 1978. 245–301.

———. Preface. *The Greening of a Red*. By Malcolm McEwen. Concord, MA: Pluto, 1991. ix–xii.

Thompson, F. M. L., ed. *The Rise of Suburbia*. Leicester: Leicester UP, 1982.

Thompson, Tony. *Gangland Britain*. London: Hodder, 1995.

Thomson, James. *City of Dreadful Night and Other Poems*. Portland, ME: Thomas B. Mosher, 1903.

Timmins, Nicholas. *The Five Giants: A Biography of the Welfare State*. London: HarperCollins, 1995.

Trilling, Lionel. *E. M. Forster*. 1943. New York: Harcourt, Brace, Jovanovich, 1964, 1971.

Tuan, Yi-fu. *Space and Place: The Perspective of Experience*. Minneapolis: U of Minnesota P, 1977.

Wain, John. *Hurry on Down*. 1953. Harmondsworth: Penguin, 1960.

Walkowitz, Judith. *City of Dreadful Delight: Narratives of Sexual Danger in Late-Victorian London*. Chicago: U of Chicago P, 1992.

Ward, Stephen V., ed. *The Garden City: Past, Present and Future*. London: E & FN Spon, 1992.

Waugh, Evelyn. *Brideshead Revisited: The Sacred and Profane Memories of Captain Charles Ryder*. 1944. Boston: Little, Brown, 1972.

Weinberger, Caspar. "Good Economic News from the United Kingdom." *Forbes* 25 Mar. 1996: 33–34.

Weissman, Judith. "*Howards End*: Gasoline and Goddesses." Forster, *Howards End* 432–46.

Williams, Raymond. *The Country and the City*. New York: Oxford UP, 1973.

———. *Culture and Society: 1780–1950*. 1958. New York: Columbia UP, 1983.

———. *Marxism and Literature*. Oxford: Oxford UP, 1977.

———. *The Politics of Modernism: Against the New Conformists*. London: Verso, 1989.

Williamson, Elizabeth. *London Docklands: An Architectural Guide*. London: Penguin, 1988.

Wirth-Nesher, Hana. *City Codes: Reading the Modern Urban Novel*. Cambridge: Cambridge UP, 1996.

Wood, Andelys. "Walking the Web in the Lost London of *Mrs. Dalloway*." *Mosaic: A Journal for the Interdisciplinary Study of Literature* 36 (2003): 19–32.

Wood, Ellen Meiksins. *The Retreat from Class: A New "True" Socialism*. London: Verso, 1986.

Woolf, Virginia. *Between the Acts*. San Diego: Harcourt Brace, 1941.

————. *The Diary of Virginia Woolf.* Vol. 2, 1920–24. Ed. Anne Olivier Bell. New York: Harcourt Brace Jovanovich, 1978.

————. *Jacob's Room.* 1922. San Diego: Harcourt Brace, 1923.

————. *The London Scene: Five Essays.* New York: F. Hallman, 1975.

————. *Mrs. Dalloway.* 1925. San Diego: Harcourt Brace, 1997.

————. *Mrs Dalloway's Party: A Short Story Sequence.* Ed. Stella McNichol. London: Hogarth P, 1973.

————. *Orlando.* San Diego: Harcourt Brace, 1928.

————. *To the Lighthouse.* San Diego: Harcourt Brace, 1928.

————. *The Voyage Out.* 1915. New York: Bantam, 1991.

————. *The Waves.* San Diego: Harcourt Brace, 1931.

Wyndham, Francis. *The Other Garden.* London: Jonathan Cape, 1987.

————. *Out of the War.* London: Duckworth, 1974.

Young, Robert. *White Mythologies: Writing History and the West.* London: Routledge, 1990.

Young, Terrence. "Social Reform through Parks: The American Civic Association's Program for a Better America." *Journal of Historical Geography* 22 (1996): 460–72.

Zwerdling, Alex. *Virginia Woolf and the Real World.* Berkeley and Los Angeles: U of California P, 1986.

INDEX

Ackroyd, Peter: *Albion,* 211; *Hawks-moor,* 212; *London: The Biography,* 211

Adorno, Theodor, 227n32

affluence, 78, 115–16, 120–24, 128, 141–42, 190, 196–97, 217, 219. *See also* class

Ali, Monica, 198; *Brick Lane,* 214

Allsop, Kenneth, 117

Althusser, Louis, 21, 23–24, 141, 221n4, 223n26; on denegation, 80; on ideology, 24, 80; on interpellation, 80–81, 94. *See also* ideology

Americanization, 222n14

Amis, Kingsley, 112, 167–68; *Lucky Jim,* 113, 125, 232n21; ——, and elite culture, 218. *See also* Angry Young Men

Amis, Martin, *London Fields,* 212

Anderson, Perry, 11, 20, 22, 56, 222n13. *See also* New Left

anger, 30, 117, 120, 125; and masculinity, 132, 141; as reaction to class system, 114, 126, 140, 142. *See also* Angry Young Men

Angry Young Men, 30–31, 73, 111, 121, 141–42, 146, 167–68; and Arts Council, 119–20; class difference, 116, 143–44; and domesticity, 114–16, 125–36, 143–44; and Englishness, 116, 124; and homophobia, 118–19, 143, 230n7; and masculin-

ity, 117; modernism, rejection of, 112–13, 118–19, 125, 143; political ambivalence, depictions of, 136, 139–43; politics of, 112–14, 117, 120; provincial themes in, 123, 143; and sexuality, 115, 131; and welfare state, 114, 120. *See also* Amis, Kingsley; Lessing, Doris; Osborne, John; Sillitoe, Alan

anthropology. *See* ethnography

Architectural Review, 45

architecture, 68, 90, 130; architectural painting, 64; bungalow, 2–3, 5, 45, 211; and imperialism, 30, 44, 77–85, 87, 88, 98, 102, 195; and postmodernism, 174; two-up, two-down, 127–28, 136; vernacular, 116, 127. *See also* cities; Docklands; domesticity; geography; public parks

Arden, John, 112–13, 119, 231n11

Armstrong, Nancy, 115

Arnold, Matthew, 36

Arts Council (Britain), 118–19, 231n11

Ashcroft, Bill, 212–13

Baden-Powell, Robert Stephenson Smyth, 79, 81, 227n2

Baker, Herbert, 45

Balibar, Etienne, 21, 223n26

Barrell, John, 69

Baucom, Ian, 7, 27, 111, 200